Advance Praise

The notion that for-profit business ca[illegible] d isn't foreign, but that doesn't mean all busi[illegible] nd civic engagement meaningfully and str[illegible] yatt's wisdom and experience, presented in a manner that's realistic and relatable, makes **Strategy for Good** *a must-read for business leaders wishing to create greater impact in the world.*

– **Jeffrey Swartz**, President & CEO, **Timberland**

If your company wants to do well by doing good, **Strategy for Good** *offers the comprehensive "how to" you need. Nonprofits can also benefit by understanding the complex factors behind corporate giving. This book tells all in an easy to understand, well-documented format.*

– **Shirley Sagawa**, Author, *The American Way to Change* and *Common Interest, Common Good*

Philanthropy and community engagement once shared an office next to the corporate mail room. Today they reside in the executive office. Susan Hyatt gives business leaders a guidebook for re-imagining how giving can energize corporate culture, sales, and brand.

– **David Batstone**, Ph.D., President, Not for Sale Campaign and Author, *Not for Sale* and *Saving the Corporate Soul*

The marriage of philanthropy and the corporate world is not only good business practice it is the right thing to do. In this book you will learn: how to give and how to grow your business using timely, tested principles. Susan Hyatt is the Queen of Giving and the most trusted, non-biased resource in North America on corporate giving strategies.

– **Barry Spilchuk**, Founder, **You're My Hero® Books** and Coauthor of *A Cup of Chicken Soup for the Soul®*

Strategy for Good *provides a step by step guide for how corporations can align their unique assets to positively affect communities and impact the lives of individuals. This is an important roadmap for anyone who wants to ensure that the tremendous human capital, resources, and know-how of the private sector is harnessed to maximize social good.*

– **Michelle Nunn**, CEO, **Points of Light Institute**

Strategy for Good *is a compelling and comprehensive guide on how business and non-profit leaders can create strategic partnerships that create mutual value and benefit. It's chock full of helpful resources, real world examples and a practical seven step plan for strategic business giving that will help business leaders reap new dividends for their company and society.*

– **Kim Frawley,** Director, Corporate Responsibility, **Pfizer Inc**

Finally, a guide that provides real-life examples and decision-making tools for companies of all sizes seeking to make strategic investments in communities. ***Strategy for Good*** *provides concrete guidance for how an organization can move from 'checkbook philanthropy' to modern strategies that can benefit communities, customers, co-workers and companies themselves, all at the same time.*

– **Brooke Smith**, Director of Strategic Partnerships, **City of New Orleans**

Unsure as to what your small business should do regarding the new business imperative called Corporate Social Responsibility (CSR)? This book will solve your problem. It will gently take you through the thinking and steps to creating a feasible giving program. The writing is accessible, almost conversational and the plethora of company stories are illuminating and encouraging. Reading this book will make you feel as if you had your own personal adviser on corporate giving.

– **Bea Boccalandro**, President, **VeraWorks** and Instructor, The **Boston College Center for Corporate Citizenship**

We all want to make a real difference in the world. ***Strategy for Good*** *provides serious advice on how to do so not only in your personal life, but also by involving your business. It's been a core value in my life, and it can be in yours too.*

– **Craig Newmark**, founder of craigslist and craigconnects

Starting a new business? ***Strategy for Good*** *is a must read. A 'Strategy for Good' should be in your toolkit along with business and marketing plans. Today's global economy makes doing "business as usual" obsolete. Forming relationships with nongovernmental organizations benefits the community and gives your business the differentiation that ensures success. Susan Hyatt's straight-forward and practical approach makes it easy to see how strategic partnering is an essential part of strategic planning. Her non-judgmental, common sense guidelines are easy to follow, and help businesses start where they are. Don't recreate the wheel. Even small efforts can make big impact.*

– **Christina Bara**, Professional Integral Coach & Owner,
All Things Connected, Alice Springs,
Northern Territory, Australia

Strategy for Good: Smart Business Giving for the 21st Century *is a must read book for organizations looking to maximize the impact of their giving and entrepreneurs who desire to become 'conscious capitalists'. Practical tips provide companies of all sizes specific game plans to ensure their giving makes a difference, while supporting the organizations long-term goals. The case studies offer excellent tips for social entrepreneurs who are seeking to build a business while making a sustainable difference.*

– **Vince Shorb**, Founder,
National Financial Educators Council

Susan Hyatt explores the business advantages and mutual benefits of what we termed "Worthy Cause Marketing". Giving non-profit supporters

a social reason to buy your product is one of the most efficient ways to build brand loyalty. ***Strategy for Good*** *is a must read for today's entrepreneurs and start-ups.*

– **Michael Houlihan and Bonnie Harvey**, Authors of the *Barefoot Spirit*, BarefootWineFounders.com

Every business leader should read this book before they commit to donating another dime to charity. Susan Hyatt provides the road map for business and nonprofit partnerships that will improve business bottom-lines while increasing the impact of doing good in our communities.

– **Ted Hart**, ACFRE – CEO, **Hart Philanthropic Services Group;** Host, T**he Nonprofit Coach Radio Show**

Strategy for Good *gives businesses, leaders, philanthropists and visionaries a road map toward ethical responsibility. All of Sue's recommendations come from understanding the consumers and investors alike based on strategic planning, training and most important "passion" for conscious capitalism. It works...and it's important for our future.*

– **Rosie K. Mauk**, Co-Founder and past Chair of **Association of State Service Commissions** and Past Director of **AmeriCorps**

Whether aiming to get started or deepen existing investments, small companies will find Susan Hyatt's approach to and ideas for community investment a useful tool to create positive impact for both business and neighborhoods.

– **Anna Cunningham**, Manager, Global Responsibility, **Starbucks Coffee Company**

Strategy for Good *fills an important gap in the literature of social impact marketing: practical information for small-to-medium size businesses. In this very readable, well-organized book, Susan Hyatt shares tons of insights, case studies and practical advice sure to inspire companies to do well by doing good.*

– **David Hessekiel**, President, **Cause Marketing Forum**

This is exactly what I need to help coach businesses on how to become better "corporate citizens" and grow their companies too. ***Strategy for Good*** *has just given me the gift of a great toolkit packed with knowledge and advice to motivate business leaders to make a real impact with a strategic engagement plan for good. This is no book to let sit on a shelf...this is a toolkit to success! Every business leader who implements what they learn from* ***Strategy for Good*** *will not only help their community but will grow their company from the benefits of becoming more altruistic.*

– **Wendy Spencer,** CEO, **Florida Governor's Commission on Volunteerism**

Strategy *for* Good

Business Giving Strategies for the 21st Century

How Your Company Can Give Back, Make a Difference, and Do Well

Susan A. Hyatt, M.S.

Book Title Strategy for Good: Business Giving Strategies for the 21st Century

Publisher's Cataloging-in-Publication Data
Hyatt, Susan A.
Strategy for good : business giving strategies for
the 21st century : how your company can give back, make
a difference, and do well / Susan A. Hyatt. — 1st ed.
p. cm.
Includes bibliographical references and index.
LCCN 2011920874
ISBN-13: 978-0-9761948-8-0
ISBN-10: 0-9761948-8-0

1. Corporations—Charitable contributions—United
States. 2. Social responsibility of business—United
States. I. Title.

HG4028.C6H93 2011 658.15'3
QBI11-600023

Published by GoodWorks Publishing
1305 South Elm Street, Suite 211
Denver, CO 80222
Toll-free 866-512-0808
www.GoodWorksPublishing.com

Printed in the United States of America

Cover design: Angela Werneke, River Light Media
Editing: Elizabeth Wolf, Good Medicine Consulting
Book layout and design: Andrea Costantine
Author photograph: Carl Studna Photography

First Edition

To my family

Liz and Steve, my parents
Because of the values they taught me—especially integrity, generosity, and dedication to the common good—and their unfailing love and support, I grew up to be the person who could write this book.

And
Karen, my sister, and Annie, my niece—two of the best cheerleaders on the planet.

Table of Contents

Acknowledgments

I am truly grateful to the many people who generously gave of their time to be interviewed for this book and share their companies' philosophy and practices of community involvement. Some have since moved on to new opportunities and I wish them well. More information about these companies can be found in the Appendix.

Clayton Adams
State Farm

Aaron Azari
Colorado State Bank and Trust

Chip Bair
Beau Jo's Pizza

Jeanie Barnett
Tweezerman

Gregor Barnum
Seventh Generation

Matt Bauer
BetterWorld Telecom

Mark Berzins
Little Pub Company

Lisa Bowen
Tweezerman

Ron Brumbarger
BitWise Solutions

Bená Burda
Maggie's Organics

John Curtis
Energy Products

Karl Dakin

David Eisner

Ramon Elder
Virginia Village Texaco

Gary Erickson
Clif Bar & Company

Eileen Feeney

Seth Goldman
Honest Tea

Priya Haji
World of Good

Amy Hall
Eileen Fisher

Mike Hannigan
Give Something Back Office Supplies

John Harris
Belcaro Paint and Decorating

Bonnie Harvey

Michael Houlihan
Barefoot Wine

Gary Hirshberg
Stonyfield Farm

John Joseph
Josephs Jewelers

Kathryn Keslosky
Annie's Homegrown

Andy Lambert
Peace Coffee

Niki Leondakis
Kimpton Hotels & Restaurants

Jason Linkow
Metafolics Salon

Cheri Lutton
CCQH

Diane McIntyre
Nestle Dreyer's Ice Cream

Zhena Muzyka
Zhena's Gypsy Tea

Jessica Newman
Rock Bottom Foundation

Rodney North
Equal Exchange

Judith O'Neill
Landscapes Within

Beau Perry

Rachel Phillips
Sambuca Restaurants

Karla Raines
Corona Insights

John Sage
PuraVida Coffee

Amy Schilling
World of Good

Frederick Schilling
Dagoba Organic Chocolate

Leslie Sheridan
The Added Edge

Maria Simone
Signature Accents

Chelsea Simons
Annie's Homegrown

Bryan Simpson
New Belgium Brewery

Jennifer Stander
Endangered Species Chocolate

Mary T'Kach
Aveda

Tracy Ulmer
The Denver Post

Tony Waller
State Farm

Jody Weiss
PeaceKeeper Cause-Metics

Tom White
SE Reporter

Judy Wicks
White Dog Cafe

Mike Williams
State Farm

Nita Winter
Nita Winter Photography

I am so very grateful for all the many people who have supported me during the writing of *Strategy for Good*. Without each and every one of you, this book would still be an unfulfilled dream. Thanks for helping me find my voice and get my message out to the world.

Andrea Costantine, book strategist/mentor:
www.andreacostantine.com
I first met Andrea during her workshop, Soulful Marketing Experience. I was drawn to her basic message of be who you

are and share that with the world in all that you do. Andrea really helped get me back into action on the book. I so appreciate her energy and can do attitude. She never sees the limitations I sometimes see about myself and has pushed me to shoot higher than I sometimes have courage to do on my own.

Elizabeth Wolf, editor: *www.goodmedicineconsulting.com*
Elizabeth and I attended a Real Speaking workshop in Santa Fe years ago. I loved her authenticity, energy and spirit immediately. She totally understood my book's message and had experienced my passion for the topic through the speaking exercises we did. She was instrumental in helping me believe I really could write a book and that I had something worthwhile to say. Elizabeth is a truly masterful editor and has been a great supporter – always ready with kind words of encouragement.

Thanks to Angela Werneke, graphic designer, River Light Media in Santa Fe, for her beautiful cover design based on a deep understanding of my message.

A special thanks goes to Anita Halcyon, who gave me the initial push to write this book and who arranged for all the original interviews. Also to Christina Bara, Shirley Tafoya, and Jennifer Schneider for their transcriptions so I could honor accurately the thoughtful words generously shared with me by the companies I interviewed. Thanks to Liz Evans for drafting and Nicole Hansen for updating all the company profiles you find in the Appendix. My sincere thanks go to all the trusted people who generously gave of their time to review the book and offer their feedback: Karen Wan – Sustaining Stories, Robert Denison – Dinner for Six, Scott Degraffenreid - N2Millennials, Rebecca Saltman – Foot in the Door Productions, Justine Murray – JBS International,

Dalene Smith – 180 Degree Design, Karen Hyatt – State of Iowa, and Dr. Elizabeth Hyatt and Stephen Hyatt – Professors Emeritus, University of Maine. It is a better book based on all your input!

Special thanks go to Judi Terrill of Jade Woman Enterprises, Brendon Burchard, and Gail Larson, author of Transformational Speaking.

Last but not least, a huge thanks to Christina and Maggie as well as all my many other friends and colleagues not mentioned by name who offered me ongoing enthusiastic support and shared my joys and frustrations at each step in the road. I am blessed to know each of you! Thanks!!

Foreword

We live in a time of great uncertainty. Terrorism, war, economic hardship, and environmental degradation are constant threats. When security outside eludes us, we are forced to look within—to search our hearts and souls for fresh answers and new directions. Indeed, as I discovered in researching *Megatrends 2010: The Rise of Conscious Capitalism*, the quest for spirituality is the greatest megatrend of our era.

Spirituality means thirsting for something beyond ourselves—for peace, wholeness, and fulfillment, those qualities that, as Grandma eloquently observed, "money can't buy." Millions of us today are seeking those qualities. We look for greater meaning in our day-to-day lives. We ponder: how can we come from a place of compassion, consciousness, and service *all* of the time, not just after hours?

Susan Hyatt's *Strategy for Good* answers these critical questions, and many more.

In the aftermath of the boom-and-bust 1990s, many question the unhappy results of a business ethic whose primary goal is profit at any cost. For more and more of us, the moral consequences of unconscious capitalism are intolerable. As a result, Conscious capitalism—reinventing free enterprise to honor shareholders and *all* stakeholders—has dawned.

Some believe the goal of capitalism is to invest capital to create *more* capital. Okay, but that does not require greed. Self-interest and greed are not the same thing. Self-interest, says Merriam Webster Dictionary, is "concern for one's advantage or well-being." Greed, on the other hand, is "excessive or reprehensible" acquisitiveness. What a difference!

Greed is self-interest run amok. Suppose you insist that greed spurs capitalism in part. There are plenty of other motivations to succeed or invest. Like achievement, success, satisfaction, security, and a desire to be of service and create a better life for your family.

Conscious capitalism holds that business bears ethical responsibilities beyond short-term profit for shareholders. That said, businesses that embrace socially and environmentally responsible practices and operate from enlightened self-interest consistently outperform their less-conscious peers.

Enlightened self-interest is not altruism, which values helping one's neighbor or society in general rather than profiting one's self. Enlightened self-interest asks: *What are the ramifications of my choices in business and in life? Which acts—which might look justifiable right now—might come around to injure me and others in a year? Or 10 years? Or 25 years from now?*

The future of capitalism lies not in the hands of "Big Business." It rests in the hands of ordinary business people like you and me doing extraordinary things. *We* have the power to transform capitalism.

And who are "we"?

"We" are the millions in business who passionately embrace vision and values and demand meaningful work in companies that contribute to society. We create businesses that make a difference. We are a dynamic mix of "ordinary" managers, small-business people, change agents, innovators, activists, socially responsible investors, women entrepreneurs, and visionary CEOs and executives. We are a powerful force for social change, yet we are almost invisible to the *Wall Street Journal* and its ilk. At the same time, people like us, once considered "visionary," are moving into the mainstream.

Millions of us — managers, investors, consumers — are

lining up behind that vision—and transforming business. As managers, we value the Triple Bottom Line of people, planet, and profit. As consumers, we buy products only from companies and retailers whose values reflect our own. As employees, we work only for companies that value their people, customers, and the communities where they operate as much as their shareholders. As shareholders, we invest only in those companies we deem socially responsible.

Susan Hyatt's book, *Strategy for Good,* powerfully illustrates the force of business as a partner in creating social change and enhancing the lives of people in local communities and around the world. Her step-by-step approach teaches you to act on the values you hold dear while bringing your business assets to the table "for good." Giving back and being actively engaged in the communities that support you not only helps meet your peoples' deep need for more meaning in life, but can strengthen your financial performance over the long term as well.

In the end, that means more good—more spirit—in every interaction we have. *Strategy for Good* is a blueprint for the path Grandma counseled: how to live a life of purpose, generosity, and fulfillment. A life well lived, of many gifts well given.

We the people have the power to heal capitalism. Capitalism has the power to change the world. Isn't it time we got started?

– Patricia Aburdene
www.patriciaaburdene.com

Introduction

Every time I speak of my passion it serves as a reminder of the deep commitment I have to business philanthropy and partnership with nonprofits that is strategic, intentional, makes a real difference, and benefits all involved.

This book is designed to help you, the small and mid-size business owner, do more good for the planet, your community, *and* your company, no matter your industry or profit margin. This book will show you why implementing your own Strategy for Good is not only essential to thriving in the 21st century, but a necessary factor for setting yourself apart, attracting loyal customers and employees, and making a lasting impact on the world around you.

While I believe that doing something in the local community is better than doing nothing, offering up your scarce resources on a first-come, first-served basis can be a missed opportunity to synergize a greater impact in the community and to strengthen your business. One pack of hotdog buns to every nonprofit that asks has no real impact—for the community or the company! Having a strategy about how to best use your company's resources, skill sets, and overall comparative advantage in service to the causes you choose to support with a link to business goals only makes sense to me. That insight is the foundation of my company, CORE THOUGHT, and the subject of this book.

Strategy for Good grew out of 20 years of experience working with nonprofits in their efforts to make a difference in the world. The last 10 years I've focused intensively on strategic business-nonprofit partnerships.

I became committed to this work as a result of consulting for the national network of Governors' Commissions on National and Community Service and the AmeriCorps programs they fund in their respective states. In my trainings for nonprofit program staff, I stress the importance of measuring the impact of their services and programs. Most of them agree it's critical for decision making and continuous improvement of their programs and to share with community stakeholders (including businesses) to leverage additional resources and grow their support base.

However, when rallying these nonprofit troops I often hear loud laments from program staff. They speak of the difficulty connecting with businesses even when they have personal connections and strong data to show why supporting their program is a good investment. I could clearly see the value of the work they were doing—because I helped them measure it—and I knew that added resources would help them serve more people and ensure a strong enough "dose of services" for positive impact. Yet as often as I saw their enthusiasm over receiving a $500 check from a local business, I heard nonprofit staff people complain that they never got another penny in subsequent years. Or that they sent out a hundred appeal letters to businesses they knew were friendly to their cause, and received not a single response.

Clearly something wasn't clicking with the businesses these nonprofits approached. What was the cause of this disconnect, I wondered? If good programs weren't able to connect with businesses with which there should be an affinity, that I knew believed in being good community citizens, what was really going on?

Over time I realized the problem was that many nonprofits were trying to connect with businesses like yours by basically begging for donations. If there were no dollars available, the conversation shut down. With so many needy and worthy nonprofits out there also making requests, their voice got lost in the crowd.

To address this issue, I designed a new training curriculum for state service commission board members on how to develop strategic partnerships with businesses. Eileen Sweeney, former head of United Airlines Foundation and now with the Motorola Foundation, partnered with me on this initiative. We focused on shifting the old "checkbook philanthropy" paradigm to connect businesses and nonprofits for mutual benefit.

Our work proved very successful. The nonprofit staff and board members "got" the distinction between asking for a handout versus proposing a partnership with a business. Many retooled their requests to present themselves as assets helping companies address their goals while enjoying the satisfaction of contributing to their communities.

My company was founded to provide training and consulting to help both types of organizations work more effectively and with greater impact. That work, passion, and desire to help businesses and nonprofits strategically partner led to the creation of this book.

Since those early days, I've continued to hear success stories from nonprofit leaders I've trained about their partnerships with businesses. However, I still hear about plenty of challenges as well—from the businesses' point of view as well as the nonprofits'.

For one thing, most of the recent books on business philanthropy (often presented as part of *corporate social responsibility*) focus on the noble efforts and accomplishments of big dogs like Nike, HP, Levi Strauss, and Target. Inspiring though these stories can be to us as fellow business people, investors, and consumers, I often hear frustration from small business owners and executives trying to translate the lessons of the Fortune 500 to their own situations: "How do *we* do this?" they ask. "What steps should the little guy take?"

After all, our resources are limited, both financial and human.

Small business people feel we are already pedaling as fast as we can. We feel we don't have the luxury to slow down, ponder philanthropic possibilities, and invest the time and dollars for an activity that at first glance seems like a fluffy "nice to do" rather than a "must do." It's easy to think, "Sure, Starbucks can help save the world, but I'm just worried about making payroll next week!" So, we sigh with envy and wish we could give back, too.

Guess what? We can! Better yet, this book will show you that strategic giving benefits your company as much as your community if done wisely and well. After all, if the big guys are doing it, it must improve their bottom lines. There *is* business value in addition to making a difference.

The primary audience for this book is small business, from entrepreneurs and single-shingles to small and mid-market company owners and executives. When resources are tight, as they are for businesses like yours, creativity and innovation are essential. Companies, especially smaller ones, need to learn about effective strategies and approaches for their business giving to ensure impact. Mutually beneficial business-nonprofit relationships are not a "no-brainer." They require intentional strategies that build on both organizations' strengths, connections, and needs in order to make a real difference in the community and grow the business' bottom line.

My purpose in writing this book is not to convince you that your company should do good in the world. My hunch is, if you're reading this book, you've already heard and responded to the call to step up and be a better corporate citizen. In my experience, most people who either go into business for themselves or run small to mid-size companies seek much more than profit at any cost. One reason to have chosen this career path is for the flexibility and the ability it allows you to craft your destiny in a more direct way than being a cog in the wheel of a behemoth company. You had a desire to feel the impact of your work through dollars and effective use of your skills and abilities to make something positive happen and fill a need in the marketplace.

At the same time, this book is not for those companies angling for a little good press or seeking to "mooch" off your partnership to better your bottom line. The company must have a passion behind their giving in order for it to be effective; the media and customers can smell a rat a mile away. The strategies covered in this book are for a win-win-win approach.

This book is geared for decision makers who feel the weight of needing to be successful and are always trying to figure out how to pull ahead of the pack to move the business forward while not sacrificing the values you and your company hold dear. It is designed to show you how you can make a more significant impact with your giving, how you can be strategic about your partnerships, and how both your nonprofit partner and your business can profit from the relationship.

Strategy for Good seeks to inspire and affirm progressive, avant-garde business people like you who are committed to conscious capitalism and doing business in ways relevant in the first decades of the 21st century. My aim is to offer ideas and solutions that aren't pie in the sky but are doable now for mainstream business owners.

Business giving can take many forms. Companies can adopt or support schools, school clubs, neighborhood groups and other community efforts sponsored by local government or other businesses, as well. However you choose to get involved is great. *Strategy for Good* focuses almost exclusively on one subset of community involvement, that of business and nonprofit connections and partnerships. This is the aspect of community involvement I know and love best, and I want to share my expertise and passion with you.

Business giving goes by a lot of different names these days. Terms I hear regularly include *business philanthropy, corporate social responsibility, business social responsibility, corporate citizenship, community involvement, community investment, charitable giving, giving back, paying forward, strategic partnerships with nonprofits, social entrepreneurism, venture philanthropy, "philanthropreneurism"*—and the list goes on! While there are subtle differences between these terms, I use them interchangeably in this book. Generally I favor the terms *community involvement* and *investment, strategic partnerships,* and *business nonprofit connections* because they suggest partnership not paternalism, "trade not aid," all-win solutions, and mutual benefit. For the same reasons, I prefer to use the words *nonprofit* or *social sector organization* as opposed to *charities.*

For this book I interviewed dozens of successful, generous companies on how they give to their communities and the lessons they've learned. *Strategy for Good* gives you specific examples of how other companies have strategically partnered with nonprofits to increase the impact of that organization and also improve their own bottom line—both through tangible and intangible measures. Some of the examples may serve as great strategies for your own business. Others might simply give you food for thought or show how a little outside the box thinking can make a big impact.

While the majority of the research cited in this book and the companies interviewed are based in the United States, the principles easily can be expanded beyond our borders. Some countries are further ahead in their thinking and actions about strategic business giving so we in the U.S. have things to learn from them; others lag behind our efforts. The interviews with thought leaders I conducted as the initial research for this book yielded timeless perspectives on the role of business in society even as the details of their giving no doubt continue to evolve.

This book has three purposes. First, it celebrates the many creative and generous ways that the business community already supports and partners with local and global causes to address the social issues they are most concerned about. Second, it seeks to inspire companies of all sizes to revisit their current community connection philosophy and actions to determine where they can tweak their efforts to go to the next level and maximize mutual benefits. Third, this book aims to demystify and simplify the process of creating strategic community connections by providing examples and best practices, food for thought, and "how to" guidance.

Strategy for Good will give you the tools, expertise, and best practice examples you need to envision, design and effectively manage your community initiatives locally and globally. This book will help you:

- Identify the specific community impacts resulting from your efforts;
- Create a community investment plan to strengthen the "people" portion of your triple bottom line;
- Develop a communications strategy that speaks credibly about your commitment, actions and impacts; and
- Manage your community investment according to your values, vision, and business goals.

This book includes three main sections. Part I provides an overview of strategic business giving. You'll learn how it has evolved from an "alms for the poor" mindset to today's focus on strategic alliances with community partners for mutual benefit. Along the way we debunk myths about business giving and look at the range of business models for community involvement. You'll learn the four powerful ways your company will benefit from strategic community involvement.

Part II guides you step by step through the exciting process of developing your own Strategy for Good. Examples from dozens of companies with proven, successful community giving programs are included to guide and inspire you.

Part III offers a smorgasbord of ways to give. Companies have so much more to offer than cash. This section covers the four main categories of resources businesses can leverage in partnership with the community. These are funds, in-kind contributions, people's time and skills, and commerce arrangements.

The Appendix is chock full of useful tools and resources. You'll also find profiles of the companies interviewed for this book, along with a glossary of terms related to business giving. For additional resources for creating your Strategy for Good, visit my website, *www.StrategyforGood.com.*

I fully stand behind the principles in this book. With a few small changes to your philanthropic strategy you will quickly see how not only your bottom line will improve, but so will the relationships with your employees, customers, vendors, and the planet. So start wherever you are—through intentional, collaborative action, we can all leave a positive legacy and be part of something much bigger than ourselves.

While reading this book, be open to seeing how strategic giving can not only "do good" but also play a significant role in the success of your company. Nonprofit partnering should be fun, purposeful, and profitable. Get ready for a new journey in business giving.

Susan A. Hyatt

Part I: *Strategic Business Giving*

Business philanthropy "is a relatively simple thing, but it is a very powerful action. It sends a huge message into your particular community of interest that says, 'We are more than just an earnings machine. We are a partner with you. We are in it with you. We care.' And that makes a difference."

– Aaron Azari, Executive Vice President,
Colorado State Bank and Trust, Denver[1]

The Nuts & Bolts of Community Involvement

At a recent Chamber of Commerce function, a small business owner asked me what I did for a living. I told him I help companies like his be more strategic with their business philanthropy to increase their impact in the community and to grow the business itself.

"That is an oxymoron!" he exclaimed. "There is no way *giving* money will help me *make* money." Before I could explain that businesses that invest in their communities typically outperform those that do not, he was hightailing it to the hors d'oeuvres table.

Little did he realize it but this fellow's attitude spelled competitive *disadvantage* for his company. Good business used to be equated with simply providing a quality product or service at a fair price. Not so today. Americans' expectations of companies are at an all-time high. To be truly competitive in the 21st century marketplace, companies are increasingly expected to consider the "triple bottom line" of profit, people, and the planet. Community investment is becoming widely recognized as an essential part of business strategy for companies of all sizes.

Entrepreneurs like you who are committed to the long-term sustainability and profitability of their companies understand that success is based on a lot more than earnings. Not only is profit important, but also how people (employees, producers, suppliers, and communities) and the environment are affected.

Companies that thrive today develop deep and meaningful connections with their stakeholders. They take a stand on issues that are relevant to both their business and their target audiences.

Sharing resources—whether dollars, time, expertise, products or services, or networks—is a powerful way to be a "good business citizen" and show your commitment to being part of the solution to the issues of our day.

Part I of the book covers the basics of strategic business giving—what it is, what it's not, and how your company can benefit powerfully from community involvement in which everyone wins. A new paradigm is emerging in business giving, and a continuum of involvement with the community. We'll explore these subjects in the following pages.

What is Community Involvement?

Community involvement refers to the myriad ways businesses can draw upon their unique expertise, resources, and connections to actively engage with organizations to address local and global issues. Most commonly, companies provide contributions of cash, in-kind product and service donations, and people power to support the work of nonprofit organizations. However, companies are increasingly engaging with nonprofits through commerce-based alliances that foster win-win relationships.

Community involvement is one of the five essential components of **corporate social responsibility**, or CSR. No longer are companies that are wildly profitable but harmful to people or the planet deemed truly successful—especially over the longer term. Consumers and investors increasingly demand that companies engage in ethical business practices. Combined with the growing awareness that socially responsible businesses tend to be more successful over time, companies of all sizes are pursuing socially responsible business practices as a proven way to improve their profitability and competitiveness in the marketplace. You should too, if you are not already.

Over the past 50 years, issues of corporate social responsibility (also called business social responsibility and corporate citizenship) rose exponentially in the business world. Media exposés, activist pressure, protester riots, and criticism from unions and non-governmental organizations (NGOs) helped corporations realize that a diverse range of stakeholders was demanding socially responsible decision making at the highest levels.

Yet CSR is not a matter of management simply stating it is socially responsible. Rather, enlightened corporate leaders today spend significant time and effort grappling with CSR to avoid placing their companies at a competitive disadvantage.

Many entrepreneurs and smaller businesses mistakenly believe good corporate citizenship concerns only Fortune 500 giants. Likewise, many nonprofits have never even heard of the term. As a result, the way they approach businesses for support often falls short of addressing the company's concerns and interests.

Nevertheless, the crusade for corporate accountability has garnered immense public support. Today, some 70 million Americans make choices in the marketplace as "values-driven consumers." Internationally, a full two-thirds of 25,000 people polled in 23 countries said they want business to "expand beyond the traditional emphasis on profits and contribute to broader social objectives."[1] A McKinsey global survey published in 2008 found that 84 percent of corporate executives from around the world "believe that society now expects business to take a much more active role in environmental, social, and political issues than it did just five years ago."[2]

CSR accountability, while misunderstood or even denied by some businesses, is a new business risk that companies large and small must address, according to Jim Kartalia, the president of **Entegra Corporation**. His company specializes in software solutions for risk management. "If not addressed properly and sincerely, CSR issues can create substantial operating, financial, and competitive risks," Jim explains. "Activity perceived as 'non-CSR' business activity can put at risk the most fragile of corporate assets: its reputation."[3] Once reputation is damaged, a company's profitability and sustainability are in jeopardy.

What does corporate social responsibility look like for your company? For starters, there are five main components of CSR, described in Figure 1 below. This book focuses primarily on community involvement.

Figure 1. The Components of Corporate Social Responsibility

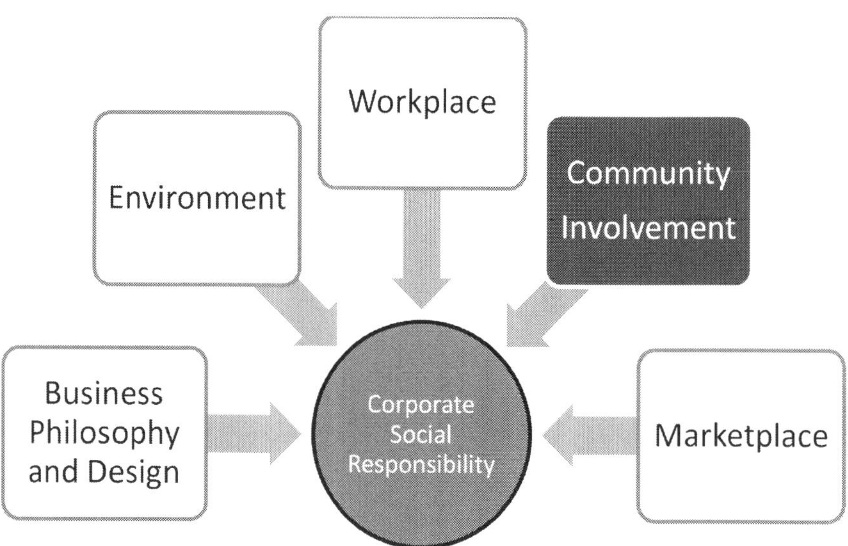

- **Business Philosophy and Design** relates to business structure, vision, mission, values, ethics, transparency, board composition, and governance.
- **Workplace Policies and Practices** include employment policies, employee compensation, promotion, benefits, diversity, work schedules, professional development, issues of work/life balance, and health and safety.
- **Marketplace Policies and Practices** include human/

indigenous rights, migrant labor, supply chain issues, wages/living wage, codes of conduct, sale of quality products and services, marketing, honest advertising, customer and vendor relations, and consumer privacy.

- **Environmental Policies and Practices** include green office practices, minimizing waste and environmental harm from manufacture, use or disposal of products, pollution prevention, and energy/water efficiency.
- **Community Involvement** refers to the ways businesses can connect or give back to communities to help address community development and local social issues.

To be considered socially responsible, a company must successfully address each of these categories. Companies that shine in all five categories are considered CSR stars. If you are just getting started, you can begin working on one area at a time. Your overall goal may be to excel in all areas eventually—truly the upper echelon of CSR.

With more than 1.2 million nonprofits in the United States today (up from 819,008 in 2000)[4], companies need to be intentional about the causes and organizations they support. There may be worthy organizations best supported through individual philanthropy that may not be an optimal choice from a business perspective. This is not to suggest businesses support causes they don't really care about just to make a buck, but rather to advocate "all-win" partnerships. For example, if you want to strengthen employee teamwork, supporting a group volunteer project for a local nonprofit is a better choice than a silent auction donation. It's all about finding the intersection between your company's goals and the community's needs.

Exciting and innovative changes in business are on the winds. Now is a great time for you to analyze your own market position, growth potential, and sustainability. Being more strategic with your give-back, making the conscious link between business goals and what most people think of as philanthropy, can reap abundant rewards for you *and* the causes you deeply care about. It takes only a little more effort to get a lot more bang for your buck.

Unfortunately, persistent myths about community involvement can confuse and mislead even the best-intentioned. Buying into these untruths means lost opportunity for both your company and your community.

Debunking the Myths

Let's dispel these myths once and for all so you can start developing your own Strategy for Good.

> **MYTH #1: Business social responsibility is for large companies only.**
>
> **FACT:** Business social responsibility is for companies of all sizes. In fact, small businesses account for *99.7 percent of American employers,* according to the U.S. Census Bureau. Our potential for community impact is huge.

"You don't have to be a big company before you can do much in the community. Even as a small company, there are many ways you can support community organizations. The smaller businesses around here have made a lot of difference."

—Chip Bair, Owner, **Beau Jo's Pizza**,
Idaho Springs, Colorado[5]

Many believe that CSR is only for behemoths like Nike, Starbucks, Philip Morris, and ExxonMobil. It is true that global companies can significantly impact the communities or countries in which they operate—for better or worse—and thus need to be mindful of their business practices. However, the reality is that in the United States, small business is the backbone of the economy. (Small businesses, as defined by the U.S Small Business Association, are companies with fewer than 500 employees.)

American small businesses employ more than half of all private-sector workers and generate 60 to 80 percent of new jobs annually. In 2009, there were 29.6 million small businesses in the nation, according to U.S Small Business Association. Of this number, 5.7 million firms had employees, and 16.5 million were owner operated, without employees.

In light of such numbers, it is clear that small business is a powerful force in the United States today. Ensuring that small businesses act according to the principles of business social responsibility in order to "profit with values" is as essential as influencing large companies with a global reach to operate in ways that are friendly to people and the planet. We are all in this together.

In 2008 over 627,200 new businesses started up, yet 595,600 closed the same year, nearly the equivalent number. Seven out of 10 new employer firms survive at least two years, and about half at five years. Only about one-third of the companies that folded reported that they were successful at closure. Factors influencing business success include ample capital, being large enough to hire employees, the owners' educational level, and the owners' reason for starting the business in the first place, such as freedom for family life or wanting to be one's own boss.

Considering these failure rates, small businesses that employ CSR practices from day one give themselves an added advantage toward long-term profitability and sustainability.

MYTH #2: Community involvement is a "do later" activity to add after my business is established and profitable.

FACT: Integrating socially responsible business practices from the beginning is easier and more cost-effective than trying to tack them on later.

"You don't have to be Microsoft or have a huge foundation with millions and millions of dollars. You really can plan to give back right from the beginning and step into it. I think every company should look into doing things right from the beginning."

—Maria Simone, Co-Founder, **Signature Accents**, Scottsdale, Arizona[6]

The entrepreneur starting a business needs to consider a million things—company structure and mission, developing the business plan, identification of products and potential customers, effective marketing and sales, securing investments, and more. Each of these areas demands choices that can help or hinder start-up. Integrating socially responsible practices, including community involvement, from the beginning helps strengthen the business and increase its profitability. Later in this section we'll explore the numerous proven business benefits of strategic community involvement.

MYTH #3: Community involvement is a fluffy, feel good side activity that would consume my company's valuable resources for little or no return.

FACT: When undertaken strategically and integrated into overall company strategy, community involvement can be an essential component of growing your business and boosting your bottom line. Studies show that companies that give strategically consistently outperform those that do not.

"We started worthy cause marketing as a way to sell our wine because we didn't have money to do anything else. We couldn't afford to put ads in the newspaper, magazines, radio, television. But [it worked] so we kept it that way as time went on and it's still being done that way."

—Michael Houlihan and Bonnie Harvey,
Co-Founders, **Barefoot Wine,** Modesto, California[7]

Community involvement activities offer an important opportunity for "doing well by doing good." In fact, many businesses no longer use the word "philanthropy." Instead, in recognition of the returns such activities provide, they use the term "community investment." Community giving can have a significant impact on a company's reputation and sales, employee satisfaction and productivity, in addition to making a valuable contribution and being part of the solution to local social issues.

MYTH #4: A company's community involvement should be motivated solely by altruism.

FACT: Community involvement based on all-win partnerships is more successful, effective, and sustainable than the charity model of giving.

"There is no one out there giving things away just to give them away—that's the reality. It can be tricky to understand business goals when you are the on cause-marketing side and to understand the cause side if you're in the finance department."

—Chelsea Simons, National Cause and Event
Marketing Manager, **Annie's Homegrown**,
Napa, California[8]

Some companies are in fact motivated by altruism and a

sincere desire to help communities. As a result, they generally make contributions anonymously to support the issues and organizations that matter to them. However, these companies are in the minority. Most companies expect their community contribution will have a business upside for them…if they are truly honest with themselves.

Some business leaders confess they are hesitant to consciously align their company's give-back actions with business goals. They worry this looks self-serving and will harm their reputation in the community. The practice of what I call "goodwashing" (also called "smokescreening" or "greenwashing")—giving solely for the sake of positive public relations—is the exact opposite of their intention.

Sincere companies that give back to their communities need not worry. A clear difference exists between self-serving behavior and enlightened self-interest with an "all-win" mentality. You can spot the difference, can't you? Trust that people in your community can, too.

A strong business community improves the local economy. A strong local economy enhances the quality of life and access to services for all members of the community, including employees of the company. To effectively improve local conditions, government, community organizations, and business must partner to make it happen. Business is an essential and powerful component, without which change is hampered.

In the spirit of true partnership, both the business and the community partner organization should benefit from their collaboration. Ensuring that the relationship is mutually beneficial helps guarantee that it can deepen and endure over time. Both sides need to feel there are benefits from their perspective or the relationship will be short-lived—a missed opportunity for all.

MYTH #5: It is self-serving for my company to tell the community about our business giving.

FACT: In actuality, sharing your story serves your customers, your employees, and the nonprofits you partner with, as well as your company.

"Getting the word out is not to just toot your own horn. It has the key goal [for us] of further engaging people: here's what we are doing and what you can do to help keep it going. It's all in that word 'engaging' as opposed to talking at people. You have to make what you do visible."

—Tracy Ulmer, Director of Promotions and Community Relations, ***The Denver Post***, Denver, Colorado[9]

Research shows that customers *want* to support businesses that give back, and employees *want* to work for philanthropic companies. And of course nonprofit partners gain valuable exposure from your company's PR.

Shameless self-promotion is of course undesirable, but getting the word out about your support of community organizations lets employees, customers, and citizens know that your company cares and is doing its part to improve the community. Many companies voluntarily develop annual CSR reports and post information on their website to be more transparent about their efforts.

Why shouldn't your company be acknowledged for the good you do addressing and supporting the local issues or needs in your community? How will non-involvement or keeping quiet about your giving help you? It won't. It is a huge missed opportunity to improve your image, strengthen customer loyalty, boost employee satisfaction, and even attract investment.

Read on to discover the abundant rewards that come from strategic business giving.

The Business Benefits of Community Involvement

"It's good for any business to have ties to their community. The community supports the business so I think it is only fair that the business supports the community. Once our customers get to know us, they understand that we are genuinely concerned about our local community as well as the communities of the coffee farmers that we work with. So it just makes sense to do it."

—Andy Lambert, Sales Manager, **Peace Coffee**,
Minneapolis, Minnesota[1]

Strategic business involvement with community organizations can offer you powerful "all-win" opportunities that benefit your community, your company, your employees, and your bottom line. Many businesses already engage in some form of philanthropy, either as a company or through the efforts of their individual executives or staff members. These businesses and those who work for them are actively involved in their immediate communities. They say they feel it is their responsibility to be involved and want to make a difference. For some, community investment offers a sense of belonging and a purpose contributing to the greater good. Overall, those involved in their communities say they experience a higher quality of life as a result.

As Frederick Schilling, Founder of **Dagoba Organic Chocolate**, puts it, "Integrity in the heart is so important. When you stay true to your heart and do what you believe in and really give back—it's a beautiful thing. It really makes you feel good inside, and gives you the desire to keep doing what you are doing."[2]

Along with the intrinsic, heartfelt rewards we naturally feel from giving back and making a difference, there are powerful business benefits available to any philanthropic company that engages with communities in authentic, meaningful, and strategic ways. Especially during these difficult economic times, the need for doing "double duty" with your scarce resources has never been greater. You need to be able to "do good" *and* "do well."

The Corporate Giving Standard Survey conducted by the Boston College Center for Corporate Citizenship surveyed companies in the U.S. Nearly half (48.8 percent) of the respondents identified their community giving as being "charitable"—that is, the company anticipated no business benefit. Another 35.9 percent identified their efforts as "strategic," expecting both the community and the business would benefit from their contributions. Only 15.2 percent identified their involvement as "commercially motivated," prioritizing business gain above community benefit.[3]

Yet more and more businesses are moving from charity to strategic giving. According to a McKinsey global survey on the state of corporate philanthropy, nearly 90 percent of companies now seek business benefits from their philanthropy programs. Desired business benefits include enhancing corporate reputation or brand, building employee and/or leadership capabilities and skills, differentiating themselves from competitors, managing risk, and building knowledge about potential new markets and informing innovation. Eighty percent of those surveyed say finding new business opportunities should play at least some role in determining which philanthropic programs to fund, as compared to only 14 percent who felt finding new opportunities should have no weight.[4]

Your resources are not unlimited; it only makes good

business sense to give to a smaller, well-selected group of causes or nonprofits to make a bigger impact. By adding focus and strategy to your giving, companies like yours can gain powerful advantages while doing good in the community.

"From my point of view, the most effective way for a business to go is to have a business model that is pro social and then use its philanthropy as an extra push to catch up its constituencies and innovations where the business model may not be realizing its full social impact," according to David Eisner, former CEO of the **Corporation for National and Community Service**. "When I was at AOL, the whole point of the company was to benefit citizens by making this new media work. The theory was that new media was going to democratize information and enable things that had previously only been available to the super rich. The core benefit AOL provided was baked into its business model and had nothing to do with philanthropy or social policy. What evolved was an understanding that the business couldn't effectively benefit society only through its own business model—it needed a philanthropic push to help. The AOL Foundation was created to help ensure [in part that] nonprofits weren't falling behind. If nonprofits are behind, then the people and constituencies they represent would also be behind, creating a digital divide. So the foundation focused on catching nonprofits up to the benefits of the internet."[5]

Forward-thinking companies view community investment as part of standard operations. Not being involved is not an option. For some companies, it is a way to demonstrate their values statement.

Judy Wicks, owner of the **White Dog Cafe** in Philadelphia, admits it is difficult to measure the financial results of community investment. Nevertheless, she strongly feels it positively affects business. "We are known not only for our good food but also for our social activism," Judy told me. "I joke that we use good food to lure innocent customers into social activism, because we do extensive programming at the White Dog." The café sends out a newsletter announcing their program calendar, which includes everything from storytelling and after-dinner discussions to international tours, community service days, and film series. "People come to the White Dog because they feel their values are aligned with us. They come here not because they are hungry for food but because they are hungry for a sense of community and being involved in something bigger than themselves. Because we are involved in so many different issues, almost everybody will feel the White Dog is behind something they care about, whether it is the AIDS epidemic, a foreign policy issue, an environmental issue, children, or the elderly. Plus, we have a lot of fun."[6]

I eat at the White Dog every time I go to Philadelphia. The food is great and I love what they do to build community!

The benefits of business giving to the community tend to be obvious. They include:

- Improved quality of life to community members;
- Assistance with critical social problems;
- Increased access to new talent, ideas, and resources;
- Improved communication between the various segments of the local community;
- A renewed sense of civic pride and spirit of citizenship;
- A strengthened local economy;

However, the advantages to the business of community investment are equally significant—and they go far beyond a tax deduction. As pictured in Figure 2 below, business benefits fall into four main categories:

- Improved company reputation and visibility;
- Increased market competitiveness, customer loyalty, and sales;
- Enhanced employee recruitment, satisfaction, productivity, and retention; and

- Increased access to investors and capital.

Figure 2. Business Benefits of Strategic Giving

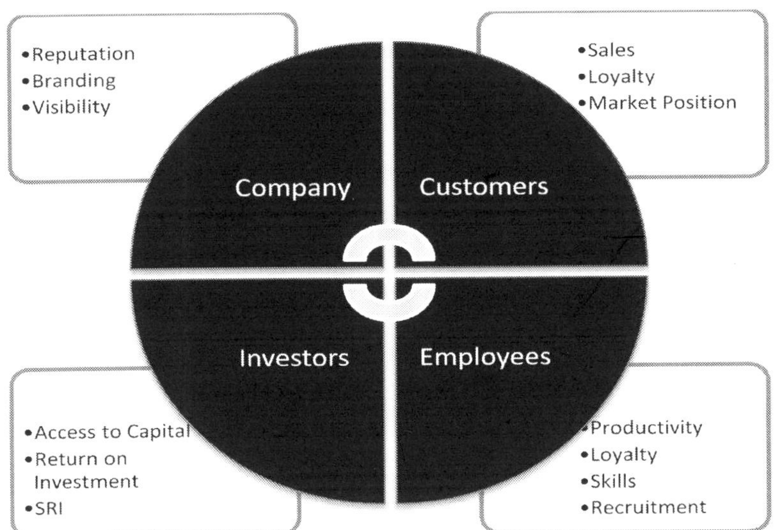

The benefits of community investment are greater than most individuals and companies originally realize. The following pages offer examples and insights from successful companies interviewed for this book. You'll also find selected research findings that make a compelling business case for strategic philanthropy. Finally, use the questions posed in "Food for Thought" to help you select the best strategies for your community investment program.

BENEFIT #1:
Giving Boosts Company Reputation and Brand Visibility

Companies associated with philanthropic activity experience an enhanced reputation with a wide range of stakeholders, including employees, customers, communities, investors, advocacy groups, and government agencies. Nearly 90 percent of companies say they seek to improve their image and reputation.[7] Why not you? Are you looking for ways to get your name out into the community and beyond to improve the your company's visibility?

The Stats

Numerous studies show that strategic giving improves business image and brand.

- 85% of consumers have a more positive image of a product or company when it supports a cause they care about.[8]
- A corporate survey found that 100% of respondents thought employee volunteering improves the company's image.[9]
- During the 1992 Los Angeles riots following the Rodney King case, looters spared all 31 McDonald's in the vandalized area because of the restaurant's positive relationship with the community.[10]
- 84% of corporate executives believe that society expects businesses to take a more active role in environmental, social, and political issues than it did five years ago. 75% believe that corporate philanthropy is one effective way to meet these new expectations.[11]
- 45% of Americans consider corporate community service a key indicator of corporate citizenship.[12]
- More than 53% of Americans see a strong link between reputation and social responsibility.[13]

From the Trenches

BitWise Solutions is a web design and development company with a history of partnering with clients to provide measurable results through digital technology. Co-Founder Ron Brumbarger had this to say about business giving:

"We know we receive brand recognition and good will from our community investments. These are two items that we can't quantify on our balance sheet but which differentiate us from the other players in the marketplace. If we are in a competitive situation with a firm that wants to use a company that has a presence in the local community, we are going to win every time as a result. I think businesses buy based on name recognition; if you can see that the firm you are working with has a lot at stake in their community, then they are probably a better fit, a better corporate citizen, and also probably a better provider of goods and services than the competitor."

—Ron Brumbarger, President & CEO,
BitWise Solutions, Indianapolis, Indiana[14]

Karla Raines of **Corona Insights** especially values the networking available through nonprofit partnerships:

"One of the great things is that every nonprofit we have a chance to work with, has a board of directors that are volunteers as well. By that one relationship with that agency, we are able to meet a whole range of people from a variety of industries and experiences and positions, than we otherwise would meet. To me it is terrific leveraging in terms of establishing networks that could really be mined for further opportunities. We are also able to reconnect with people we may not have seen in a while, in a forum that is very positive. It gives us a chance to keep our company name in front of people in a way that is not a direct sales pitch, which I think is really positive."

—Karla Raines, Principal and CEO,
Corona Insights, Denver, Colorado[15]

Food for Thought

Is one of your business goals to enhance your company's

reputation and brand? Not sure? Consider the following questions.

- How well known is your company? Could strategic community involvement help improve its visibility?
- How is your company or brand perceived? In the community? By customers?
- Do people associate your company with your community involvement? Are you missing opportunities to strengthen your reputation?
- Do you wonder how to differentiate your brand or company from your competitors to existing and potential customers?
- How can you refine your business giving to get your name out into the community and gain more visibility?

BENEFIT #2:
Giving Increases Sales, Customer Loyalty, and Market Share

Increasingly, today's consumers want to buy from companies that are active in communities and are good citizens. "Another benefit to companies is the marketplace loyalty gain," explains David Eisner, former CEO of the **Corporation for National and Community Service**, "because consumers today are more ready to differentiate between products based on companies' social engagement. It builds their loyalty."[16] Nearly 95 percent of companies say they give to improve customer relations, and 50 percent expect donations to improve sales. Why not you?

Companies of all sizes benefit from their work in the community through increased competitiveness and market positioning. Opening new customer doors ultimately increases sales. Some companies, such as UPS, intentionally use their corporate volunteer program to brand themselves and develop new markets.

The Stats

The research is clear: customers favor companies that give back to their communities.

- 88% of Americans say it is acceptable for companies to involve a cause or issue in their marketing, a 33% increase since 1993.[17]
- 41% of Americans say they have bought a product because it was associated with a cause or issue in the last year—doubling since 1993.[18]
- 89% of Americans expect companies to support causes during the holidays.[19]
- 80% of Americans are likely to switch brands, about equal in price and quality, to one that supports a cause.[20] 92% of mothers want to buy a product that supports a cause.[21]
- 75% of men and 84% of women say they consider a company's commitment to social issues when deciding what to buy or where to shop.[22]
- 61% of consumers are more willing to try a new brand or one they've never heard of if it supports a cause.[23]
- 19% of consumers are more willing to buy a *more expensive* brand if it supports a cause.[24]

From the Trenches

Sears, Roebuck offers its wide range of home merchandise, apparel, and automotive products and services through more than 2,400 Sears-branded and affiliated stores in the United States and Canada. These include about 925 full-line and 1,100 specialty stores in America. Yes, Sears is a huge company with many more resources than your company or mine, but check out their inspired idea:

Sears created a partnership with Gilda's Club, a nonprofit providing meeting places where people living with cancer come together for emotional support, social events, and laughter. The retail giant partnered with the nonprofit to promote special ties, scarves, and Levi's 550 jeans. During the promotion, Sears sold 100,000 ties and 30,000 scarves. Sales of 550 jeans increased in-store by 56 percent in Gilda's Club cities as compared to 16 percent in non-Gilda's cities.[25] Your company could do something similar!

A telecommunications company offers another dramatic example of customer loyalty. In that industry the big problem is "churn," a business term for customer turnover. **BetterWorld Telecom** is proud to have a churn of less than one percent. "This is unheard of in the industry," says Matt Bauer, the president and co-founder. "Most companies have to get people into long-term contracts so they stay. Customers are not staying because they want to; it is what they have to do to get a good price. We have proven from a customer loyalty standpoint that our model of sustainability and commitment to nonprofit partners really supports that."[26]

Jennifer Stander, Marketing Director for **Endangered Species Chocolate** in Indianapolis, Indiana, also notices promising trends in customer behavior and loyalty. "We feel very, very grateful that there are so many consumers who are consciously aware of the products they are purchasing," she says, "not only what they are putting in their bodies but the impact of their product purchasing on our environment and our world."[27]

Food for Thought

Is one of your business goals to enhance customer loyalty and increase sales? Not sure? Think about the following questions.

- Are you looking for an added edge to help you retain your existing sales base while attracting new customers?
- Do you seek access to new groups of people who are potential customers?

- How could you use your community involvement to strengthen sales and customer loyalty?
- Which causes and nonprofits could your company support to leverage sales from your key markets?
- What partnership or strategic alliance could you initiate to use cause marketing or a commerce model to boost revenue for both you and the nonprofit?
- Do you share what you do in the community with your current and prospective customers? They want to know that you are a good business citizen.
- For example, do you have a page on your website that describes your community involvement?

Think you're too small for that? Not so! All businesses that give need to get the word out, and multiple ways are best. My website describes my company philanthropy. Check it out at *www.core-thought.com*. You'll see a web page such as this does not have to be elaborate, and you don't have to disclose dollar amounts contributed either.

BENEFIT #3:
Giving Enhances Employee Satisfaction and Productivity

Along with fostering goodwill among consumers and communities, business giving can have a strong positive impact on how companies are viewed by their employees. Employees care as much as consumers about the behavior of the company they work for. Studies show that employees who perceive their companies as philanthropic or community-minded are more motivated, productive, and committed to the companies' overall goals.

Even if your business doesn't create a sexy product or service, employees can still feel proud of their work and the company they work for. It all depends on the quality of your leadership team and organizational values and culture. There are a whole host of human resource policies and procedures your company can consider to address the needs of 21st century employees. Your company's involvement in the community, your approach, and the ways you engage workers in the process can have a significant impact on employee morale, loyalty, motivation, commitment, performance, and productivity.

Community investment activities can:

- create team-building opportunities;
- improve communications and relations between management and workforce;
- generate recognition as a good place to work, an "employer of choice;" and
- enhance employee recruitment and retention.

Employee stress is due in part to the pressure and intensity of workers' daily tasks. In *I Want to Make a Difference,* author Tim Drake suggests that stress partly stems from employees feeling disconnected from the company or work they are performing. Burnout follows. If your employees feel their efforts don't matter or they experience a conflict between their values at work and at home, it is hard for them to stay motivated and productive.[28]

One way your company can develop deep and meaningful emotional connections with your employees is by taking a stand on issues important to them.

The Stats

Employees want to work for companies that invest in their communities. Consider:

- 94% of businesses thought employee volunteering provided a way to help employee morale.[29]
- 79% of employees who are involved with their company's cause programs feel a strong sense of loyalty to their company.[30]

- A company's commitment to social and environmental issues affects 69% of Americans' decisions about where to work.[31]
- 61% of Millennials, people born between 1979 and 2001, feel personally responsible for making a difference in the world.[32]
- 63% of survey respondents found volunteering has had a positive effect on their career.[33]
- Security Benefit Group, in Topeka, Kansas, found that formalizing its volunteer program reduced its turnover from 22% to 7% in five years and boosted income generated per employee from $49,700 to $79,000 three years later.[34]
- 30% of employees involved in workplace volunteering are more likely to want to continue working for their company and help make it successful.[35]
- 44% of companies seek to build employee and/ or leadership capabilities and skills through their philanthropy.[36]

From the Trenches

Aveda™, The Art and Science of Pure Flower and Plant Essences™, was founded in 1978 with the goal of providing beauty industry professionals with high performance, botanically based products that would be better for service providers and their guests, as well as for the planet. Aveda's Mary T'Kach had this to say about the impact of the company's strategic giving on employees:[37]

"I think the biggest benefit to Aveda from our community involvement to date has been internal, with our employees and our network of spas, as they hear the stories about all the things we are doing. It helps with employee recruitment: 'Everybody

wants to work for Aveda.' People are really proud to be employees at Aveda because they know we are doing such great stuff. Employee retention is also great. People see it in their promotion and bonus opportunities. If they are serving the mission of the company, that's recognized as a good thing. So it's a very positive reinforcement."

—Mary T'Kach, Executive Director of Environmental Sustainability, **Aveda**, Blaine, Minnesota[38]

At a local Chamber of Commerce networking event, I spoke with Sharon Hendricks, a small business owner, about her community involvement. Her company is a franchise of **Express Personnel Services**, which provides staffing solutions. She explained to me that she promotes volunteering for the Children's Miracle Network with their job-seeking clients as a way as to strengthen their work skills and employability, as well as to increase the visibility of the company with prospective employers and the community in general.

Food for Thought

Is one of your business goals to improve your company's employee loyalty and productivity? Not sure? Ask yourself the following questions.

- Do you have any challenges hiring, retaining, motivating, or promoting employees?
- Would you like to improve employee productivity or commitment to the company?
- Do need to support ongoing skills development in an affordable way?
- How could you use community involvement as one strategy to address these challenges?
- Do you actively encourage and reward employee volunteering? Offer paid time off, community service

days, or flextime? How could this improve loyalty to your company? Increase skills?

- Do you share your company's community involvement activities with your employees? If they don't know what management or other business units are doing in the community that they may not have had a role in, they can't support it, get involved, or feel proud. Giving back is a great way to build an internal company culture of teamwork and pride—not to mention skills.
- How can you tweak your giving to help increase employee loyalty?

BENEFIT #4:
Giving Attracts Investors and Boosts ROI

Companies committed to being good citizens and supporting communities are increasingly understood to have a greater return on investment (ROI) than the national averages. Are you looking to attract new resources to grow your company? If you are not looking for investors or to sell your company at this time, you may think this does not apply to you. However, strategic business giving will provide you an added edge down the road, so don't be too quick to discount this potential benefit to your company. Start getting your ducks lined up now!

The Stats

Strategic giving translates to higher returns, pure and simple. Check out these findings:

- 59% of Americans consider a company's commitment to social and environmental issues as they decide which stocks or mutual funds to invest in.[39]
- A 2005 study of public firms on *Fortune*'s list of the "100 Best Companies to Work For" examined how well they

rewarded shareholders: between 1998 and 2004, they returned 176%, compared to only 39% for the S&P 500.[40]

- Towers Perrin's 2005 study of 25 firms that excel in stakeholder relationships showed a return of 43% in total shareholder value compared with 19% for the S&P 500.[41]
- Nearly $1 in every $8 professionally invested in the U.S. adheres to socially responsible investing (SRI) practices.[42] SRI takes into account both the investor's financial goals and an investment's impact on society.[43]
- Of the $25.2 trillion in assets under management in the U.S. (according to Thomson Reuters), about $3.07 trillion, or 12.2%, pass the SRI test. Back in 1995, when SRI assets totaled only $639 billion, they made up just 9.1% of total U.S. assets.[44]
- A company's social, ethical, and environmental practices can make or break a brand name and affect share prices.[45]

From the Trenches

"One of the draws for the people that came on board to invest in our company was not just the beautiful products we were selling and the great returns we offer, but also our perpetual giving model where a percentage of our profits goes to support local nonprofits. Our investors liked the fact that by investing in our company, their money also was leveraging support for community groups. We invite our investors to be advisors selecting which nonprofits we will support."

—Maria Simone, CEO, **Signature Accents**,
Scottsdale, Arizona[46]

Food for Thought

Seeking capital to start or grow your business? Not sure? Ask yourself the following questions.

- Looking for investors in your company? If not now, how

about in the future?

- Does your business plan describe your current or planned strategic giving plan involving cash, stock, or other resources? If not, it should! It might be the hook you need to convince investors your company not only has a great product or service but is committed to being a good corporate citizen.
- Could a strategic giving plan add value to your pitch and/or an investor's return? How? Through your reputational capital? Sales generation?
- How could you leverage your philanthropy not only to give back in ways that make a true impact in the community but also to advance your business goals?

The New Giving Paradigm

"Business is where wealth is created in our society. There is no more fundamental institution in our society, in terms of wealth creation and distribution, than the business world. So, we're trying to build an institutional framework that captures that power of the marketplace and puts it into service to the community."

—Mike Hannigan, Founder, **Give Something Back Office Supplies**, Oakland, California[1]

The concept and practice of corporate social responsibility—the belief that companies have an obligation to help maintain the health and well being of the communities in which they do business—has existed in the United States since the early 1950s. Historically business support of the community usually took the form of charitable contributions of money or products and services.

Today, companies of all sizes are fundamentally rethinking their business giving. Pet projects reflecting the personal interests of individual senior executives or activities undertaken as propaganda for the company with little real benefit to society are no longer in the majority. Neither of these ways to engage "realize the opportunities for significant shared value creation that have been achieved through smart partnering," according to Keys et al. in the December 2009 *McKinsey Quarterly*.[2] "In such ventures, the focus of business moves beyond avoiding risks or enhancing reputation and towards improving its core value creation ability by addressing major strategic issues or challenges. For society, the focus shifts from maintaining minimum standards or seeking funding to improving employment, the overall quality of life, and living standards. The key is to tap into the resources and expertise of the other, finding creative solutions to critical social and businesses challenges."[3]

The old days of "checkbook philanthropy" based on an "alms for the poor" mentality are coming to a close. A new giving paradigm is emerging, one based on partnership between business and the social sector, not paternalism.

This section explores what this new model looks like and how it can benefit your business and maximize the good you do in your community.

Over the past two decades, a growing number of business leaders have come to view corporate social responsibility as not only "the right thing to do" but a key business imperative which, if done strategically, will generate a "win-win-win" situation for any company, its employees, and the community.

James Austin, in his book *The Collaboration Challenge,* describes the shifting relationship between business and nonprofits as a "collaboration continuum."[4] On one end are philanthropic activities characterized by the "gratefulness and charity syndromes"—the old school of business giving. These are characterized by minimal interaction or collaboration in defining activities and an unequal exchange of resources. Next are project-based "transactional relationships" based on a greater sense of partnership, shared vision, an overlap in mission and values, as well as a more equal exchange of resources and shared competencies. At the far end of the continuum are "integrated alliances," defined by a sense of "we" instead of "us versus them." Such partnerships include joint-benefit projects with shared equity investment that engage all levels of both organizations.

Today's trends in business giving stem from the growing desire among business leaders to visibly experience *and* benefit from the efforts of their support to causes.

One trend is the shift from passive support to more active involvement by the company and its employees. Business people increasingly want to be able to directly see the fruits of their labor. It is no longer satisfying enough for many to just write a check either directly to a nonprofit or to an intermediary like United Way. People want to know how their contributions were used or what difference their support made on the specific cause they care about. In response to recent trends, United Way Worldwide has modified their mission to incorporate changes in their volunteer mechanism and how they obtain donations. The new mission focuses on improving lives in three key areas by mobilizing the power of communities to advance good.

Another trend is toward more strategic giving as opposed to using a "shotgun approach." Companies of all sizes receive requests for support from many worthy nonprofits and community organizations, such as schools, every week—sometimes daily. It is easy to feel bombarded and chagrined that you can't provide assistance to the many deserving organizations that approach you. The challenge is how to choose which causes and organizations to support based on criteria that make sense for your company and its core values and competencies.

In a related trend, community investment goes beyond the individual interests of senior management or one "super volunteer" staff member to focus on strategic business interests. The company's philanthropy merges the desire to give back with the goals and directions of the business itself. Part of this trend is a greater focus on impact or ROI for both organizations.

Another new approach sees companies integrating their social responsibility and community giving into company and/or product branding. An example is (PRODUCT)RED, the effort initiated by Bono in which companies like Dell, American Express, and the Gap develop specific products for which a percentage is donated to support HIV/AIDS education and treatment in Africa.

Also gaining ground are voluntary reporting of social accountability and disclosure of community investments on company websites. In the U.S. such reporting is not mandatory, but there is increasing peer pressure on companies to engage in such transparency.

David Eisner is the former CEO of the **Corporation for National and Community Service**, the federal agency that engages more than five million Americans in service through Senior Corps, AmeriCorps, and Learn and Serve America. David explained another trend to me. "I am particularly fascinated by innovation gains [from philanthropy]. Organizations, like IBM, are using their philanthropy and employee engagement as tools to get their employees closer to their customers and to be thinking innovatively about overcoming obstacles and becoming more culturally aligned. Innovation is increasingly critical for competitive success. Philanthropy enables employees to be closer to their marketplace."[5] He feels this has always been true for smaller companies in local communities. Witness how effectively they have supported local sports teams, for example, as a way of locking in market loyalty, building employee morale, and increasing productivity.

Today, however, American society is moving away from traditional extracurricular or non-work activity (such as bowling leagues, glee clubs, Rotary, etc.) into a space that's more about our connectedness as a community. "That's the next frontier for our small businesses," David believes. "They have to figure out how to be the foundations for community connection in our communities."

Changing cultural forces also shape business giving models. In *Firms of Endearment*, published by the Wharton School, Raj Sisodia et al. describe three cultural eras in American history that have impacted commerce and the way companies operate.

First was the "Age of Empowerment," based on the notions of a free society and free markets that followed the signing of the Declaration of Independence and the publication of Adam Smith's *The Wealth of Nations,* both in 1776. "Joined at the hip, democracy and capitalism marched into the future to bring forth a whole new world," the authors write. "For the first time in history, ordinary people were empowered by codified law to shape their own destinies.... A free market economy aided their efforts."[6]

Next came the "Age of Knowledge," which transitioned the United States from an agrarian to an industrialized society. During this time, there was a focus on productivity—getting more from less. Society saw increases in quality of life and material well being, as well as decreases in the cost of living. The preoccupation with productivity and cost cutting to improve bottom lines, while initially positive for many, later took a toll on workers and their families, communities, and the environment. Corporate flight in search of lower labor and other operating costs pushed many local communities into crisis. The pro-business justification for this trend was that "to reap the benefits of capitalism, society must tolerate the pain it sometimes causes people on the lower rungs of society." However, growing numbers of citizens now wonder whether such pain is acceptable. Many people have come to view "commerce as lacking a human heart. They feel most companies see them as just numbers to be controlled, manipulated, and exploited."[7]

The third era is described as the "Age of Transcendence." In it people increasingly search for higher meaning in their lives, not just material possessions. This new age, the authors say, is being driven by the cultural evolution resulting from an aging population and scientific and technological developments.

Gregg Easterbrook, *New Republic* senior editor, makes a similar point: "A transition from material want to meaning want is in progress on a historically unprecedented scale—involving hundreds of millions of people—and may eventually be recognized as the principal cultural development of our age."[8] These transformations fundamentally alter both the marketplace and workplace as people rethink the ways businesses operate, not just to make profits but also to provide social value.

Other 21st century trends play a significant role in changing the marketplace. For one, services now make up about 80 percent of Gross Domestic Product (GDP) in most developed countries, far outweighing either agriculture or manufacturing. Also, as *New York Times* columnist Thomas Friedman asserted, the "world is flat," as evidenced by developing country companies rapidly gaining market share due to globalization, the rise of the internet, lower wages, and a host of other factors.

Given the convergence of these trends and the need to stay competitive in today's marketplace, the old rules of how business "should" operate are in flux, including the role of business in society. While some businesses still operate by the old "profit at all costs" paradigm, pressures are increasing for all companies to rethink the fundamental values built into their mission, design, operating policies and procedures, and products and services. The 2006 GolinHarris corporate citizenship survey found that an overwhelming two-thirds of Americans interviewed said:

- "doing well by doing good" is a savvy business strategy. Good corporate citizenship should be approached as an investment, asset, and competitive advantage for business that contributes to the company's success;
- business should invest significantly more money, time, attention, and resources in corporate citizenship than it does today; and
- corporate citizenship should be considered an essential, high priority compared to other priorities companies face and manage in running a profitable, competitive and

successful business.[9]

Studies show such practices are *good for business,* too. Much of the existing research on the connection between social responsibility and profitability has focused on the big dogs—the Fortune 500. While the exact numbers vary depending on the studies and companies included, the evidence is overwhelming: companies using a stakeholder model (focus on employees, community, vendors) outperform those stuck in a shareholder mentality (focus on profit and the bottom line) by anywhere from 25 percent to 700 percent. *Translation: socially responsible companies made lots of money because they invested the time and resources to set up more humane, values-based business systems.*

In his book *Giving,* Bill Clinton asserts we can "create real opportunities for each of us to be more effective givers of our time and money by simply changing our buying habits as ordinary consumers. When we support companies that do good things, the increased demand will cause other companies to follow suit."[10]

My belief is that we all are fortunate to be living in transformational times. In many ways, the current approach to transformation is much quieter than in the past. Patricia Aburdene, author of *Megatrends 2010,* talks about the rising interest in and commitment to personal and spiritual development that is beginning to spill over from personal life into the business world. These forces, or "megatrends," are shaping more enlightened approaches to how we do business. She calls it conscious capitalism.[11]

Listening to Patricia Aburdene speak at Mile Hi Church in Lakewood, Colorado, I was struck by the audience's response to her words. They were hungry for her insights. The author helped people better understand the changes they had been experiencing but couldn't put their finger on. The small business owners present also wanted to know how they could take action to operate their companies from an even higher place of integrity and consciousness.

The quiet growing mass of people Paul Hawken identified in his bestselling book *Blessed Unrest* are changing their expectations of and actions in everyday life.[12] Not only are these people in your family or neighborhood, they are your employees and customers. They—we—want more meaning and connection in our lives. As an entrepreneur, small business owner, or corporate executive, you want to make a difference while ensuring your business thrives. The new business giving paradigm can help you do both.

To summarize, the emerging model favored by forward-thinking companies replaces "checkbook philanthropy" with strategic, all-win partnerships. This "new school" of business giving includes:

- moving beyond a "cash cow" mentality to bring the full value of a company's expertise, assets, and connections to bear on critical social issues;
- linking giving to strategic business goals while authentically supporting causes that matter to you;
- two-way exchange of assets between businesses and nonprofits;
- deeper involvement with fewer nonprofit partners to maximize community impact;
- upgrading from passive to more active hands-on involvement with community partners;
- emphasizing greater ROI and impact on both the community and the company;
- integrating social responsibility into company and/or product branding; and
- voluntary social accountability reporting and disclosure of community investment on company websites and other media.

What do successful companies that practice strategic giving look like? Let's turn to the next section to find out.

The Continuum of Community Involvement

As we have seen, business philanthropy ranges from shotgun charity with little interaction with the nonprofit to strategic win-win partnerships that foster deep relationships that create significant and lasting good. In a category of their own are what I call Vision Quest companies, is a different "species" of business designed to fully embody conscious capitalism. As the level of relationship and degree of strategy increase, the number of companies involved decreases. Figure 3 illustrates this spectrum.

Figure 3. The Continuum of Community Involvement

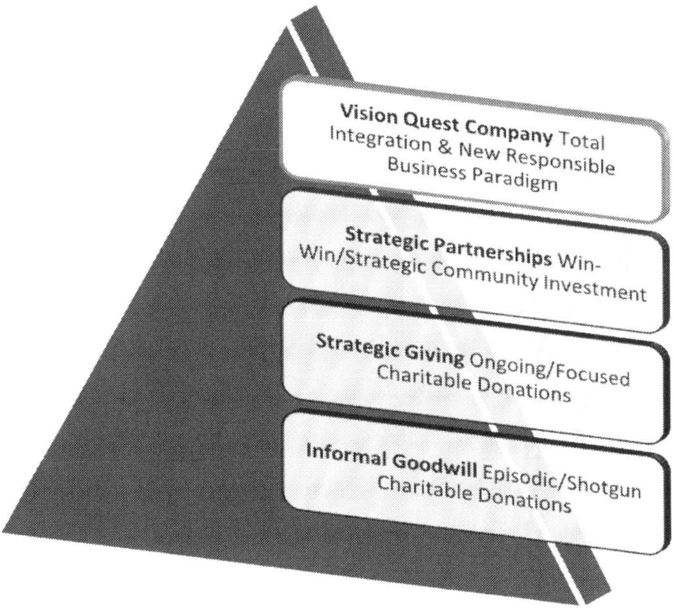

Companies engaged in **Informal Goodwill** support the community with a mindset of giving back to "help those less fortunate." Informal charity companies tend to donate money, time, and goods/services to nonprofits sporadically, often on a first come, first-served basis or based on personal connections and interests of the owner(s) and/or employees. These companies give back because they feel it is the right thing to do and have minimal expectations of a business return beyond being considered a contributing member of the community. In *Saving the Corporate Soul—and (Who Knows?) Maybe Your Own,* David Batstone writes, "charitable giving...ought to be treated as a baby step in a company's community engagement. Yes, philanthropy provides valuable funding for nonprofit groups that are attending to social needs. On its own, however, charity does not make a company a player in a community network."[1]

Strategic Giving companies support causes and communities through intentional selection and activities designed to allow them to achieve business goals while being active in the community. These companies believe they have an ethical responsibility to actively support the people and communities in which they do business. Strategic Givers select causes and organizations to support through donations of time, talent, and treasures that are in alignment with business goals and for whom they can add value. They often support co-sponsored activities or programs generally on a one-time or short-term basis. Strategic Givers are especially focused on the reputational and marketing benefits, as well as selling more goods and services. These companies are seeking to "do well by doing good."

Strategic Partnership companies use a strategic approach to community involvement to publicly demonstrate what they stand for, while improving their bottom line. These companies choose a multi-pronged, multi-layered approach engaging the resources of their various business units with a few select causes to maximize impact for the nonprofit partner(s) and the company itself. Such companies "adopt" a specific cause or organization with which to have a deep relationship. They creatively pull out all the stops to apply the full range of expertise and resources that are within their comparative advantage to make a focused impact in the community. Strategic Partnership companies often are involved in the community as part of a larger commitment to operating according to the principles of corporate social responsibility. They have cranked their community investment up 10 notches to maximize impact using the win-win model.

Vision Quest companies are designed by progressive owners from their initial conception to be not only profitable but also provide high quality socially responsible goods/services competitive in the marketplace. Through intentional development of a new paradigm and a model for business operations, ethical, environmental, and social concerns are tightly woven into the company's foundation and overall fabric and inform all business structures and practices. Community involvement is a core component of business operations and is so integral to company culture and branding that it can't be teased out; it is not an add-on. Vision Quest companies are rewriting the rules of business and working to show that new models can be very profitable and also do good for people and the planet. Vision Quest companies are changing the world and how it works by blazing new trails.

We are at a crossroads in the business world. The "profit at any cost" approach no longer flies, even among many shareholders. After the numerous corporate scandals in the U.S. came to light, affecting thousands of people as investors, employees, and consumers, public opinion of corporate America and business in general has taken a serious hit. Everyone wants a great return on investment. However, many no longer feel comfortable with a sky-high rate of return if quality has been compromised, people mistreated, or the environment pillaged. While the bottom line is what keeps any company in business, increasingly profit is viewed as only one measure of success. Also important are two additional bottom lines of people and the planet.

We have reached the tipping point concerning ethical business practices and community investment—there is no going back. Just as the motorized car replaced the horse and buggy, socially responsible business is overtaking the short-term profit at any costs driver. Instead of the old question—"Should we be doing this?"—we're asking new questions: "How do we operate as a socially responsible business?" "What are our options?" "How do we make business giving an all-win activity?" "How do we create our own Strategy for Good?"

As you read this section, consider which category best describes your company's giving right now. Where would you like it to be? For the answers, let's turn to Part II: Developing Your Strategy for Good.

Part II: *Developing Your Strategy for Good*

"I am a firm believer in the power of business. Business is the strongest, fastest change agent that we have. Businesses need to become more sustainable and create donations to support their local communities—not just their economies. Everybody's got to start working together across the lines to really spike this up as opposed to everybody just doing their own thing."

—Matt Bauer, President and Co-Founder,
BetterWorld Telecom, Reston, Virginia[1]

Getting into Partnership

Whether you are just starting your business giving program, regularly donating products or funds, or already partnering with local nonprofits, bravo! Wherever you may be at this time, give yourself a pat on the back. Doing something for the community is always better than doing nothing.

That said, there are proven practices that strengthen business giving to make an even greater difference. It all starts with a mindset of partnership.

Although a vehicle for generosity, the old school of business philanthropy was based on an "alms for the poor" mentality. It fostered paternalism, not true partnership. Today, more and more companies seek to collaborate as equals with community organizations. "We want nonprofits to look at us as a partner," explains Jessica Newman, formerly with the **Rock Bottom Foundation**, "not just as someone who is there to give to them, but to really engage with them in the things that they do."[1]

Businesses and nonprofit organizations have a common interest in working together and have much to learn from each other. For example, commercial partners can teach the social sector how to:

- create incentives for higher performance
- increase organizational competitiveness
- be "customer-driven," that is, meet the needs of clients, not just the organization
- focus on results and outcomes instead of just inputs
- think creatively about generating revenues, not just spending them

- leverage change rather than attempting to control it[2]

Likewise, business can learn important lessons from nonprofits. Says Mike Hannigan of **Give Something Back Office Supplies**, "Don't second guess the nonprofit and minimize the expertise those folks bring to the table."[3] Skills that effective nonprofits can teach business include how to:

- make decisions based on mission rather than solely on profit
- strategize ways to hold the CEO accountable to the board of directors
- be a more attractive employer by inspiring staff productivity and commitment
- engage with diverse stakeholders such as employees, board members, clients, and communities and their various interests

Consider the following example of an effective partnership between The Home Depot, home improvement specialty retailer, and KaBOOM!, the nonprofit dedicated to constructing innovative, kid-inspired playspaces, using a community-build model that improves the well-being of children and the neighborhoods they live in. Working together to build playgrounds has generated benefits for both organizations. For KaBOOM!, the partnership with The Home Depot has helped them access needed building supplies, volunteers skilled in construction, funding, pro bono services, and introductions to other prospective funders. For The Home Depot, partnering with KaBOOM! has helped the company build stronger community relationships and provided significant opportunities for team-building among their employees.[4]

Maggie's Functional Organics is a company that produces products in partnership with women worker cooperatives in Nicaragua. Founder Benà Burda recommends that companies keep an open mind when working in local communities. She believes strongly that while there may be many people in need who don't have the material wealth Americans take for granted, there is "incredible talent, incredible gifts that so many of these people have." She finds it exciting that once barriers are removed and businesses, nonprofit organizations, and local people start working together, everyone learns from each other. "Providing a vehicle is very exciting," she says. "You have to open yourself up to whatever ideas, talents, or creativity they are going to bring to the table."[5]

The following pages take you step by step through the process of creating win-win partnerships with nonprofits and developing your own powerful Strategy for Good.

The Seven Steps of Strategic Business Giving

There are seven essential steps in strategic business giving. Whether you are planning smaller-scale initial actions or a thorough multipronged community investment program, following these steps will improve your impact. Your efforts can result in so much more good with a little focus, intention, and planning. Resources are too tight not to be strategic!

The following pages cover the basic process necessary for effective community investment, but if your flow is different, that's fine. However, remember that each step is essential. Carefully considering each will help you strengthen your giving and improve the impact for both your nonprofit partners and your company. Even one small change to make your community investment more strategic can dramatically enhance the success for all involved.

If you would like help on how to focus your energy and identify areas for upgrading, visit my website to take a complementary self-assessment: *www.StrategyforGood.com.*

In a nutshell, here are the seven steps to strategic business giving:

Step 1: Build commitment within your company
Step 2: Review past community involvement
Step 3: Take inventory of goals and resources
Step 4: Select causes, partners, and projects
Step 5: Grow win-win relationships
Step 6: Measure success
Step 7: Share your story

Step 1: Build Commitment Within Your Company

"The key is not simply to show business people that corporate engagement can be financially rewarding...but that it does so in strategically important areas of business performance."

—John Weiser and Simon Zadek,
Authors of *Conversations with Disbelievers*[1]

The first two questions entrepreneurs, business owners, senior managers, and board members usually ask about business giving are "Why are we doing this?" and "What are we going to get out of it?" The quick and dirty answer to both is that business giving done strategically can absolutely help a company meet its goals and improve performance while making a heartfelt difference in the community.

One of my favorite books on the case for corporate citizenship is John Weiser and Simon Zadek's *Conversations with Disbelievers,* quoted above. To understand what would be persuasive to skeptical managers, the authors studied over one hundred businesses that had increased their community involvement activities. While they found a wide range of company-specific reasons, three general drivers of community involvement stood out.

First was the need to respond to external pressures such as regulation or advocacy groups. Second was a desire to express the core values of the company. Third was using community involvement to support or enhance a key long-term business strategy.[2]

Their findings show that for these business leaders, community involvement was not just a "nice to do" but a "need to do" as part of a broader strategy to be competitive in today's marketplace and improve their bottom line.

In the push to show quarterly profits for shareholders, business leaders often feel torn between their desire to give back and the need to provide a significant return for their shareholders or investors. However, the notion that these are competing interests is a myth. If business giving lost companies money, the case would be clear. In fact, the opposite is true.

As Part I revealed, authoritative research proves that financial performance flourishes when a company's community investment and other aspects of corporate citizenship are actively taken into account and implemented. Business giving is one important indicator of a people-centric corporate culture and a hallmark of overall good management and business practices.

Tracy Ulmer of *The Denver Post* attests that community involvement "really does add to the bottom line, if that is a concern. It relates to relationship and trust building with key customers and people they are trying to work with. It does matter to people. With some strategic focus and some thought put behind how they are investing their resources, the impact is just huge for what you put into it. That's been proven time and time again with the number of different companies who are doing it."[3]

Your business giving strategy has to come from both the top and the bottom, with buy-in and support from senior management as well as from employees. If company leaders are gung ho but employees are not (or vice versa), things can get dicey fast. To be truly successful, your community investment has to be understood and appreciated throughout the company in order to be part of your corporate culture and values. You also need an internal champion who has the respect of both management and employees, and enough clout to make your community investment program happen.

We all know from firsthand experience that projects fail or succeed depending on the buy-in from various stakeholders within the company. Of course, buy-in isn't about manipulating others to get our way. Instead, it is about the process of guiding a group of people to genuinely say yes to an idea, a plan, a step, or a project. It's about getting the green light—the agreement of everyone involved to spend the necessary time and resources either to do further investigation or to move forward with a plan.

The buy-in process encourages people to articulate their view of company needs, points of pain, values, drivers, and desires for making a difference in the community. Knowing this will help you identify how strategic community investment can help meet those needs, resolve their conflicts, coincide with their values, and help them in their quest to achieve identified goals.

Meet with your stakeholders to share information and brainstorm. Questions to ask during this dialogue include:

1. What do we as a company want to achieve through a more strategic approach to our community involvement? What are our most pressing business goals? How can we do double duty—that is, do real good in the community and have a positive impact on the company as well?
2. What are our key competitors doing in community investment? What leverage has it given them? What can we learn from their efforts?
3. What will happen if we *don't* engage in community investment? What are the potential negative impacts on our reputation in the community? Among our customers and employees? On sales?
4. What suggestions do each of us have to ensure that this effort is as successful as possible? How can each of us help?

If your various stakeholders aren't committed or convinced, you will likely see symptoms of dissatisfaction later: changes in scope, miscommunication, employee problems, and more. Just as in selling a product to someone who isn't convinced of its value, you run the risk of that person rejecting the product later.

My clients have found that sharing research findings on the benefits of community investment with the people that need to be involved is helpful. The findings provide food for thought and offer people a glimpse of new possibilities for their company. Pulling together information to share about industry competitors' CSR or community investment also helps make the case for your involvement. To download a handout on business benefits and research results to help you make your case for community investment, go to *www.StrategyforGood.com*.

Once you have all needed parties on board—management, employees, other key people—it's full steam ahead. However, remember not to put the cart before the horse. Be sure you take care of business first.

When to Start

"I think getting involved [with nonprofits] is like working out. It's always hard to go that first time, but once you get started and begin to feel the benefits of regular participation, you can't imagine how you lived without it. I hear very often: 'I'm too busy to volunteer,' 'I don't have the time,' 'I wish I had the time to do it.' Really, these are just excuses. If it's important to you, you'll make the time to do it. And once you make the time and see the rewards, it will become a part of your life."

—Mark Berzins, Owner, **Little Pub Company,**
Denver, Colorado[4]

The best time to begin thinking about how to engage with

your community is when you initially design your business. You do not need to be an established, profitable company to either start or increase your involvement with nonprofits and other community organizations. Starting your business giving activities early allows you to build community investment into your organizational values, culture, and operations so you don't have to "turn the Titanic" later.

Take entrepreneur Judith O'Neill, who founded her business, **Landscapes Within**, after burning out as a hospice worker and experiencing the death of her father, who suffered from Alzheimer's. Her desire to take beautiful, artistic photographs quickly grew into a vision of creating a national greeting card company. Judith and her employees did well by doing good from the start, donating generously to organizations that support Alzheimer's research. From the beginning the artist knew, "I would not be satisfied with just having my financial needs met. Giving back is actually going to be more fun for me—not just a 'should.' I am excited about being able to see the business supporting something I have a deep passion for."[5]

However, if setting up a community investment program was not on your radar during start-up due to the crunch of getting your business up and running, don't despair. It is never too late. Take a baby step now, get some experience, figure out what works for your company, and keep moving forward. If you have been doing unfocused checkbook giving until now—bravo for caring and doing something—think about what comes next. How can you do something that invests your company at a deeper level and makes a bigger impact?

No matter the size, age, or profitability of your company, you can make a positive difference in your community. Always remember, the efforts of one person or a small group do matter—even more so if you choose to work with an up-and-coming nonprofit. Newer organizations really need partners as they do not already have a plethora of existing business supporters. When working with a huge nonprofit like the American Red Cross or the American Cancer Society, it is easy to feel like one small drop in the ocean as your relative contribution is small and harder to see directly.

Another option is to pool your company's resources with others to jointly work on community projects either informally or through organizations designed to promote such efforts, like Social Venture Partners (SVP). Social Venture Partners International is a nonprofit network of engaged philanthropists, with over 25 local SVP organizations and 200-plus partners internationally. Collectively, since 1997, SVPs have contributed $36 million in grants to more than 397 nonprofit organizations and countless hours of strategic volunteering. I am a partner in the Denver SVP, and Social Venture Partners International is one of the nonprofit beneficiaries and partners for this book. (For more information on SVPi, see the Appendix.)

Remember Margaret Mead's words: "Never doubt that a small group of thoughtful, committed citizens can change the world. Indeed, it is the only thing that ever has." So go for it!

Take Care of Business First

Be mindful to balance your social goals with the need to build a solid base for your enterprise. If you don't, chances are you won't be in business long enough to make the difference you desire!

Mike Hannigan is the founder of **Give Something Back Office Supplies**, a for-benefit company that donates 100 percent of profits to the social sector. To people interested in his business model because of the community good it can do, Mike says, "Don't even think about it unless you really understand whatever business you plan on getting into. When you are competing every day with Office Depot and Staples, you are not going to win if you just have a 'feel good' idea. You are only going to win if you understand how your competitors are competing with you and how to run a successful business in that particular space. People who are socially oriented and see the power of the marketplace also need to understand how to control the marketplace. They need specific business skills in order to be successful in business. The nonprofit part of it is not enough by any stretch of the imagination."[6]

Mike believes his company's success is largely due to the fact that they have 14 years' experience running a solid business in a very competitive marketplace. He knows that if they hadn't focused on first things first—the essentials of running a business—the company "would have been taken out by our competitors for being incompetent and inept. Your competitors aren't going to care anything about your social goals. They are going to take you out by giving your customers better value for their dollars." So remember, focusing primarily on the social goal is not enough. Attend to business basics first.

Matt Bauer, **BetterWorld Telecom's** President and Co-Founder, agrees. "After all, we are a business. We have to spend an inordinate amount of time paying attention to the business because telecom is a difficult service to do effectively and bring to customers. I'd love to spend all my time donating money and working in these organizations, creating new paradigms and ways business can push things forward. But we are not there yet. We are doing as much as we can with what we have."[7]

Seth Goldman, Founder of **Honest Tea**, also believes a business needs to stay focused on its bottom line while doing good. He said during our interview that when Honest Tea first started, it had "a little bit of a mixed personality because we were trying to achieve some nonprofit ends through for-profit means. Even internally, we sometimes faced the question of which is more important, the mission or the bottom line. Where we usually came down to was, we have to make sure that there *is* a bottom line, and if there is, we can achieve great things. But we have to make sure we're really growing as an enterprise."[8]

Step 1 Action Plan:

- Hold brainstorming sessions with key stakeholders to get buy-in and solicit ideas.
- Develop the business case for community investment within your company.
- Research the community investment programs of other companies in your industry.
- Identify community investment champions within your company.
- Get commitment to move forward.
- Identify next steps and who will be involved and in what capacity.

Step 2: Review Past Community Involvement

"For most senior managers, the first query—Why are we doing this?—is surpassed in importance by a second query—What are we going to get out of this? Every project that hopes to be sustainable in the future will need to calculate a return."

—David Batstone, Author of *Saving the Corporate Soul & (Who Knows) Maybe Your Own*[1]

The second step in strategic business giving is to review your company's past and current community involvement. You need to look back to move forward so you can assess the return and effectiveness of your efforts.

It's important to take the time to pause and reflect on two things. First, what resources did you contribute in the past, to whom, and why? Second, what difference did your efforts *really* make—for the community and your company?

The answers to these questions give you critical baseline data to understand where you are now. You can use that information in your decision-making going forward. When you know your starting point, the positive results of the enhancements you make as a result of reading this book will be easier to see.

This step is sometimes called a "community involvement audit." However, many of my clients have a negative reaction to that term, for it conjures up visions of stern IRS agents poring over company financials. I prefer to think of this step as an exercise in self-exploration. You are simply determining what has worked so far, so you can do more of the same while letting go of actions that haven't paid off.

Track and Value Your Community Involvement

All companies need to set up internal systems that both track and calculate the value of their giving and community investment. There are two main areas here to consider. First, what was your company's total annual contribution including cash, in-kind donations, the value of employee volunteering, and other support? Second, what impact or return on investment (ROI) did you leverage for nonprofits and their beneficiaries as well as your company?

Do you have such tracking systems in place? Are you able to report to key stakeholders internal and external to your company the big picture value you contributed for social impact? If you are currently missing some of this information, this step will help you refine your tracking system to make more strategic decisions.

Due to accounting systems and banking records, dollars donated to nonprofits are usually the easiest contribution to track for most companies. If donations from customers and employees have been tracked and logged within your financial management and/or sales systems, they are relatively easy to aggregate as well. If you collect spare change or tap petty cash, you need to be sure to create receipts for your record keeping.

Hopefully you also keep accurate records of the in-kind products and services that you provide. If not, you can estimate. When giving in-kind donations, your company should always give the nonprofit some form of documentation stating the value of your donation. Not only does this help you value your contributions and tax write-offs, it is data your nonprofit partners need for grants, as they often must specify the value of in-kind donations received in their proposals.

Do you track employee volunteer hours, either on company

time or after hours, because it was encouraged by your company? If not, you should—especially if done on company time, even if it is not tax deductible. Employee volunteering is a very important component of your overall contribution to the community. I always recommend companies value that time and include it as part of annual community investment reporting.

Some companies, like **Motorola**, however, choose not to include their employee volunteer time valuation in their annual contribution figures. Eileen Sweeney, Director of Corporate and Foundation Philanthropic Relations, explained that the Motorola Foundation decided that their other philanthropic numbers from cash and in-kind donations are very strong on their own. So although employees do engage in volunteerism, Motorola chooses not to report the value of those hours.

Macy's, on the other hand, does calculate the value of employee volunteering and adds that figure to the aggregate value of their community investment portfolio. When I visited the Macy's website after seeing a newspaper ad citing $17 million donated through community investment, I was surprised to see not that figure but over $70 million! Collectively, contributions from Macy's, Bloomingdale's, the Macy's Foundation, and the Bloomingdale's Fund of the Macy's Foundation—as well as customer and employee contributions through targeted giving campaigns—was more than $71.2 million in 2009.[2]

Turns out those website numbers include the value of employee volunteer hours. Macy's encourages all its employees to be active volunteers through the company's Partners in Time program. In 2009, Macy's reported that over 28,000 participants joined 1,300 Partners in Time and other give-back projects throughout the U.S. providing over 100,000 hours of service. Since Partners in Time was founded in Atlanta in 1989, Macy's reports that thousands of associates, family, and friends from Macy's, Bloomingdale's stores, and business support functions nationwide have given about 1.8 million hours of service valued at nearly $30 million.[3]

Unclear how to value your employees' volunteering? Here are two basic figures to use based on the type of volunteer service provided.

The dollar value of general, hands-on volunteer tasks such as painting or trash cleanup was estimated to be $20.85 per hour in 2009.[4] This figure is updated annually by Independent Sector, a nonprofit that researches giving and volunteerism in the U.S.

Skilled pro bono services were given a rounded average of $120 per hour by the Taproot Foundation, a nonprofit that connects business talent with charitable organizations, in collaboration with the Committee Encouraging Corporate Philanthropy (CECP). CECP was created after Paul Newman approached John Whitehead and Peter Malkin to encourage companies to commit greater resources to charitable investments. Pro bono services include marketing/advertising/PR, accounting/financial, architecture/engineering/construction, strategic consulting /HR/ IT/ organizational design, and legal/medical.[5]

If you are looking for something more specific, the Bureau of Labor Statistics provides hourly wages by occupation that can be used to determine the value of a specialized skill if you do not already have established rates, especially for certain types of internal business services your people may be providing.[6] Independent Sector also calculates the average value of a volunteer hour by state.[7]

It is important to remember that when a doctor, lawyer, craftsman, or anyone with a specialized skill volunteers, the value of his or her time is based on the type of volunteer work, not his or her earning power. In other words, volunteers must be performing their special skill as volunteer work to value it at the professional rate. If a doctor is painting a fence or a lawyer is sorting groceries, he or she is not volunteering his or her specialized skill so the time would be valued at the lower, general rate.

How much money did you directly contribute to nonprofits through grants or other cash awards? What was the total value of the in-kind gifts you donated? How many hours did you or your employees volunteer for organizations on behalf of your company? How much of your volunteering was general versus pro bono? What was the total estimated value of your employee volunteering contribution last year using the provided dollar figures?

Calculate Total Annual Community Investment

Using information from your last fiscal year, calculate your total community investment. It might be informative to do this for the past three to five years.

The list below identifies six things to do to get a clear picture of your company's total community investment. Table 1 shows a handy way to compile the information. For a downloadable template of the table, go to *www.StrategyforGood.com.*

1. Make a list of all the nonprofit or community organizations your company supported in some way.
2. For each organization, note the specialty, cause, or type of service they provide and why you chose to support them. Was there a strategic link? Could there be?
3. Summarize the types of support you provided to each organization. Did you provide cash, in-kind donations, employee volunteer time, or some other contribution? Any trends in your general approach?
4. Calculate the dollar value for each type of support listed. Cash is the easiest to determine, if you have receipts. For in-kind donations, provide a reasonable estimate. For volunteer time, use the most recent figure from

Independent Sector. In 2009, general volunteering was valued at $20.85/hour. Specialized pro bono services were valued at an average $120/hour.

5. Total the value of all the resources you contributed to each nonprofit supported. You might also want to note other forms of support you provided including expenditures from your operational budget (such as vendor service contracts, etc.) as well as benefits accrued by both organizations.
6. Calculate all nonprofits supported for a grand total.

Table 1. Sample of Nonprofit Contribution Calculation

Name of Nonprofit	Type of Contribution	Estimated Value	Benefits to Company/ Nonprofit
Junior Achievement *Financial Education*	1. Employee General Volunteer Hours (20 @ 10hrs/each) 2. Operating Grant 3. Office Supplies Also: Paid Ad	1. 200 hrs @ $20.85 = $4,170 2. $25,000 3. $2,000 TOTAL = $31,170 Ad = $300	Company: • Improved employee morale and teamwork • Visibility among families with children and the community at large Nonprofit: • Able to offer program to more students (classrooms and schools) • Helped purchase program materials, conserve scarce $$

How does the dollar figure of your total contributions look? Are you pleased with what you found out? If you had trouble completing this exercise, you may want to consider a better method of tracking such information from this point forward.

Now, calculate your total giving as a percentage of your company's overall financial pie. To do that, divide your total contribution by your pre-tax profit. For example, using the data from the table above: $31,170 (contributed) ÷ $1,000,000 (pre-tax profit) = .031 x 100 = 3.1%. Note: some companies calculate their giving percentage using gross revenue, sales, or net profit. It's your choice. Take a look at what others in your industry are using before you make your choice. When reporting, just be sure to reference which figure you used.

Now, I bet you are wondering, *how does my number compare to what other companies contribute?* There is no easy answer to this question, but if you are in the 1 to 10 percent range you are doing very well. We will look more closely at targets for business giving in the next step.

Assess Impact

Another part of looking backwards to go forwards focuses on how things worked and what difference you made. Do you have tools or systems in place to collect impact information from your nonprofit partners or to gauge the impact of community investment on your company goals? If not, you may not have a lot of details here.

Don't be shy about asking your nonprofit partners what difference your support and involvement made for them. Measurement of social and company impact is critical to your Strategy for Good and is covered in greater depth in Step 6.

For now, to get a sense of whether your time and resources were well spent, consider the following questions.

1. What benefit were we hoping for? Did it materialize? If not, why not?
2. What benefit did our support leverage for the community? The specific nonprofit organizations? For our company?
3. Were our community involvement efforts consciously linked to any of our business goals last year?
4. What lessons have we learned about our giving and its impacts? What do we want to be sure to do again? What do we want to change?

Partnerships or initiatives that worked well may be the ones you want to continue. For those that were only minimally successful, you will either need to make some changes to ensure greater success next time or discontinue them ASAP! Time and resources are too scarce to limp along.

If a specific partnership or project experienced issues and you are strongly committed to the cause or organization, you can choose to provide additional support to help build your nonprofit partner's organizational capacity. You could also revisit your company's role in the unsuccessful partnership to create a better chance for a positive ROI the next time around.

You should also ask yourself about the quality of interaction between your company and nonprofit partner. Was the partner timely, communicative, and professional? Did they deliver what they agreed to? Did you? Were they appreciative and recognized your input(s)? How was dealing with their staff and volunteers? Were they committed to not only getting their needs met, but also ensuring your company experienced value?

What looks like a great partnership in theory may not be worth your support if it requires a high level of energy or has a minimal return. In the end, if the relationship headache outweighs the positive benefit, it's time to reconsider. Be thinking how to create better ground rules for communication and interaction the next time around, if you experienced issues.

Having completed this step, you now have a more complete view of what you have been doing, why, and what difference it has made.

Step 2 Action Plan:

- Track all community contributions (cash, in-kind, volunteer time, and other resources).
- Calculate last year's (or three to five prior years') total financial investment.
- Calculate your estimated annual give-back percentage based on before-tax profit.
- Assess the difference your efforts made.
- Note lessons learned and preliminary ideas for how to strengthen your efforts.

Step 3: Inventory Your Values and Goals

"It is fun, exciting, and also very challenging at times to operate in a financially and socially responsible manner. Any company that takes that on, you have to have a great amount of respect for."

—Jennifer Stander, Director of Marketing,
Endangered Species Chocolate, Indianapolis, Indiana[1]

At this point in the process it's time to pause and honestly reflect on where your company is—right now. Take a look in the mirror: what are your company's values, motivations, needs, and goals? This critical step in building a Strategy for Good is often postponed or skipped entirely by companies, especially smaller ones. People get excited and blindly dive in, spending company resources to do good things without forethought.

However, it is essential to slow yourself and others down. Get clear on your values, motivations, needs, goals, and available company resources *before* you develop the specifics of your community investment program portfolio. Clarity about your needs and expectations allows your perspective to shift to "win-win." Accept the fact that your Strategy for Good will bring business benefits in addition to the satisfaction that comes from knowing you are doing good.

Clarify Values and Motivation

"The only reason your business survives is because the community is supporting you by buying your product or service.

Since you have benefited from that community support, you have a moral obligation to give support back to that community. It is not something that is nice. It is not something that is convenient. It is a moral obligation."

—Aaron Azari, Executive Vice President, **Colorado State Bank and Trust**, Denver, Colorado[2]

The moral obligation and "feel-good factor" are the primary reasons most entrepreneurs and business leaders give back. Community investment is a great way to demonstrate goodwill, and both personal and company values. But, do you also have some other motivations, either explicit or implicit?

It is easy to default to our shared values (and political correctness) and say "we should" and "it's just the right thing to do." Of course these are (and should be) strong and critical drivers for business giving. For many business owners, giving back or tithing is one way they express their values and heartfelt and faith-based commitment. For others who consider themselves more spiritually minded than "religious," business giving reflects their belief in karma, the Law of Abundance, and/or the Law of Generosity. How can your strategic community giving reflect your company's values?

The majority of us do have greater-good motivations for our community investment. That said, I am asking you to dig a little deeper and be completely honest with yourself. Remember one of the myths of community investment is that your giving should be totally altruistic. But does your company actually give anonymously or do you use your company name? There is a way to do double duty with community investment. You can have a Strategy for Good that simultaneously impacts causes positively *and* helps the company thrive—losing nothing in the process.

Some entrepreneurs and business leaders, especially from small and mid-size companies, shy away from thinking they should get any "return on investment" from their business giving. They dismiss the concept of receiving any direct or indirect benefit as crass and self-serving. Instead, they donate valuable resources without much thought and hope for the best. Any benefit the company realizes is considered a "happy accident," an added bonus but not the point.

I strongly encourage you to leave such thoughts behind, if you have a tendency to go there. A Strategy for Good is designed to help your company do good *and* do well. If you leave your company's potential benefit out of the equation, you will miss out on significant opportunities to boost your reputation, visibility, and bottom line while you are making a difference.

Consider the example of Denver's **Little Pub Company.** Early on they decided their business model would be based on developing customers from the neighborhood immediately surrounding their bars. "We realized that traditional advertising and approaches to promoting our business was not going to work because we didn't want to draw people from outside the community. We wanted to draw nearby neighbors, pedestrian traffic, that type of thing," says Owner Mark Berzins.[3]

So, they came up with the idea of getting involved in the neighborhoods through their nonprofit work. "In lieu of an advertising budget, we really started dedicating our financial and personnel resources to helping out with various events and philanthropic activities," Mark explained. "It's neat because while we are good citizens within the neighborhood, at the same time it promotes, and is very consistent with, our company's desire to be a neighborhood player. Doing good always feels good and having had the additional benefit of making us fit into the neighborhood better, it was really a doubly rewarding strategy."[4]

Determine Company Needs and Goals

How healthy is your company and bottom line, especially in this challenging economy? Honestly, what key issues have you been dealing with? Is there anything you are concerned about in the workplace, marketplace, or elsewhere? How has the bottom line fared? What do you really need right now to help move things forward and increase profitability?

Given your "health status," what specific business goals do you have now? Are you open to supplementing your standard solutions to achieve business goals/growth with heartfelt yet strategic win-win community investment? Be very clear about this and remember to always take care of business first. Realize that your giving should be strategic so it does real good *and* can help grow your business and boost your bottom line. Remember, win-win community investment is by no means a panacea to address all company challenges or a way to save a failing business.

Do you have at least one business goal to which your community investment could add value if done strategically? I believe that the overarching desire here is to find ways to give back and be part of the solution to the issues of our times...and have both sides of the equation benefit. Nonprofits get resources and clout to do more of their good work and businesses get to build their brand, reputation, and bottom line and be contributing members of society—strengthening their positive image inside and outside company walls. Think enlightened self-interest and strategic involvement. Unless both partners benefit, the relationship will probably be short lived and superficial. Give yourself permission to explore possibilities for what your company could gain from your community investment.

"One of the top five overarching goals that were put in place for The Denver Post when we first formed was certainly community service and touching the lives of thousands in our community. It is critical to us."

—Tracy Ulmer, Director of Promotions and Community Relations, ***The Denver Post***, Denver, Colorado[5]

Think back to your original reasons for getting involved in business giving and reading this book. What were you interested in? Was community investment or giving already written in as part of your company mission or values statements? Did you have a Strategy for Good? Is community investment something you consciously have integrated into your corporate culture? Study the following list and see if any of these reasons ring true for your company.

We wanted to:

- Make a difference in the community
- Be good business citizens
- Expand our business contacts
- Develop our employees' leadership skills
- Promote our company to the local community
- Have fun and/or get together outside work
- Meet new people with similar values
- Create a stronger sense of teamwork within our company
- Lend our support to a cause or issue
- Address our responsibility or expectations of us
- Something else?

John Joseph of Josephs Jewelers based in Des Moines explained to me that as a general philosophy, his company believes in giving for giving's sake; if they get something back, that's all the better. However, part of their community investment is done in ways to ensure the business interacts with potential customers.

"Obviously we're in business and want to create business; anything we can do obviously helps, so I have to admit there's always a bit of a selfish aspect to some of it. There are some of the larger charities that tend to draw a lot of the people in the community who tend to be our customers. So to have a presence there, to be out and see those people socially, and have an opportunity to spend time with them and get to know them and have them get to know us on a personal level is a long-term thing that is good for the company and our business. But, our philosophy is just giving because we feel it is a responsibility to give and so we don't just pick those charities to support."

—John Joseph, Vice President, **Josephs Jewelers**, Des Moines, Iowa[6]

Table 2. Potential Business Needs and Goals

Which of the needs or goals below could be strategically linked to your community involvement to provide benefits for your company?		
Market penetration	Shareholder value	Talent recruitment
Customer loyalty	Technical expertise	Employee retention
Sales volume	Effective contribution to community	Employee skill/ teambuilding
Brand building	Solve a community issue	Community relations
Media coverage	Employee motivation	Other:

Use the bulleted list and Table 2 above as food for thought to clarify your current business interests. Do you have specific goals that could be strategically linked to your community involvement to provide benefits for your company? You might want to revisit the four main categories of potential business benefits outlined in Part I as you think about your company's current needs and goals.

Now that you have assessed past community investment and

are clear on company values, motivations, needs, and goals, you are ready to develop (or refine) your Strategy for Good.

Put Together an Advisory Group

You will need to assemble an advisory group for your community investment. Advisory groups are usually comprised of employees and perhaps senior managers representing the different divisions of the company. Outside experts can also be involved, if you so choose. The advisory group helps set the direction and then implement the company's Strategy for Good. Specific roles and tasks can include developing action plans, conducting an inventory of the company's available resources for supporting community investment, reviewing requests from nonprofits, making funding/resource decisions, soliciting employee engagement, and helping spread the word within the company. If you are a solo-entrepreneur you could ask trusted colleagues, friends, and family members to help with tasks and provide a sounding board.

The Denver Post's employee advisory group meets monthly to review nonprofit requests for volunteer activities and selects 8 to 10 projects per year. These generally take place on weekends or after work hours to encourage family participation. The advisory group promotes the selected projects to other employees to get them excited and involved.[7]

Dreyer's Ice Cream Foundation has two advisory groups that make their community investment decisions. One is a large grant committee that makes funding decisions on annual grants between $3,000 and $50,000. It is comprised of employees and community members familiar with what's going on in Oakland, where Dreyer's headquarters is located, to help focus resources and make impactful investments. This committee reviews grant proposals and conducts site visits with applicants to identify which organizations to fund. The smaller employee-only grant committee reviews product and other smaller in-kind donation requests throughout the year.[8]

New Belgium Brewing Company also has an employee philanthropy committee comprised of a cross segment of production and administrative employees. Bryan Simpson shared, "The way we have constructed the philanthropy committee has been really beneficially to our corporate culture. Anybody that chooses to step up and be involved can. This gives them an ownership mentality. We are an employee-owned company so we try to empower our folks to be active in decision making. I think it is very healthy for our internal environment that employees can see the good that the business is doing."[9] In addition, in all states where their beer is distributed, they have a sales team called "Beer Rangers." The eyes and ears of the company on the ground, the Rangers research local nonprofits to identify eligible organizations in the company's funding priority areas.

Take Stock of Company Resources

The advisory group can help catalogue the variety of company resources available for community investment. Some may be less obvious and either overlooked or taken for granted, but could be very helpful to a nonprofit partner.

Think way beyond the dollars allocated to your charitable donation line item on your annual budget. As you remember, one of the myths of community investment is that if a business doesn't have dollars available to donate, they should wait until they are a more established and profitable company before giving back. Having dollars to contribute is great and cash donations are often what nonprofits request first from businesses, but they are only the tip of the iceberg. Since a large portion of individual giving is through financial contributions, many nonprofits and businesses alike forget there are many other resources to which companies of all sizes have access and could leverage for good. Part III: Ways to Give, offers an extensive menu of ways to engage with nonprofit partners through contributions and commerce.

Think outside the box. Innovate. What makes your company unique? What is your comparative advantage? How can you leverage your resources and networks to make the most difference possible?

Table 3 lists common business resources for community investment. Which of these items do you have? As you dialogue with a potential nonprofit partner later, additional ideas may come to mind about ways to add value; this list gets you started.

Clarity about what your company does and doesn't have to offer helps narrow partnership and project choices to those that make the most sense based on company assets and conditions. For example, if a nonprofit seeks after-school volunteer tutors, you might feel you can't commit to regular release time for your employees for a whole school year. Yet if you really like this nonprofit's mission and their people, you might offer up vehicles and employees as drivers for a special field trip instead.

Creatively thinking about what resources you can offer a nonprofit results in a different conversation and opens up exciting new opportunities to do good. Your resource availability influences the types of organizations you consider partnering with from the get go, as well. Often nonprofits are stuck in a narrow view of fundraising. As a result, many will approach companies first for dollars. Therefore, you may need to help guide the dialogue into a deeper exploration of what they do and their current needs to uncover the best ways to support them. Tony Waller of **State Farm Insurance** says, "It's always been very important to us to make sure we are not known as checkbook

Table 3. Company Asset and Resource Options

What resources does your company own or can leverage in support of your community investment and nonprofit organizational needs?		
Cash donations	Brand value	Marketnig reach
Product	Stock value	Sponsorships
Volunteers	Web presence	Financial systems
Meeting rooms	Telephone banks	Suppliers/vendors
Community influence	Newsletters/ publications	Professional associations
Used equipment	Monthly statements	Information sources
Recycable waste streams	Line item to buy services	Vacant property/offices
Professional skills	Expired inventory	Down time
Networks/contacts	Technology	Customer traffic
Parking lots	Ideas	Office supplies
Legal tools/services	Restaurant - food	Training programs
Advertising venues	Vehicles	Equipment loans
Media professionals	Community leaders	Furniture/equipment
Technical services	Mailing lists	Loaned executives
Endorsements	Management tools	Software
Banks - ATMs	Source of board members	Retail stores - discounts
High tech - services capacity	Communications - airtime	Other

philanthropists but as a company very much involved in the things that we make contributions to."[10]

Rachel Phillips, formerly of **Sambuca Restaurants**, explained to me that she is not a big fan of pure cash donations for two reasons. First, as a small restaurant group, it's not feasible given tight margins. Second, she says, "it just doesn't deliver as much benefit to us as the product giveaways we do, which bring people in for a direct experience of the atmosphere, food, and service in our restaurants."[11]

Be focused and strategic. Instead of throwing resources at a range of causes or organizations, think about how you can get a multiplier effect from focusing your varied resources on a narrower range of causes or organizations. Be selective. Be strategic. Instead of sending company volunteers to help renovate a homeless shelter, giving cash to support a youth-serving organization, buying advertising space in the community orchestra program, and giving product donations to senior centers, why not leverage and integrate your resources to make a greater impact? Perhaps helping one organization in multiple ways through volunteers, cash, and product?

If you spread your company's resources too thin by giving one pack of hotdog buns to every nonprofit that asks, it may help them in a pinch with their cookout for Saturday—but is there any real lasting impact? For them? Or for your business? Probably not. If your scarce resources were being allocated to any other business function, you would certainly question yourself about ROI. However, if you are a company like ***The Denver Post***, with a business goal of serving the entire community as they are your customers, your approach will be broader naturally to be in alignment with company business goals.

While many people consider the return from community involvement to be "soft" and difficult to measure, that doesn't mean you shouldn't think how to best allocate your activities and resources to maximize impact as much as possible. If your efforts are really not going to make much or even any difference, why bother? The more you can get involved with activities for good that do double duty by having impact on both the community and your company, the better, more effective use of your resources.

Think About Actions Outside the Box

> *"There is a real trend over the last 10 years for every nonprofit to have some big gala dinner event in the fall. You look at your calendar and there is one every single weekend. Those days are done. Maybe the big fancy dance appeals to some people...but how much do you spend on that? And is that really representative of your mission? For a homeless shelter to have one of those big fancy dinners ten years ago was a way to get [businesses] and people to the table and learn about their organization. But, it's getting old. They have to change with the times."*
>
> —Ellen Feeney, Corporate Social Responsibility Expert, Boulder, Colorado[12]

Ellen Feeney suggests instead that companies work with their nonprofit partners to come up with some new project or event that could produce greater benefits for both organizations. "Maybe do a health fair in the park for families that people may actually go to with their kids," she suggests, "as opposed to one more rubber chicken dinner on a Saturday night."[13]

There are so many other ways to support nonprofits besides event sponsorships and checkbook philanthropy. Think outside the box to make your involvement strategy innovative and fun. More people will want to be involved and the buzz will be bigger. Creative approaches can help cement the branding of an event or program and provide greater mileage for all organizations involved. Unusual is good and will likely result in free media coverage, which neither organization could afford to pay for with their advertising dollars. Such events will generate greater interest as well as credibility.

Set a Contribution Target

> *"We are tempted to do too much. There are thousands and thousands of organizations; a lot of them are very good. It's really hard because we get a lot of great letters from organizations asking for support. We often have to say 'no.' It is hard to go backwards if you start donating and then say this year we can't because we're doing this or that. Be careful at the start to do what you can without overshooting. Think long term."*
>
> —Gary Erickson, Founder, **Clif Bar & Company**, Emeryville, California[14]

Target levels for company contributions to nonprofits vary significantly by industry, geographic region, business size, and core philosophy. On one end of the spectrum are those businesses that contribute nothing or little. Perhaps they give a few bucks to the Salvation Army at the holidays, Trick or Treat for UNICEF, or the March of Dimes, and call it a day.

On the other end of the spectrum are the "for-benefit" (also called "all-benefit") companies such as **Newman's Own** that dedicate all of their profits to the causes they support after operational expenses, taxes, debt repayment, financing costs, and reasonable working capital reserves. For-benefit companies are still in the minority within the business community, but their numbers are growing. In doing the research for this book, I found more companies operating this way than I knew about previously. Examples include **Pura Vida Coffee**, **Give Something Back Office Supplies**, and **Untours**.

Jodie Weiss, Founder of **PeaceKeeper Cause-Metics**,

encourages entrepreneurs starting a business to seriously consider the for-benefit company model. "You earn a good salary, pay your staff, but give your profits away," she explained. "How much money does a person need to live? People ask me all the time, 'Jodie, are you nuts? How can you invest the energy and make the effort to build this company and not make money on it?' I say to anyone trying to move into this sector, be bold. Don't give 50 percent, don't give 30, don't give 10, give all. Give 100 percent."[15]

For-benefit companies, while inspiring, were designed from inception to operate using this unique business philosophy and model. However, these companies are part of an elite club, so to speak. While we can all learn from their experiences and success, most of us will never be like them. However, as part of our Strategy for Good, we might consider a for-benefit product in addition to our other offerings.

Most businesses fall within the middle of the spectrum. As a basic guideline, I recommend companies give a minimum of three percent of pre-tax profit from a mixture of cash, equity, product/services, and volunteer time. This is a great goal, especially if you are just getting involved or have not thoroughly tracked past community investment expenditures.

In their book *Compassionate Capitalism: How Corporations Can Make Doing Good an Integral Part of Doing Well*, Marc Benioff, Founder of Salesforce.com, and Karen Southwick suggest a similar figure. They encourage companies to donate three percent annually, one percent each from equity, employee time, and profits.[16]

Gary Erickson, Founder of **Clif Bar & Company**, makes a strong case for giving a percentage not of profit but of net sales. "You have to ask, what is our profit? What if you don't profit that year?" he asks. "Ten percent of zero profit is zero, but one percent of net sales is one percent of net sales. That is our sweet spot.

We are there and want to stay there for the indefinite future."[17] The Committee Encouraging Corporate Philanthropy (CECP) Corporate Giving Standard Report for 2010 also raises the issue. "Giving budgets set by arbitrary percentages of pre-tax profit may restrict innovation and collaboration."[18]

If you can commit to giving more, go for it!

As you track the ROI on your contributions and cause marketing over time, you may find that it makes good business sense to increase spending on giving rather than traditional advertising or branding activities. Just be careful not to go overboard. Careful assessment will ensure you don't let partners down or create frustration inside the company if you can't deliver as promised.

Overall, the amount companies dedicate to their community involvement usually ranges from 1 to 10 percent. It gets confusing fast because sometimes just looking at percentages is comparing apples to oranges. Some companies calculate their giving targets based on gross revenue, while others use gross profit or after-tax profit. The most successful U.S. companies generate only 10 to 13 percent after-tax profit; 4 to 5 percent is more typical. That profit is used not only for giving but also to cover reinvestment for growth, dividends to shareholders, bonus structures, and other business expenses. Many companies, even highly profitable ones, are not as cash flush as many nonprofits believe. Therefore, figuring out ways to commit resources beyond cash is essential to a sound community investment.

One percent may not sound like much, but if you are a very small company, this amount can seem like a significant commitment—and it is. For Fortune 100s or multinationals, one percent is a *very* large number due to sheer size of the company and its revenues. So whether it's one percent of a small or large number, every bit your company invests in support of communities makes a difference.

As an example, Yvon Chouinard, environmental activist and Founder of Patagonia, Inc., and Craig Mathews, Owner of Blue Ribbon Flies launched **1% For The Planet** in 2001. Its mission is to be "an alliance of businesses committed to leveraging their resources to create a healthier planet. Members recognize their responsibility to and dependence on a healthy environment and donate at least one percent of their annual net revenues to environmental organizations worldwide. The alliance aims to prove that taking environmental responsibility is good for business."[19] Members include businesses of all sizes.

Each company selects and supports the environmental group(s) of their choice reporting annually to 1% Percent For The Planet to maintain membership rights. Part of their purpose is to increase the funding available for environmental nonprofits and by leveraging one percent from many companies, they not only raise awareness of environmental issues but make a big impact with significant dollars.[18] My company, CORE THOUGHT, is a member. In fact, 1% For The Planet is one of the nonprofit partner-beneficiaries of the sales of this book.

Regional differences exist in how much businesses commit to their community investment. Research your own geographic location and industry. In the Denver area, where I live, two percent has become an informal local benchmark due to the **Two Percent Club**, a coalition of business executives ranging from small companies the size of mine to larger local players like Miller Coors, Xcel Energy, and Qwest Communications. As members we agree to donate annually a minimum equivalent of two percent of company profits to charitable organizations in the community.[20]

In contrast, many Minneapolis businesses commit five percent. Companies that embody the principles of business social responsibility or that build community involvement into their brand commit as much as 10 or 20 percent on an ongoing basis.

So do many companies whose owners view their give-back as tithing from a faith-based or spiritual perspective.

For now, I recommend you stick with three percent as your overall strategic giving target. However, do the math based on your situation and adjust up or down accordingly. Usually, three percent is doable for most companies, especially when you total all resources contributed together (cash, in-kind, volunteer service, etc.). It won't break the bank and it is enough to make a significant difference if invested strategically.

Write Your Strategy for Good

Now that you've inventoried resources and set giving targets, it's time to begin drafting your company's Strategy for Good. Just as a good business plan helps you grow your business and avoid mistakes, a written community investment plan will help your company stay focused, make strategic decisions, and leverage the greatest difference.

Begin with a mission or vision statement specific to your community investment. Next describe the desired company and community goals, focus areas and priorities, partnership selection criteria and decision-making process, and timelines. You'll fill in details about focus areas when you complete Step 4. Nonetheless, it is essential to take the time up front to decide company priorities and write down your strategy—even if it is only one paragraph.

Your Strategy for Good can be as simple as the one for my company, below. Other examples are available for free at *www.StrategyforGood.com*.

Having a written strategy helps you stay clear about company priorities and aids in decision making. It is also easier for interested, potential nonprofit partners to understand your priorities and to help them determine whether to contact you for a partnership or not.

As you craft your strategy, consider other factors. Where will you focus your community investment efforts? Near headquarters, regional offices, or all local locations? National or international? Research has shown that 46 percent of Americans believe companies should focus on issues that affect quality of life in local communities, 37 percent on U.S. issues, and 17 percent on global issues found in countries around the world.[21] What is best for your company?

Where will primary decision making on community investment occur, centrally, locally, or a mixture of both? For example, **Kimpton Hotels & Restaurants** uses a two-pronged approach to their community investment. All of the company's hotels are affiliated with local nonprofit organizations, including those that benefit the arts, education, and neighborhood beautification. In addition, Kimpton Restaurants are involved in their local communities, working to help support food and hunger organizations, as well as underprivileged children, by hosting and teaching cooking classes along with other charitable events and promotions throughout the year. Additionally, Kimpton headquarters has selected five primary national nonprofit partners to support: EarthCare, The Nature Conservancy, Trust for Public Land, Dress for Success, and Red Ribbon.[22] Local hotels and restaurants are encouraged to engage with the local affiliates of those national partners as well.

Give Your Community Investment a "Home"

Which company department will manage your community investment? Who will be responsible for day-to-day operations? It is preferable to have a staff person dedicated to managing your community investment. If that is not possible at this time, clearly identifying which employees will include community

CORE THOUGHT
Strategy for Good

CORE THOUGHT actively supports nonprofit/NGO organizations locally, nationally, and internationally. Our integrated approach moves beyond "checkbook philanthropy" alone and includes engaging with nonprofits in a variety of ways. We believe small businesses like ours can "do well by doing good."

OUR COMMITMENT

- We will participate in at least one volunteer service project per quarter.
- We annually donate 10% of our pre-tax profits to our nonprofit partners engaged in the following four areas:
  1. microbusiness and social enterprise development,
  2. world peace and intercultural understanding,
  3. the environment, and
  4. youth development.
- We select one nonprofit annually to receive pro bono services in one of our areas of expertise, such as program evaluation.
- We donate our used equipment, office supplies, and other items to local nonprofits offering services in one of our four priority areas.
- We actively seek nonprofit partners for joint program development and implementation, cause marketing, and as vendors.

investment among their ongoing responsibilities. Write these responsibilities into one or more job descriptions to ensure it happens consistently. If you use a "tack on," "in your spare time"-type approach, too many variables can get in the way of doing consistent, good work, and your company's reputation will suffer. The following are options for "housing" your community investment activities.

Company Foundation: Many larger companies create a private foundation to handle their community investment. Grantmaking funds are derived primarily from the contributions of the profit-making business. Such company-sponsored foundations usually maintain close ties with the donor company, but it is a separate, legal organization, sometimes with its own endowment, and is subject to the same rules and regulations as other private foundations. According to the Council on Foundations, there are more than 2,000 corporate foundations in the United States holding some $11 billion in assets.[23]

Creating a foundation may be the optimal choice for some bigger companies, but most smaller companies would be ill advised to split their focus to dabble as a foundation. So many times when talking to entrepreneurs and start-up business owners about what I do, they lean in and tell me, "in confidence," that when they have successfully grown their business, they plan to start their own foundation to give back. They have no conception of what it takes to start a foundation, how to capitalize it, requirements for annual payouts, the intricacies of running an effective grant program to distribute funds, and the accompanying responsibilities of the foundation to its grantees. There is a reason there are only 2,000 corporate foundations in the U.S. as compared to over six million businesses! Many people do not realize all the other available options, so it limits their thinking and action. Countering this view is one reason I wrote this book!

There are many other ways to bring business resources and expertise to bear on the community and the causes you care about. Community investment can often be done more simply in-house or out-sourced to a community foundation or a consulting organization like mine. Other options, at first glance, may look like more work to you. Instead think about them as an opportunity to join forces to engage the comparative advantages of all involved to make a more significant impact. Running your own foundation should be an option for later—as it is always time consuming if you do it right!

Corporate Social Responsibility (CSR) Department: Larger companies often include community investment as part of CSR department responsibilities to oversee the company's inclusion of public interest into their decision-making action and the triple bottom line of people, planet, profit. The CSR department focuses on the impact of company activities and seeks to eliminate potentially harmful environmental and social practices, as well as supporting the communities in which they operate.

Human Resources: Volunteer activities sometimes are run through the human resources department due to the company policy link with annual performance reviews and staff development. Some companies consider volunteer activities an employee benefit.

Community/Public Relations: Grants and cash donations, volunteer activities, sponsorships, and other types of connections may all be made through the community/public relations department.

Marketing: Advertising, cause marketing, or event sponsorships are usually housed in the marketing department as they are more commercial than strictly charitable. Do you have one department handling all of these or are they separated by type?

CEO or Owner's Office: In smaller companies without a

department structure, community investment may be based in the office of the owner, CEO, or senior manager so they can oversee activities and ensure it remains a priority for the company.

Where will you house your community investment program? What department makes the most sense for your company structure? Will all components of your community investment be co-located or split out by type? If split, how will you ensure integration and a common direction? Who will have primary responsibility?

Develop Basic Support Systems

To do quality and effective community investment, you need basic systems for decision making, resource and activity tracking, communication, and fostering employee engagement. For example, how will you get the word out within your company about what you are doing and opportunities for employee involvement?

The Denver Post uses their mass employee email system to send out notices about the company's service projects. They also assign captains to each of their projects. Captains are responsible from a grassroots perspective to get the word out to their fellow employees at meetings, by putting up posters, etc. to encourage active participation. "On an annual basis, when we announce our projects for the year, we actually go around and have little special events where we hand out ice cream, t-shirts, and other things along with a listing of what's coming up for the next year so people can get excited about it," explains Tracy Ulmer.[24]

Step 3 Action Plan:

- Put together an advisory group.
- Inventory company resources.
- Set a target for how much to contribute.
- Write a strategic plan for your community investment program.
- Give community investment a "home" within the company and on your books.
- Set up basic systems.

Step 4: Select Causes, Partners, and Projects

"We get requests every day. Every day without exception, either by mail, phone or email. At a meeting someone will ask if we would sponsor an event. So, you have to be extremely selective about what you undertake and what you can invest in because the pie is pretty limited, obviously. Our goal is to invest in events where both the decision makers and decision influencers that either recommend or buy our services are present. That's where we try to focus our money, try to focus our efforts."

—Ron Brumbarger, President & CEO,
BitWise Solutions, Indianapolis, Indiana[1]

One of the most rushed steps in the process of community involvement is the strategic creation of your community investment portfolio: selecting the cause(s) and the specific nonprofit partner(s) that most appeal to you. Basically there are two options. Either nonprofits seek you out or vice versa. When nonprofits approach your company, they are either on a blind yet hopeful "fishing expedition" or they are responding to your specific guidelines and criteria for support. Having a clear, accessible Strategy for Good helps weed out many requests that wouldn't be the best matches anyway.

Often, especially for smaller companies, the first nonprofit to call or stop by with a request "wins." First-come, first-served superficially may appear the easiest and "fairest" way to select what causes or organizations to support. However, while it may require less of your valuable time up front, with no criteria for selecting what groups to support, it is easy to end up feeling pressured and stressed by the sheer volume of incoming requests from deserving organizations.

Using this non-strategy, there is a high probability that you will either spread yourself too thin trying to make everyone happy (with minimal real impact for them or you) or you will feel guilty for having to refuse a request with no reason other than "we've committed all our resources for now." Things can easily spiral out of control and leave you feeling like you are only viewed as a cash cow or resource warehouse and the sharks are circling.

"When you first get involved with the community and find out the depth and breadth of the need for help, it can really consume you. As organizations find out that you are philanthropic-minded, you are suddenly solicited on virtually all fronts,"[2] Mark Berzins, Owner of the **Little Pub Company** explained. "Our first couple of years we really overextended ourselves because there were so many good causes and so many people in need. We overspent and overcommitted in a lot of ways. A few years later, we decided to revisit our community giving strategy, and to focus our major resources of time and money on one slice of the philanthropic community and to participate more broadly through the use of gift certificates and donations of product versus our time and cash. We made the decision to focus on the arts and culture arena specifically because I think it is a tougher area to fundraise in while still being a very, very vital part of the community. It is very important thing for my children and the next generation to keep the arts vibrant and thriving. So, that was a decision that we reached. So, since 1996 or 1997, we have been primarily focused on arts organizations and most of my board work has been with art organizations."[3]

Don't skip this step and choose a nonprofit partner purely for convenience. Your company needs to be strategic, not reactive.

With over 1.2 million nonprofits in the U.S. alone—and dozens, hundreds, or even thousands in your city—you can't help them all. You have to narrow the field and identify the cause(s) you care most about, hopefully that align in some way with your business mission.

To be strategic, develop and post your selected focus areas and criteria for selection. Then your advisory group will review requests that come in to determine which the company will investigate further and/or support. Or, you can proactively seek out nonprofits whose missions and services fit your focus and develop a relationship with them. Perhaps what works for you best is a combination of both.

Choose Causes or Social Issues

> *"Don't just pick something to support because you think, 'oh, that sounds good' or 'someone I know believes in it.' You have to have a vision of what you want to do."*
>
> —Judith O'Neill, Owner, **Landscapes Within**, Boulder, Colorado[4]

What current social issues truly matter to you, the company, and your employees? What causes relate in some way to your business mission, products, or services? There are countless worthy causes in the U.S. and the world; you can't support them all. Making a strategic link with business goals is essential, as is choosing a cause that really matters to you and your company can get behind. Where can you have the most impact? How can you create new approaches to meet needs?

> *"Your community involvement "has to match your passion. You have to feel like it is a calling. Don't ever get involved with a nonprofit that you don't, in your heart, believe in…just because*

you were asked to. That is a lousy reason. You have to believe in its mission, you've got to believe it is doing good things, you have to want to advocate for it."

—Aaron Azari, Executive Vice President, **Colorado State Bank and Trust**, Denver, Colorado[5]

You want an authentic and genuine commitment behind your community investment. Don't just go through the motions to look good by doing something in the community. People can sniff that out a mile away and it can end up damaging your reputation instead of building it, as you intend. Grand gestures are just that and may not have much impact.

In addition, connecting for business building with no heart can make community involvement feel like a chore, a time waster, and corrodes the intrinsic value that such activities can deliver down the road. If you don't really care, it is easy to put community involvement last on your to do list of "important actions" for each day. The results will reflect your ambivalence and "prove" to you that it wasn't worth doing in the first place. Instead, pick something that matters, relates to your business in some way, and go for it wholeheartedly.

According to Cone, Inc., when choosing an issue to support, 91 percent of consumers believe companies should consider one that is important in the communities where they do business. Another 91 percent feel they should consider one that is consistent with responsible business practices or the way they make and distribute their products (e.g., impact on the environment, treatment of employees, financial transparency). In addition, 89 percent said the cause should be one that is important to their consumers; 88 percent said where the business can have the most social and/or environmental impact; and 85 percent one that is important to their employees.[6]

"The [community] work you are doing has to align with your company's core values... If you are going to say you support women, then you better do it in your backyard first. It has to align with your values and it has to be real. It can't just be a marketing thing and your people have to be passionate about it."

—Niki Leondakis, President, **Kimpton Hotels & Restaurants**, San Francisco, California[7]

Make sure the day-to-day operations of your company and employees do not contradict the face you present to the community. You must operate with both internal and external consistency and integrity; everything needs to be in alignment. Remember, doing great things in the community is nice but it is only part of the package. If you treat your employees poorly or are damaging the environment to fuel your profits, all the community involvement in the world won't erase a tarnished reputation or help you be viewed as a good corporate citizen.

I always recommend you link your involvement directly to the expertise or interests of your company. What can be the concrete link between your company values, core products or services, and your giving? For example, Andrea Costantine, the book strategist/mentor and freelance writer that has been helping me with this book has changed the focus for her community volunteering as a result of learning more about strategic giving through our work together. She used to volunteer at the local botanic garden but now has chosen for her company to support a nonprofit that promotes literacy. A great choice for a company all about books and writing!

Equal Exchange, a fair trade, organic coffee and chocolate company, partners with such faith-based groups as Lutheran World Relief because their commitment to local people in developing countries and social and economic justice aligns with company values. To have the most impact, **Zhena's Gypsy Tea** chooses to support peace and greening initiatives like Code Pink and Bioneers.[8]

BitWise Solutions encourages community involvement across the board. However, the company intentionally chooses to support the organizations or events that fit with the company's goals and objectives. Ron Brumbarger says, "We certainly would not discourage anyone from participating with an organization they feel passionate about. However, we probably would not feel inclined to support their membership in the rabbit club or something like that. I am all for good rabbits, don't misunderstand me, but that's probably not going to further our cause here as a company."[9]

The following table lists selected causes and nonprofit focus areas as food for thought; however, it is not an exhaustive list. What issues or interests resonate most for you? Are there causes which clearly link to your business mission and products?

What causes can your company get juiced up about and excited to support? Does your selection make sense based on your business mission, expertise, and available resources? Is there a link with some business goal?

Research Potential Nonprofit Partners

Once you narrow down the cause(s) you want to support, you need to go one step further to think about program approaches. There are often many ways to address a given social issue; you need to decide where you have the greatest interest and can have the greatest impact.

For example, say you decide after surveying your employees that your company wants to support breast cancer. The next thing to consider is, as shown in Figure 4, which of the existing approaches to breast cancer-related action makes the most sense

Table 4. Possible Issues to Select as Your Company's Cause

Cause	Sample Nonprofit Focus Areas
Aging/Senior Services	senior centers, meal on wheels, nursing homes, in-home assistance, assistance with daily living including home and yard work
Animal Rights & Welfare	humane societies and veterinary services; no-kill shelters, protecting animals from cruelty, exploitation, and other abuses; animal training and specialty services, such as seeing-eye dogs; zoos and aquariums
Arts, Culture, & Humanities	performing arts, museums, public broadcasting and media, libraries, historical societies, landmark preservation
Children and Youth	childcare, early childhood education, health, adoption, foster care, family counseling, parenting education, advocacy, neglect and abuse, after-school and other out-of-school-time programs, leadership, mentoring
Civic Engagement & Volunteerism	service learning programs, voting, community development
Civil and Legal Rights	legal aid
Community Beautification & Development	community centers, parks and neighborhood clean-ups, community organizing and advocacy
Criminal Justice	prisoner re-entry programs
Disabilities	support services, job and life skills, housing, accessibility, independent living
Disaster Services	relief, preparedness, response, remediation, recovery
Diversity	racial, ethnic, cultural, gay/lesbian/bisexual/transgender rights, cultural competence
Domestic Violence & Victims Assistance	shelters, counseling, legal aid, mediation, support services
Economic Assistance, Business & Workforce Development	microenterprise development, job skills, job search assistance and coaching, mentoring
Education (K-12, Higher Ed, Trade) and Literacy	schools, reading, math, arts, athletics, digital divide, after-school and other out-of-school-time programs, leadership, mentoring, adult, children and youth, English as a second language (ESL) training
Environment, Conservation, & Sustainability	environmental protection and conservation; botanic gardens, parks, nature centers; fish, wildlife, and bird refuges and sanctuaries, wildlife protection and conservation; organic farming and gardening, local food
Health Care	Access, diseases and disorders, patient and family support, treatment and prevention, medical research
Hunger, Housing, & Homelessness	affordable housing, green building, shelters, counseling, job skills, food banks and pantries, food distribution, prepared-meal programs
International Development	water, population, health, nutrition, agriculture, small business development, women's issues, fair trade, refugees
Mental Health	call centers, counseling, crisis centers
Peace and Tolerance	conflict resolution, intercultural understanding, international exchange programs, refugees
Substance Abuse	drug and alcohol treatment, counseling and other services
Transportation	bike to work, public transit, senior services, youth programs, carpooling, high-occupancy-vehicle lanes (HOV)
Veterans	support services, counseling, homeless services

for your organization. Are you more interested in supporting research, advocacy, education and community outreach, screening, treatment, or support services for women with breast cancer? What organizations have that focus? For example, if you chose research, what are the best nonprofit partner choices?

Figure 4. From Identifying Cause to Nonprofit Selection

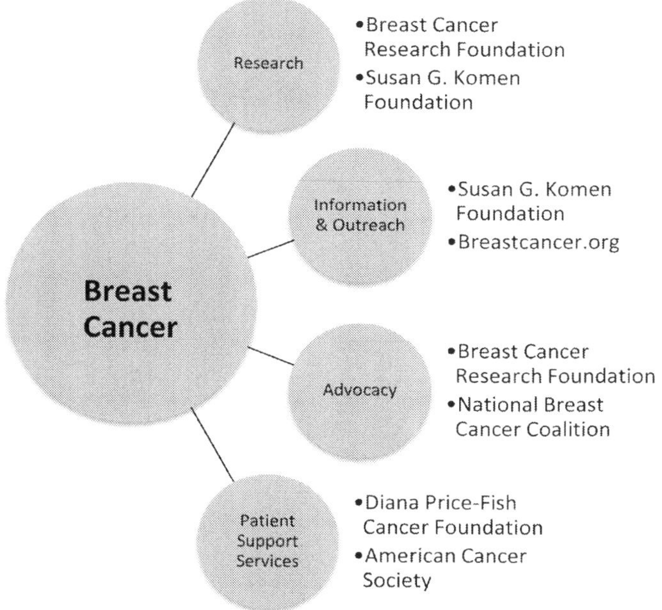

Identifying where your company wants to focus helps you to be clear in the community investment guidance and selection criteria you develop and share. It also provides you criteria for identifying potential partners.

Choosing a Nonprofit Partner

"We provide organic and fair trade products. Our partners are members of the faith-based community as we have seen we have many shared goals. Our first faith-based partner was Lutheran

World Relief (LWR) which had been doing great work over decades helping people similar to those we traded with. We saw that by partnering with them, we could get the story of these farmers out in a more powerful way...LWR had been doing good education and outreach. However, their work was augmented as a result of their partnership with Equal Exchange because then they could actually point to a bag of coffee, something very tangible. . .to demonstrate how their parishioners were connected to people all around the world through coffee, cocoa, and other items they purchase."

—Rodney North, *"The Answer Man,"* **Equal Exchange,** Bridgewater, Massachusetts[10]

If you are seeking a specific partnership based on how you want to make a difference, you will need to research potential partners to identify those with missions and programs in alignment with yours. Consider the example of **Equal Exchange**, a company selling fair trade certified coffee, tea, cocoa, chocolate, and sugar. In addition to their commitment to direct purchasing from small-farmer producers in developing countries at a fair price, they also donate 10 percent of their profits to other Fair Trade organizations as a way to strength the network.[11]

The following are tips for locating potential nonprofit partners:

- Contact your statewide nonprofit association, Better Business Bureau, state service commission, local volunteer center, United Way or community foundation, or other local funders to ask if they know of any nonprofits that could be of interest
- Do a Google search
- Ask your community connections/networks for referrals

Also, check the resource section in the Appendix for a list of selected organizations that can help in your search for nonprofits working in key areas in which your company is interested in making a difference.

After making your prospect list, you need to do some research. Look at the organization's website to review their values, mission, and objectives to make sure they are a good match with your company. Review their press releases and do an internet search to see what other information is available besides what they provide on their website. You may also want to call and request written materials, such as annual reports or program evaluation summaries, as well.

Some things you may want to pay attention to include the following.

- Do they match your company priorities?
- What is the program model they use? Does it make sense? Does it address root causes?
- Do they have information on their beneficiary/community impacts?
- Who are their current partners/supporters? What is your relationship with those businesses or organizations? Do you have any contacts you can call and ask questions about their experience? Is anyone else from your industry a partner? Does not being sole source minimize your exposure? Any other conflicts of interest?
- Does the organization have the staffing/capacity to handle the grant, donation, funding, and/or your employee volunteers?
- How much will the program cost your company in time and other resources?
- Do they potentially need what you have to offer?
- How strong are they organizationally? Financially?

"I believe it's important that nonprofits who come to us for money, support, or partnership be able to show how a gift to

them or a partnership with them is actually going to sell more yogurt. In other words, how will it help to get Stonyfield's name out there, how can it generate more enthusiasm and support for our brand and our approach? I am not the least bit bashful about that. I think this kind of inquiry helps the nonprofits themselves to be more business-like and better at marketing themselves and, of course, it helps us to figure out who is really serious."

—Gary Hirshberg, *CE-Yo,* **Stonyfield Farm**,
Londonderry, New Hampshire[12]

Remember, true partnership is a two-way street with both organizations sharing resources and expertise and reaping benefits as well. Nonprofits also have assets they bring to any business partnership such as connections, specialized skills (content area, program design and management, volunteer recruitment, retention, and recognition, etc.), and a positive reputation and credibility in the community. What nonprofit assets could benefit your company?

However, many nonprofits are so focused on what they need, they never consider that they have assets and can be part of a solution to a business need. Some are stuck in a needy, charity mentality and can't simultaneously see their strengths clearly outside their service delivery model.

Often, they are not alone in their tunnel vision. Many times businesses also forget to think about what assets nonprofits bring to the table and ways to leverage those to help meet their social and business goals. Instead of thinking solely about what you offer to the nonprofit partner, consider also how engaging in a meaningful way with a nonprofit could reinforce your business objectives. Not acknowledging that both partners have assets to share can color interaction and set up the relationship to be distorted and unequal from the start.

The following is a sample of typical assets that nonprofits

have. This is not an exhaustive list but meant to give you food for thought. Nonprofit assets can be subtle so you need to listen carefully or ask probing questions as you have preliminary dialogue and negotiations with your potential partners.

Table 5. Nonprofit Asset and Resource Options

What assets might a nonprofit have to share with your company that would be useful in helping you meet your business objectives?		
Market penetration	High-profile events	Advocacy programs
Credibility	Community presence	Community leader access
Media appeal	Values systems	Information/databases
Community relations	Publications	Web traffic
Emotional connections	Creativity	Service opportunities
Membership base	Service delivery capability	Educational opportunities
Brand value	Celebrity spokespeople	Passionate staff
Technical expertise	Political connections	Board members
Local focus/global reach	Business relationships	Other:

After you identify and research prospective nonprofit partners and have developed your "short list," you can contact them and set up a meeting.

Contact the Nonprofit and Make a Pitch

If you do not already know a staff person at the nonprofit, you may be wondering who you should speak with. Depending on the size of the organization, there are four main potential points of contact: the executive director, development director, volunteer manager, and program staff. For larger projects, it is always a good idea to have contact with the board chair or other board members as well, as they are usually part of the decision-making process for most major initiatives.

First is the executive director (ED) or chief executive officer (CEO). In an incorporated nonprofit 501(c)(3), the ED or CEO has the primary responsibility to carry out the organization's strategic plans and policies as established by the board of directors, as well as oversee the day-to-day operations of the organization and its programs. The ED reports to the board of directors.

The second potential point of contact is the development director. The development director of a nonprofit organization provides leadership, strategic initiative, and management of all fundraising efforts. The director creates and coordinates programs to increase the organization's support base among individuals, corporations, foundations, and additional sources. In smaller nonprofits, the ED may play both roles.

The third way in is to contact the volunteer manager, if you are primarily interested in employee volunteer opportunities. Volunteer managers establish and operate the organization's volunteer management system including volunteer recruitment, identification of volunteer opportunities, and matching volunteers with opportunities that best utilize volunteer skills to meet organizational needs. One thing to note is that some volunteer managers are best at identifying general volunteer opportunities and have less experience identifying and managing pro bono service to improve organizational capacity. If you are interested in offering pro bono services, you may also need to talk with the ED and/or development director.

The fourth, though less frequently used, entrée point is program staff. Program staff oversee the various programs and services the organization offers. If you are looking for information about program details or sites, they are a great source of information.

After a preliminary phone conversation, set up a live meeting to continue the dialogue. Conducting the meeting at their location can give you a deeper sense of who they are as an organization, as well as their clients and programs. Go to the meeting with a clear preliminary sense of how and why your company wants to get involved, your needs, as well as the resources you can leverage. Be sure to introduce who you are and your role within the company, an overview of your company and its products or services, and a description of the company's community investment interests and how and why you are looking to get involved. Make a list of questions and/or concerns you want addressed and then prepare an agenda to ensure you cover all items.

Include any specific ideas you have for an existing or a new program or service your company can fund or support. However, I strongly advise against having a project or plan completely prepackaged to present at the meeting. From my experience, working to together to co-create whatever activity or program, fleshing out the specifics jointly leads to a more solid relationship and foundation for the long run. Together you can figure out what the project will look like, how it will run, and what results it will produce for both organizations.

As Gary Hirshberg of **Stonyfield Farm** explained, "More often than not, somebody will bring up an idea and then we'll get together with them and mutually we'll work together to improve it. In other words it will be a collaborative effort. They will think of something that we haven't thought of, we'll think of something they haven't thought of. We often find that one plus one equals three."[13]

After your dialogue ask yourself some questions. Did you sense enthusiasm on their side and were you excited about possibilities for good and working with this organization? Did you get your questions answered? Are they a good fit for your company, now that you know more? Is there "chemistry" and compatibility between your organizations on the level of formality, ethics, work style, communications, etc.? Do any items require follow-up by you or the nonprofit?

Listen for What the Nonprofit Needs

During initial conversations to explore partnering with a nonprofit, you need to ask targeted questions to help you better understand the programs and clientele of the organization. As mentioned previously, the most common request that businesses receive from nonprofits is for a cash donation or grant. While all nonprofits can use dollars, many are stuck in the old paradigm of fundraising or charity donations—not building partnerships or alliances that involve engaging in ways to benefit both organizations. Unfortunately, this short-term focus on cash can limit a nonprofit's ability to both ask for and receive other resources that could be very useful to their organization in the longer-term.

Sometimes "begging for dollars" is an indicator of the nonprofit's self-focus, limiting beliefs, poverty consciousness, fiscal crisis, or other form of instability. Other times, it simply shows they don't understand business enough to know how else to engage with you and ask for anything else.

Consider the example shared with me by David Eisner, former CEO of the **Corporation for National and Community Service**. "Nonprofits can be skeptical of business," David explained. "You find a lot of them...feeling like they are holding their nose to accept help. When I was at AOL, we would speak to nonprofits and offer to help them be more effective on the internet. Basically, we would often hear, 'That's nice. Thanks a lot, but why don't you give us a check and we can manage ourselves.' It missed the whole point of what we could have helped them with."[14]

There is a bias among some donors that their support to nonprofits only be used for direct program costs, in the mistaken belief that will mean more benefit in the community. When coming from this perspective, donors and business partners place a disproportionate weight on the percentage of the budget for administrative costs in their decision making. Also, be sure to compare nonprofits that do similar work, if you are looking at their finances. The type of work done by a nonprofit can affect its operating costs dramatically.

Many times what keeps a nonprofit operating below their potential level is that they do not have the internal capacity or operating capital to hire people with the skill sets necessary to really take the organization to new levels.

If you are seeking to develop a relationship deeper than providing cash, you may need to listen carefully and read between the lines to identify ways you can offer unique and significant support. You know your company's strengths and assets. As you listen, you may uncover ways to address needs they may not see fully because they are so close to them. Or together, you may co-create new and innovative ways to help address their mission in the community.

There is a fine line between listening for needs to see what an organization truly needs and being a "know it all." Remember, it's all about partnership, not paternalism. Consider this example and make sure it doesn't describe you.

A consultant colleague shared her excitement with me about joining the board of a nonprofit focused on leadership and self-esteem for girls. She understood firsthand the challenges of being a female senior executive in a predominantly male industry, so their "girl power" programs totally resonated with her. It was clearly a great fit and way for her to offer support she didn't have at a similar age. However, in her enthusiasm to do good, she unintentionally crossed a line. Before even attending her first board meeting, being introduced to her fellow board members, or learning more about the organization through participating in their work, she developed a proposal to present at her first board meeting for a leadership program she had been dreaming about for a long time.

A better approach would have been to put the program idea on hold for a while so she could first get immersed in the organization, learn how it operates, and better understand their needs and current situation. From 20-plus years working with nonprofits and their boards, I know from direct experience there is always a learning curve to really understand the structure and dynamics of any organization. No two are exactly alike. Relationship building is key to ensuring the great ideas and resources your company can offer are relevant to further the nonprofit's mission and will be embraced and implemented.

Ask for What You Want

> *"Don't be afraid to demand reciprocation. You are putting something on the table. Don't be timid about laying out what you need as a business. I think when both parties know clearly what they each need then you can get it done."*
>
> —Gary Hirshberg, CE-Yo, **Stonyfield Farm**, Londonderry, New Hampshire[15]

Just as important as listening to the nonprofit is asking for what you want. Openly discuss both organizations' expectations of the partnership. By doing so, you both learn about each other's needs and can work together to meet them. Dialogue up front allows any inflated expectations to be dialed back to more realistic goals.

Many businesses worry that they shouldn't be direct with their expectations either because they are still subconsciously clinging to the old 100 percent altruism model or they don't want to further burden an already stretched nonprofit. As a result, it is amazing how many businesses ask for no report on how resources were used and what impact they had. Sometimes they don't even get a thank you note! Not acceptable.

Be clear about what you need on your end to rationalize the company's expenditure of resources and to show your model is working and helping you get closer to reaching business goals. Then discuss what is realistic and negotiate how it will happen. You might need to invest some employee time to work with their staff to enhance the capacity of the organization to meet your needs the first time—but that can be part of your contribution.

For example, if you want to know how many of your employees volunteer and for how many hours for an after-school mentoring program, the nonprofit could have a sign-in sheet to track your staff at the program location. If their organization doesn't already have a way to do that, you could have someone on your end set up a Word document to share with them, as well as work with their most appropriate staff person to determine a system that works for both of you—a way for your volunteers to sign in, track their hours, and share the data back with you on some periodic basis.

If one of the business goals for your community involvement is to enhance visibility, discuss with your partner ways to achieve that goal. For example, do you want to be featured on their website, in newsletters, in a press release to local media, signage at the event, etc.? Hoping the nonprofit will "figure it out in their own" and get it right, probably won't happen. Make your request clear and you will avoid disappointment.

Jason Linkow, the former owner of **Metafolics Salon**, advises companies to speak up for themselves when dealing with nonprofits. Realize it is okay to say "no" if you don't think your company can benefit from a specific partnership. The nonprofit may be asking for your support just because you are well known in the community. "If you really don't think you can benefit your company or their nonprofit, you may not be doing a service to the cause and you may actually cause more problems than good," said Jason. "It's alright sometimes to decline involvement."[16]

Now that you have identified your nonprofit partner(s) and ways you will engage with each other, write an annual implementation plan. Tracy Ulmer of ***The Denver Post*** shares that "we try to figure out a year in advance what our set volunteer projects are going to be. But there is always room for added opportunities and increased outreach to our employees, so we review requests on an ongoing basis as well."[17]

Step 4 Action Plan:

- Select a cause(s) you care about.
- Research nonprofits with related missions and programs.
- Identify what nonprofit assets could benefit your company.
- Identify your community investment partner selection process.
- Identify potential partner organizations.
- Have a preliminary meeting and make your pitch.
- Clarify expectations for both partners.
- Write a plan for the agreed-upon project or activity.

Step 5: Grow Win-Win Relationships

"It comes down to the relationship between the two key players. It is real important to find somebody that you can have good dialogue with and where you are really looking for a win-win. Both sides have to feel this is a real positive—what I am getting is worth what I am giving, if not more. It's really looking at the nonprofit organization and seeing, what is their mission and focus; who are they trying to reach? Are they trying to reach some of the same audience and potential markets we are?"

—Karla Raines, Principal and CEO,
Corona Insights, Denver, Colorado[1]

Successful partnerships manage the relationships, not just the deal. It is critical that there is a specific point of contact within both organizations for consistency and clear communication. This lead person understands that it is his or her responsibility to manage the relationship with the nonprofit, communicate and coordinate the activities, and oversee both the overall implementation of the project and the participating employees.

Start small to grow big. Begin with a pilot, a small, manageable project to enable both organizations to get to know each other, establish relationships, and experience early success. Undertaking a big project for which you lack adequate capacity can spell disaster and jeopardize your partnership with the nonprofit.

"These types of partnerships don't happen overnight," explains Gary Hirshberg, CE-Yo of **Stonyfield Farm**.[2] "You can't think of it as a campaign for a semester, a term, or quarter. Usually partnerships require multi-year commitments to be successful."

Developing quality relationships with a nonprofit partner takes time. So you also need to start slow to begin developing a solid working relationship with your partner, letting both organizations build trust while getting to know each other. The best partnerships are those that have developed over time.

For example, **Equal Exchange** had a long courtship with Lutheran World Relief (LWR), their first faith-based partner. As Rodney North explained to me, "I think a lot of credit goes to LWR, because they too were taking it slow and steady, doing their research, getting to know us, and making sure we got to know them. The lasting lesson is to go slow and steady."[3]

Coming to understand and work with differences in organizational culture can involve a few bumps along the way, due to assumptions on both sides about how the other should behave. Get to know your potential partner and what they need to be comfortable, not just what they need in the transaction. Both partners need to get clear on what the other organization expects. Rodney recalled, "We knew we needed to keep in mind what would make this relationship work for Lutheran World Relief, our partner, and never forget that."[4]

Equal Exchange's partnership with LWR started with a pilot in one region of the U.S. Each organization had one champion thoroughly dedicated to making the partnership work. After the first partnership was fully established, thriving, and growing, it was easy to replicate the model. Equal Exchange was better prepared to engage in similar partnerships with the Methodists, Quakers, Unitarians, and other congregations because they already had been through all phases of developing a win-win faith-based partnership.

Think going deeper for the long term. Starting fresh every year with new partners takes a lot of work, so investing in keeping the ones you've got now is a good strategy. Over time see how you can evolve the partnership to have new and deeper ways to engage together to make an even bigger difference. Gregor Barnum, Director of Corporate Consciousness for **Seventh Generation**, put it this way: "Strategically, one of the things [we] think about is how can we begin to engage organizations we think are doing a good job; how can we form deeper partnerships that have a more long-lasting effect."[5]

State Farm is proud of its long-term view of the company's community engagement. The insurance leader chose its philanthropic focus based on what it believes is vital to a prosperous and successful society. As Clayton Adams, Executive Vice President of Community Development, explains: "In order to have a workforce that can continue this society, we think it is incumbent that we be competitive in this global economy. Interestingly, over the past decade, we have been falling further and further behind on the education front as compared with other countries. Therefore, State Farm has committed to supporting educational excellence focusing on both student and teacher achievement. No matter what you do in a community—whether it's creating affordable housing, making the community safer, or creating jobs—if you don't have people who can read, do science, and handle eighth grade algebra, then you won't have a community that will continue to prosper. It's fundamental as far as we're concerned to have a good educational system."[6]

Foster Partnership, Not Paternalism

"It takes paying attention to both the work and the relationship aspects to make a successful partnership. As you start a new partnership or enhance an ongoing one, consider the time spent on fostering relationships compared to planning work tasks. It is critical that attention be paid to the development of

skills, knowledge, and training that helps partners balance the relationship building needs with the work of the partnership."

—**Points of Light Foundation**,
Building Partnerships that Work[7]

Your goal is to make a difference. Toward that end, remember that joining forces with other organizations, each offering varied skills, creates synergy and impact beyond what any entity could do alone. Your business brings important resources and assets to the table, such as business savvy, technical skills, networks, and more.

It is important, however, to focus on the partnership. Some commerce leaders slip into the "business knows best" mindset. They assume (often unconsciously) that the for-profit sector is more sophisticated and effective than its charitable cousin. While differences between the two sectors do exist, a paternalistic attitude that says "we will save you poor people" is off-putting and counterproductive to developing mutually beneficial relationships. Take care to respect the assets, skills, and insights that good nonprofits bring to bear on service to their communities. They are experts in their content area and service delivery models—and can use your support to do an even better job.

Here are some guideposts for developing a win-win relationship with a nonprofit partner:

- Identify common interests;
- Develop a vision statement and define desired outcomes;
- Design the terms of engagement of the project;
- Develop a written work plan or memorandum of understanding that details the project purpose, scope, roles and responsibilities for each organization, timelines, points of contact in each organization, and benchmarks;
- Foster a mutual-benefits perspective to ensure both

organizations receive value from the working relationship;
- Be flexible, communicate clearly and regularly, and ensure accountability; and
- Consider how your employees can be engaged in meaningful ways.

Think about how to institutionalize your joint efforts. Although project champions are necessary, if your partnership depends too heavily on specific people, the project can falter or crash if key people leave. While most partnerships begin as a meeting of the minds between individuals from each organization, growing beyond that ensures broad support and engagement. Otherwise, it can be difficult to stay true to the original agreement and foundation for the partnership.

Avoid Pitfalls of Partnering with Nonprofits

Businesses and nonprofits often experience challenges when beginning to work with each other. Each has misconceptions about the other based on stereotypes and cultural differences between the sectors. However, if the business anticipates potential challenges and discusses them early with the nonprofit, the organizations can design their partnership to minimize the issues and strengthen the relationship.

During the interviews for this book, I asked business leaders if they experienced any challenges working with nonprofit organizations. The following is a list of ten bugaboos mentioned.

1. Nonprofits are often not receptive to engaging in creative programs with higher levels of business involvement beyond just asking for checks.—*Niki Leodankis, Kimpton Hotels & Restaurants*[8]
2. Many nonprofits cannot succinctly describe their mission or message. They can't get to the point and spend too much time describing their program models. Also,

many don't follow the submission instructions for grant applications.—*Amy Hall, Eileen Fisher*[9]

3. Nonprofits often don't give us back any information on the impact of the support we provided.—*Gregor Barnum, Seventh Generation*[10]
4. Many nonprofits are risk-averse. They are playing not to lose rather than playing to win. Such risk-aversion has a negative impact on innovation.—*John Sage, Pura Vida Coffee*[11]
5. There can be profound cultural difference between nonprofits and businesses in how work is approached. Nonprofits sometimes have trouble understanding business demands.—*Seth Goldman, Honest Tea*[12]
6. Timing and organizational culture difference can be challenging. The business focus on business often is hard for nonprofits to understand as is the fast pace of business and the push to meet quotas. Also, both partners may have stereotypical beliefs about each other that can get in the way.—*Mary T'Kach, Aveda*[13]
7. Many nonprofits are not savvy about marketing their partnership with a business to their supporters and the community at large. Although one business motivation to engage in relationships with nonprofits is to enhance visibility and marketing efforts, nonprofit partnerships don't necessarily lead to a direct sales opportunity.—*Seth Goldman, Honest Tea*[14]
8. Nonprofits may not have the patience required to build the relationship with a business. You need to start slow. —*Rodney North, Equal Exchange*[15]
9. Getting nonprofits to understand where the company is coming from and differing definitions of deadlines can be challenging.—*Clayton Adams, State Farm*[16]
10. So few nonprofits take inventory of their power. For

> example, their supporter networks and communication tools are an asset of great value to businesses. Mentioning your business in their newsletter, on their website, a thank you at a board meeting, or bringing their board to your restaurant for a meeting can all be ways to help you get increased exposure.—*Jessica Newman, Rock Bottom Foundation*[17]

Lastly, Leslie Sheridan of The Added Edge is astounded that some nonprofits even forget to say thank you to their business partners! [18]

Keep your eyes open for potential challenges as you begin to work together, as well as throughout your relationship. With communication and planning, nothing is insurmountable.

Step 5 Action Plan:

- Define a pilot activity or project to work on with the nonprofit.
- Develop clear roles and responsibilities; consider drafting a memorandum of understanding with key partners.
- Assess the success of and benefits from the pilot.
- Manage the relationship—be open, transparent, and communicate regularly.
- Be proactive to avoid the common pitfalls of working with nonprofits.

Step 6: Measure Success

"Every single fundraising effort has got to have an ROI on it. You've got to look at what it costs in terms of invitations, food, rental, mailings, and staff time to plan that event and what we [as a company] get out of it. It's like a business. If that event doesn't more than pay for itself and justify six months of staff time, then why do it? If it is for information sharing or awareness raising for the community, that's one thing. Otherwise, it's just not worth it."

—Ellen Feeney, Corporate Social Responsibility Expert, Boulder, Colorado[1]

The sixth step in strategic business giving is measuring success. This is where you assess impact to figure out what's working and what's not. Your company is generously investing scarce resources to do good—is it happening? To really know what's working, you need to track your resource inputs and estimate a rough return. Figuring out if you truly are making any difference is key to any Strategy for Good, for both your company and your community.

Measurement of community impacts by U.S. corporations and businesses is spotty. Just over one-third report having any kind of system to account for resources provided to the community (for example, grants, in-kind donations, and employee time). Only one in seven companies has a process to assess the internal impact of their community programs, and only one in eight evaluates the impact of corporate engagement on the community.[2] Few companies thoroughly report on their social initiatives, and even fewer use third-party verification for their information—a crucial element in building trust and credibility among stakeholders.

Let's face it, if your company resources were allocated to any other business function or unit, such as labor or marketing, impact would be tracked with a fine-toothed comb. What's different about community involvement? Nothing.

The findings above reveal that the majority of businesses fail to practice *strategic* community involvement. As author David Batstone writes in *Saving the Corporate Soul—and (Who Knows?) Maybe Your Own*, "There's lots of room for improvement here, but it's not a matter of incompetence. The results of the study more likely point to a lack of priority."[3]

Smart businesses track their community investment—and it's not difficult. You'll want to consider two types of outcomes for any partnership effort: the difference made for the nonprofit and its clients ("the community") and the difference made for your business. The following is food for thought on what each entails.

Assess Community Outcomes

> *"We want to work with organizations that are having an impact."*
>
> —Gary Erickson, Founder, **Clif Bar & Company**, Emeryville, California[4]

Many businesses shy away from expecting nonprofits to let them know how their resources were used and what difference those resources made to the organization. Some worry they are burdening already overstretched nonprofits or believe incorrectly that such things "aren't measurable" anyway.

The reality is that effectively run nonprofits already track both the number of people served and the difference those services make. Or, if the nonprofit runs an environmental program, for example, it may collect data on how many trees were planted or miles of trail were refurbished. Federal and foundation grant programs have strict requirements for nonprofits on reporting results. For example, any nonprofit receiving federal dollars to run an AmeriCorps or VISTA program, takes performance measurement very seriously; it is one factor in receiving future grant funds.

By the same token, it is entirely reasonable for contributing businesses to ask for performance reports from nonprofit partners. Many of them already collect the information you seek, at least in the aggregate. Ask what they measure and the results they have been achieving. You don't need to recreate the wheel or think your company must measure the community outcomes yourself to justify your investment.

That said, in some cases your nonprofit partners are unable to isolate the impact of your *specific* contribution from that of other supporters. Unless the partnership was designed so that your company's resources were clearly the only new inputs into a project or event, it can be difficult to say with total precision what your specific impact was. However, it never hurts to ask.

Changes in the social world involve many variables. Sometimes the measurements taken to show progress and impact seem imprecise, especially when compared with results measured in a chemistry lab or in business ROI calculations. The expected standard for measurement is different in the nonprofit world, but don't be quick to judge it "inaccurate." Many nonprofits use rigorous and sophisticated measurement systems to document impact.

However, even if your partner can't tell you details of your direct impact, you can definitely say that you were an essential part of making a given result happen. In a partnership you are working together to achieve community goals, so it is appropriate to share credit for the results your contribution helped leverage—

especially if you were integrally involved. While it might be a stretch to pinpoint the impact of a $50 check invested in a gala charity dinner, that same amount invested more strategically might allow one more child to participate in a mentoring program. Contributions like that make it easier to see the impact.

Asking for nonprofit results on the activities you partner on allows you to make good decisions about what organizations to support and the best ways to do so for your company. In preliminary discussions, be sure to ask how they measure impact and what results they have found from their work. If they are unclear or can only speak in generalities, either help them upgrade their data collection tools using your employees' skills, hire a company like mine that has years of experience in social program measurement—or look for another partner.

Ron Brumbarger of **BitWise Solutions** stated, "I am not terribly crazy about funding an event just because someone wants to have an event. There better be a return in it for us. Even if it's somewhat difficult to calculate, there needs to be a return."[5] Any business person knows they will eventually need to answer the question, "what was the return on investment?" A "good" answer is typically X percent increase in sales for every X dollar spent on the program. However, there are no standard metrics and dueling points of view on how best to capture the impact of social action. Having trained nonprofits nationally for 20 years in performance measurement, I have seen firsthand that part of the issue is semantics. Most of the nonprofits I work with talk about performance measurement and evaluation—not metrics.

Most nonprofits have good systems in place to track their output results such as the number of client contacts or unique people served. So, getting at numbers that benefit from various programs or activities is not difficult. Often, all you have to do is ask. Historically many businesses have not asked them to share such information, so they may not think to offer it to you.

Many nonprofits also have systems in place to measure the difference their services made, at least in the medium term. It is always difficult to measure the long-term impact of some nonprofit services. For example, efforts focused on improving reading ability for third graders as a way to improve school performance with the long-term goal of improving high school graduation rates requires tracking students long after their participation in the program ends. Financial constraints combined with high mobility rates, especially among lower income at-risk youth, exacerbate the long-term measurement issue.

Frequently, the best a program can do is to show within a one to three year timeframe that they are creating the intermediate outcomes that are necessary prerequisites for longer-term changes. Finding that students have improved their reading to grade level and have improved performance in school is valuable. While not a guarantee of high school graduation, such results do show a child has a better chance of "making it" there. So measurement efforts in the here and now are extremely valuable indicators of the potential for the desired long-term outcome.

Many businesses and nonprofits are actively working to take their measurement systems to the next level. One current trend involves measuring "social return on investment" (SROI). However, in my experience, going this next step to make a financial estimate of the impact of social programs is still relatively rare in the nonprofit sector.

Another great example of an emerging trend in nonprofit measurement comes from **LifeQuest World Fund**, a nonprofit organization founded by T.J. Agresti in 2009 to provide charity-to-charity (C2C™) support, services, and funding for other nonprofits primarily through Charitable Legacy Accounts™. LifeQuest's mission is to increase the long-term financial strength of its charitable partners without impairing their current ability to support those in need. Ted Rusinoff, the fund's executive director, told me about the innovative "LifeQuest Index" to measure social value.

"When an organization receives a dollar from a donor, it can often deploy that dollar or some portion of it in such a way to increase the real, absolute value of the gift. If a $100 gift to an organization can be used to bring more than $100 of good to a certain group of beneficiaries or society as a whole, then a new way of defining accountability and measuring outcomes is possible," Ted explained. The LifeQuest Index provides a standardized means of considering the cost of delivering a nonprofit's service with the impact leveraged by investments in that service. "This ratio offers a new multiplier that helps define those nonprofits that are the most impactful with the resources that they have been given."

Ted stated that "this approach tends to quiet those who feel efficiency is the most important measure of an organization's operations. If the same dollars are given to two different organizations providing the same service to similar beneficiaries, then the real issue becomes effectiveness. When an organization measures effectiveness, it shifts the perspective to how much was enabled, instead of what percentage was deployed. As this concept continues to grow in its acceptance, more organizations will report on the way they can magnify the effective value of your gift."

Food for Thought

- Have you asked your nonprofit partners about the impact of their programs?
- Do you request such information? Routinely? Inconsistently?
- What can your partners tell you about outcomes? Can they provide the kind of detail you seek?
- What are your expectations for community impact?

Are they realistic? Have you discussed them with your nonprofit partners?

- Are you pleased with the leverage to do good in the community that resulted from your investment?
- How can you assist in improving your partners' capacity to measure impact?

Assess Company Outcomes

As discussed earlier in Step 6, few companies measure the business value of their community involvement initiatives. Measuring and quantifying improved reputation, faster permitting, or customer loyalty, for example, is not easy. Initially you may need to rely on estimates as you begin to develop internal systems and identify indicators, data collection tools, and processes for determining how community investment affects your company. Your efforts will be well worth your while.

This section offers guidelines on what your company might begin to measure to assess the impact of your community investment. Due to the complexity of defining and measuring the impact of community investment on your company, you may want to consider hiring an external consulting group like mine that specializes in measurement to provide assistance and help you get started.

To begin, consider two things. First, think back to the business goals you hoped to achieve and included in your Strategy for Good. Measuring something other than an intentional focus for your efforts is ill advised. For example, say your goal was to improve employee morale. To achieve this end, you sponsored a series of service projects with your favorite nonprofit partner. Clearly it makes sense to measure success with an employee survey of morale and loyalty. However, measuring the impact of those service projects on company sales, for example, especially if you did not strategically position the projects to maximize company exposure to potential or existing clients, can lead to disappointment. If you desire specific outcomes, be sure to design the joint action with your partners—and its measurement—strategically.

Second, consider what results would make the strongest case and be of greatest interest to your stakeholders. I believe companies should launch social initiatives for reasons beyond just the fact that it "feels good." Social programs, like any other corporate or brand program, need to prove their worth. However, I would challenge you to create trackable metrics beyond sales figures that demonstrate the value of such programs. This means examining the impact of your social programs on all of your company's stakeholders.

How does your community investment impact your company's customers, employees, community, suppliers, and shareholders? Community outcomes are directly related to the program or activity in which your business is involved. Company outcomes relate to how you have chosen to be involved and the goals you identified in your Strategy for Good. The following table provides food for thought about outcomes various stakeholders might be interested in.

Remember, to track a metric you must benchmark it *before* the program launches. You won't know how far you've gone unless you know where you started!

As you know, ROI is a common business metric or performance measure. It is used to evaluate the efficiency of an investment or to compare the efficiency of a number of different investments. To calculate ROI, the benefit (return) of an investment is divided by the cost of the investment; the result is expressed as a percentage or a ratio. For example, if you invested $10,000 in an event and it generated $25,000 in sales your ROI would be 1.5:1 (or x 100 = 150%).

However, for most community investment efforts, it is difficult to make clear links to ROI, in part due to how the terms of engagement were initially designed. However, remember the old saying: "What gets measured gets done." Even if you can't fully quantify the ROI of your community investment or a specific partnership, having a mindset of effectiveness and making a difference is important.

Table 6. Sample Outcomes of Interest to Stakeholders

Stakeholder Type	Sample Outcome Indicators
Customers	• Customer connection and loyalty • Exposure to new connections/networks • Sales • Generation of new business • Enhanced reputation • Brand recognition • Other
Employees	• Skills: teamwork, public speaking, project design, communication, management, leadership, etc. • Attitudes: morale, job commitment, company loyalty and pride, peers, community, diversity, etc. • Behaviors: absenteeism, lateness, productivity, etc. • Recruitment, Promotion, and Retention: new hires, turnover effects, cost savings, etc. • Other
Shareholders	• Value of risk avoided or mitigated • Sales • Market share • Other
Suppliers & Vendors	• Trust in company • Enhanced reputation • Other
Community –Nonprofit Partner(s)	• Total value of services or goods provided? • What difference did this activity make to: individuals, organizations, neighborhoods, community as a whole

There are four things you need to do to assess the results or performance of any business-nonprofit partnership:

1. Develop a logic model for your community investment activity. Before attempting to measure your results, get clear on the community and company results you desire. A great tool for this is a logic model. It is a planning matrix that helps you clarify your theory of change. Think of it as a roadmap for your community investment program, highlighting how you expect it to work, the sequence of activities, and the desired outcomes—both for the nonprofit/community and for your company.

A logic model also gives you the framework to do a reality check on the results you seek: do they make sense based on your level of investment? For example, if ten employees will each mentor one at-risk youth three hours a week, odds are good you will not significantly reduce the crime rate in your city. In a given neighborhood… maybe. Talk with your nonprofit partner about setting realistic targets.

Table 7 presents the five components of a logic model and an example to give you a flavor of how to use it.

2. Create measurement tools, processes, and timelines based on your desired results. Identify which ones you will do and which ones will be done by your nonprofit partner. Then implement the planned program/activities your business is supporting that will result in your desired outcomes. Use the Sample Partnership Measurement Plan, Table 8 below to identify things you need to consider.

3. Follow your plan. Collect the necessary information to measure the performance of your program/activity and its results.

4. Use the information you collect about the results of your partnership to improve the program/activity and/or the partnership itself. Share the results with your stakeholders to demonstrate how your resources helped create real good in the community, and to show that your nonprofit partnership

was a sound investment. Finally, use your results to promote what you and your nonprofit partner are jointly doing in the community.

Table 7. Sample Logic Model

Need	Inputs	Activity	Outputs	Outcomes
What identified local need is the program trying to address with its resources?	**Resources available to be invested**	**What the program does with its resources to address community needs and make a difference**	**Counts of the amount of services delivered, work completed, or products created** Note: *Outputs* do NOT provide information on changes or benefits for beneficiaries	**Changes or benefits that occur as a result of services delivered Changes or benefits that occur as a result of services delivered**
At-risk middle school youth who lack positive adult role models are at greater risk for delinquency	*Employees Paid release time for volunteering*	*15 employees will mentor at-risk middle school students through XYZ nonprofit one-on-one 3 hours/ week*	• *# of employee mentors recruited* • *# of middle school students mentored* • *# hours of mentoring*	***Community:*** *At-risk middle school youth mentored have lower delinquency rate (than not mentored peers)* ***Company:*** *Employees are more loyal to company*

In addition to measuring the difference your efforts made, it is also important to take an intentional look at how the partnership process worked. Be sure to develop a process for soliciting feedback from employees involved in the activities. After an event or program is completed, it is highly recommended that you have a debriefing with your nonprofit partner to discuss how things worked from both of your perspectives. Reviewing each joint project or activity helps you proactively build on strengths and minimize issues in the future whether with this partner or others.

Table 8. Sample Partnership Measurement Plan

Component	Example
Activity *Describe what you plan to do. Tell who is involved, what they will be doing, where, when, for how long, etc.*	10 employees of CORE THOUGHT will participate as a team in the annual Denver Partners Superstars Fundraising event, where teams compete in a series of fun sporting events, on Saturday, July 9, 2011, 9 am to 3 pm, to help raise money and show support for mentoring.
Desired Result(s) *Describe what you hope will happen as a result of this activity*	**Business:** To increase visibility in community **Employee(s):** To increase teamwork skills To increase pride in company **Community:** To raise money for mentoring programs
Nonprofit Beneficiaries *Who directly benefits from this activity? How many benefit?*	Denver Partners nonprofit organization and their 50 Senior and Junior mentoring partnerships
Indicators *What are the visible things that show you are moving in the direction of reaching your desired result?*	**Outputs (What gets done?)** Company logo displayed at event Public thanks given at event Number of employees participating Money raised by CORE THOUGHT, by event **Outcomes (So what? What changes?)** Intentional use of teamwork skills during event Increased pride in the company
Targets *How much will you consider to be "enough"? How many will change by how much?*	Outputs: Company banner will be displayed at event Company featured in 3 media spots reaching 500,000 people At least 10 employees will participate At least $1,000 will be raised **Outcomes**: 80% of participating employees report intentional use of teamwork skills during event 80% of participating employees express increased pride in the company
Data Collection Method and Instruments *How will you collect information to show you are reaching desired result?*	Log: Event Summary Report and Employee Sign-In Sheet Survey: Employee Follow-up Email Survey

Food for Thought

- Did you do what you said you would with the joint project? Did your nonprofit partner?
- How well did you do it? What worked?
- Were internal deadlines met?
- Was the project and/or relationship well managed by both organizations?
- Was the communication timely and clear?
- What could be done better next time? Any lessons learned?
- What feedback did you receive from participating employees? From those not involved?

Step 6 Action Plan:

- Discuss the data collection system your nonprofit partner uses to measure impact.
- Identify the community outputs and outcomes your investment will affect.
- Identify the desired company outputs and outcomes of your investment.
- Develop data collection systems and tools to measure company effects.
- Collect and aggregate company-related data.
- Summarize community and company results.
- After the project or activity, hold a debriefing session with participating employees and nonprofit representatives.
- Assess overall success; identify lessons learned and next steps.

Step 7: Share Your Story

"There is nothing wrong with making sure that your company is adequately acknowledged for your contribution to different causes and events."

—Jason Linkow, Former Owner, **Metafolics Salon,** Denver, Colorado[1]

Congratulations! You've created and implemented a business giving program. You've begun developing win-win relationships with valued nonprofit partners. Your community, the nonprofit, and your company are all starting to see the results of your Strategy for Good.

The final step in engaging in mutually beneficial partnerships with nonprofits is celebrating your success. Share the story of your community involvement with stakeholders both within and external to your company. Spreading the word about your positive connection with a nonprofit adds value and builds reputation for both organizations. For small or low-profile nonprofits, partnering with a well-known, respected business can cause people to stop and take more interest in them and what they do. For businesses, sharing the story of an interesting way you have supported a nonprofit can affect how the company is viewed by employees and current or potential customers, helping to cement loyalty, as discussed in Part I: Strategic Business Giving.

Some business leaders worry that sharing information about their community investment is distasteful self-promotion—they don't want to appear crass or self-serving. Others fear being accused of "goodwashing" or overinflating their efforts.

Remember, there is a huge difference between boasting for self-gain and raising awareness of mutually beneficial partnership between business and the nonprofit sector. In these times of increasing employee and consumer expectations concerning give-back and accountability, sharing the story of your community involvement is an essential step. Don't skip it!

Communicate with Employees

Employees are key stakeholders for your community investment efforts. You need to have a transparent and timely way of sharing how the company works with nonprofits and how the community has benefited. Employees that were involved firsthand know of the company's efforts, but others may not. Don't overlook sharing even modest support provided to nonprofits. Think about ways you can go beyond sharing after-the-fact announcements of your involvement. For example, you could host a festive, celebratory lunch or break-time to show company commitment to both your employees and the community. The more employees know about the company's community investment and experience it as a positive, the more likely they will become involved themselves, helping leverage even more good on your behalf. Be sure to follow up and share results as soon as possible after the activity to acknowledge your employee's participation and ensure they feel successful so their passion will continue.

Consider the following possible approaches to sharing and celebrating your successes with employees:

Share reports of the company programs and activities and their results. Consider the best ways to get the word out and build buzz. These can include interoffice memos, email, intranet, bulletin boards, posters in the break room, and status updates on the company Facebook page.

Invite employees who participated to act as spokespeople telling the story of what they learned and how they experienced the work of the nonprofit partner.

Host company-sponsored events or parties to celebrate participation and achievement of community investment goals and/or encourage future participation.

Plan field trips or site visits to your nonprofit partner's location(s). Establishing a personal connection and seeing firsthand the work being done in the community is powerful and helps engage passion and commitment.

Give awards or prizes for excellent service in the community, such as certificates of appreciation, gift cards, a free lunch with the CEO, etc. for employees or the department.

Make a donation in the name of an employee or a department on top of whatever good they already provided.

Have a "big check" presentation ceremony using a mock poster-size check made out in the amount of the donation when providing cash or grants. Invite employees, nonprofit representatives, local dignitaries or elected officials, the media, etc.

Tell Customers and the Community at Large

Your customers and the community also want to know about your community investment. Effective communication can provide you a competitive edge and cement loyalty. According to Cone's 2010 Cause Evolution Study, "90 percent of consumers want companies to tell them the ways they are supporting causes. Put another way: more than 278 million people in the U.S. want to know what a company is doing to benefit a cause."[2] Therefore, effective, well-rounded communications is an essential ingredient of effective community investment.

In addition, Americans want to experience and make direct

contributions to their communities not only through their own participation, but also through their buying power in partnership with companies they know are actively giving back. If you minimize or withhold information about your community investment, in effect you are giving ground to competitors who *do* publicize their giving program openly and effectively. Put simply, *if you don't share your story, you stand to lose valuable business.* What's more, research shows that if a company offers consumers scant information about how a specific cause-marketing purchase benefits the issue, 34 percent will either choose another brand or walk away entirely.[3]

Gary Hirshberg of **Stonyfield Farm** explained, "We get a lot of media attention when we leave the typical ivory tower of corporate activism and mobilize and energize around causes." Several years ago, as a father frustrated by the quality of food offered his children in schools, Gary and Stonyfield launched "just a simple little 30-machine demonstration effort to put healthy vending machines in schools around the country" to see if kids would use them. "It was just a modest little attempt to ask, 'Hey, can't we come up with something better than what we are presently doing?' Just the act of asking the question and posing one hypothetical answer caused an avalanche of media and consumer interest. We received something like 50 million media impressions."[4] Not only was this an innovative project designed to "do good," it generated valuable attention the company never could have afforded through advertising.

Some businesses are concerned if they let people know what they have supported, they will be bombarded by even more nonprofit requests—and they already feel stretched. This is where having a solid Strategy for Good, clear community investment priorities, strong selection criteria, and an established process makes all the difference. The benefits of transparency to your bottom line outweigh the issue of increased requests.

Before embarking on any promotional plan, think about how you want your company represented in promotional materials, including how you will use your logo. Logos are a very important marketing and branding tool. Having invested thought and money in designing your logo, it is important to control its use by your nonprofit partners since it is synonymous with your business. Therefore, it's wise to establish some rules for use of the company logo in community activities. Consider the following questions and then write a page or so explaining your parameters for logo use. Share this document with your employees or partnering nonprofit organizations as you ask for publicity and recognition for your company's community investment.

1. Do your employees need written permission to make the company logo available to a partnering charitable organization?
2. If so, do employees also need approval for the volunteer activity they wish to perform before logo use is allowed?
3. Are there any instances where company logo use is prohibited?
4. Where will the employee obtain the logo? (CD? Website?)
5. What are restrictions on the modifications of the logo?
    a. If it is in color, can it be used in black and white or grayscale?
    b. Do you need to ensure that a trademark (e.g., TM, ®, or ©) be included with each use?
    c. Can the logo be combined with other symbols or trademarks?
    d. Are there size restrictions (maximum or minimum)?
    e. Must the company name always appear with the logo?"[5]

It is important to talk with your nonprofit connection to determine mutual expectations and roles and responsibilities not only for engaging in the specific project but also in sharing the word of your joint efforts. Many businesses people expect the nonprofit to get the word out to their constituencies on their behalf and are disappointed when that doesn't happen as they'd hoped. If this is one of your expectations, discuss clearly and directly with your partner how to make the desired result happen.

In the rare case where you truly do not want your story shared publicly, be sure to make your wishes plain to your partner. For example, a nonprofit developed a partnership with a large national membership warehouse company to put together backpacks with school supplies for a back-to-school event for low-income children. The company donated significant resources to help make this happen. The nonprofit wrote a nice piece in their annual report thanking the company for the support, thinking it was the "right thing to do." However, company representatives were unhappy about the publicity—although they did share other community investment efforts. The oversight almost nixed the possibility of repeating the activity a second year. Don't make assumptions! You need to be clear about your expectations and communicate them to your nonprofit partners.

Most businesses appreciate the good press. Additionally, they expect the nonprofit to take the lead in getting the word out to the community about the partnership, and to share the benefits of the joint efforts. Having the nonprofit send out press releases under its name greatly increases the likelihood that it will be picked up by media outlets. People generally have greater trust in what a nonprofit says about a company than what the company says about itself in the media. If publicity is a weak area for your nonprofit partner, your company can assist in preparing articles and press releases, perhaps through your public relations unit. Preferably the release should go out under the nonprofit's name. Let them toot your horn.

Businesses often complain that the nonprofit was unable

to deliver on their promise of getting the word out. If that is an expectation agreed upon by the partners, be sure both organizations follow through. Remember, sharing success is a two-way street. Your company has various ways to publicize your nonprofit partnerships to help get the word out about the programs/activities you supported and your nonprofit partners, which will raise awareness for your joint efforts and encourage others to get involved.

Getting the word out is "not to just toot your own horn," says Tracy Ulmer of ***The Denver Post***. "It has the key goal [for us] of further engaging people: here's what we are doing and what you can do to help keep it going. It's all in that word 'engaging' as opposed to talking at people. You have to make what you do visible."[6]

The Denver Post communicates what it does in multiple ways: through quarterly giving reports distributed to subscribers and other key stakeholders, on the company website, and through full page ads announcing grant recipients. All of these describe how the money will be used, plus nonprofit recipient descriptions and website addresses so interested people know where to go to learn more or get involved themselves.

"Giving back to the community is a very neighborly thing to do, so we don't like to run around patting ourselves on the back," says Mark Berzins, Owner of Denver's **Little Pub Company**.[7] "But at the same time, we like people to know within the communities where we operate that we are good citizens and support causes in their neighborhood; we're donating services to their children's schools and to organizations they enjoy."

One way the Little Pub Company lets people know about their nonprofit work is by periodically putting information out on the tables at their pubs. They frame it as thanking customers for supporting the company, which in turn supports patrons' neighborhoods by giving time and money to the local organizations. The table placards list the organizations that have benefited from Little Pub's community work. Mark states, "I think that's an intangible benefit. I have people come up and say all the time, 'Thanks for helping out with this or that event.' I think people are a little surprised because often times, in my business, people don't take the time to give back."[8]

Below are ways to share your community investment story with customers and the community at large:

- Post a community involvement page on your website highlighting your Strategy for Good mission, strategy, and criteria.
- On your website's community page, present which organizations were supported, perhaps with logos. Provide basic information on your nonprofit partners' work, and always include a link to their websites. Consider offering ways customers can participate with you in support of these organizations.
- Develop a calendar or timeline for media exposure by working backwards from the day of your event or announcement.
- Provide statistics on your community involvement's reach and impact, e.g., "50 middle school students were tutored by employees who provided over 500 hours of time" or "90% of mentored students showed improved commitment to school." Include dollar values (actual or estimated) for resources, donations, or leveraged assets, if you choose.
- Post a sign in a visible location in your store or office highlighting your partnership and promoting their organization.
- Print a summary of your community giving on customer bills or include an insert either with the statement to save postage or as a separate billing.

- Prepare press releases, calendar listings, and public service announcements either directly or in collaboration with your nonprofit partner.
- Write an opinion editorial, guest column, or letter to the editor highlighting the work of your partner and/or the issue they are addressing and its impact on the community.
- Make presentations about your partnership featuring the work of the nonprofits to professional and community groups. Identify employee spokespeople or service beneficiaries to talk about their experience participating in your community investment.
- Put an ad in the local newspaper honoring your nonprofit partners.
- Invite the media to attend an event or do a special interest story.
- Include a section on community involvement in your annual report or prepare a stand-alone report.
- Send holiday or greeting cards to customers announcing donations to a nonprofit in their name or by your company.
- Include customers on your distribution list for press releases on your community investment.
- Leverage industry publications, trade magazines, and other communications tools to become a community investment champion—both to create a competitive advantage and to serve as a role model for other companies.
- Follow-up with thank you notes and outcomes of projects to the media.

Keep in mind the following four important questions when sharing your successes.

1. WHAT is the message?

- WHAT do we want to share?
- WHY do we want to promote our story?
- WHO do we want to promote to?
- HOW do we plan to do it?

2. What avenues do we have for sharing the successes of our partnership and publicly acknowledging the contributions of both organizations?
3. What are the expectations of our nonprofit and other business partners concerning telling the story?
4. How can the nonprofit support our efforts in getting the word out? (e.g., press releases, connections, etc.)

Discover Award Opportunities

Few businesses engage in community involvement simply to receive an award for their efforts. However, honors bestowed by business peers, chambers of commerce, industry associations, nonprofits, and other community groups are an added side benefit that enhances your reputation as an exemplary corporate citizen. Usually, a nonprofit partner, peer, or community member familiar with your community investment nominates you by filling out the necessary paperwork detailing your contribution and its impact. Alternatively, you may nominate your own company, although I always think it is better if someone else toots your company's horn. To find out about local and national awards, the easiest thing to do is keep your ears open or run an online search.

Examples of award sponsors include National Philanthropy Day, the *Denver Business Journal*'s Partners in Philanthropy, CECP's (Committee Encouraging Corporate Philanthropy) Excellence Awards in Corporate Philanthropy, and the *San Francisco Business Times*' Corporate Philanthropy Awards.

Step 7 Action Plan:

- Create a promotional plan and determine ways to get the word out.
- Work with your nonprofit partner on sharing your story within your company and in the community.
- Celebrate your success with various stakeholders, especially employees.
- Investigate relevant awards for which your efforts might qualify.

In Part II we walked through the overall process of strategic business giving, from planning to realization to celebrating success. The section offered questions for reflection, action steps, and real-life examples from companies to get you on your way. Before moving on to Part III, which covers the key categories of business giving, let's summarize the seven essential steps to developing your own Strategy for Good.

- Step 1 is all about building commitment for business giving within your company. It's important that all stakeholders—senior management, employees, and investors—buy in to community involvement and understand the many business benefits of giving.
- Step 2 looks backward to move forward. Review past philanthropic efforts to get a sense of which contributions and actions brought a meaningful return for both you and the causes you supported.
- Step 3 helps you identify your company's values, needs, and resources so you can link community involvement to key business goals.
- Step 4 covers the process of selecting causes, partners, and

projects that are a good match for your company and the business ends you hope to achieve.

- Step 5 guides you in cultivating win-win relationships with nonprofit partners that last and provide mutual benefit to both the organization and your company.
- Step 6 shows you how to measure the impacts of your giving on your nonprofit partner, the community, and your company—a critical piece of an effective Strategy for Good.
- Step 7 encourages you to share your business giving story both within and outside of company walls. Remember: people *want* to support companies that make a positive impact in their communities and in our world.

For dozens of ideas on ways to give—of dollars, in-kind contributions, people's time, and commercial arrangements—let's dive into Part III.

Part III: *Strategic Ways to Give*

"It's amazing...when you transform the fundamental goal of business, what other opportunities emerge as possible ways to serve the interests of the community—without compromising the ultimate goal of being a successful [and profitable] business."

—Mike Hannigan, Founder, **Give Something Back Office Supplies,** Oakland, California[1]

Dollars, In-Kind, People, and Commerce

Although financial resources are an important option to consider as part of your business giving portfolio, there are many other ways to support nonprofits via both contributions and commerce. The following pages cover the main categories of engagement, represented in Figure 5 below:

- Charitable dollars (cash) from the company, customers, and employees;
- In-kind contributions;
- People's time and skills; and
- Commerce

Figure 5. Ways to Give

Cash
Commerce
Strategic Community Investment
In-Kind
People

Most companies pursue a range of ways to support nonprofits as part of their giving portfolio. Pick the ones to try that most resonate with you and your employees and build upon your company's strengths. This section of the book offers you a menu of options on ways to give. However, although extensive, it is not an exhaustive list. Some of the examples presented are well-known proven tactics for good; others are more innovative. Let this section provide food for thought as you consider how best to support nonprofits and their missions. Hopefully, the examples and ideas in the following pages will help spur creative thought as you design the unique ways your company can be involved in the community.

In Part III we'll look at the main categories of business giving. Dollars, in-kind, and people all constitute a company contribution of one kind or another. Commercial approaches are a different animal, covered last in this section. Under charitable dollars, you'll find ideas for ways to leverage your networks of employees, customers, vendors, and business colleagues to raise money beyond what might be available in your own philanthropy budget. (Generating cash through cause marketing is covered under commerce.) Next we'll look at in-kind donations of both goods and services. Last in the contributions section, you'll find ideas and strategies for engaging people and their time. Finally, moving beyond company contributions, we'll cover engaging with nonprofits based on commercial approaches that help both organizations achieve their goals.

Part III explores each of these options, explaining what they are, providing real life examples of how companies have done them, and offering up food for thought questions for you to consider if you are interested in trying it out or fine-tuning what you are already doing in each area.

Pick ways to get involved that make sense based on the community where you want to be involved but also on your company's goals, assets, comparative advantages, and available resources. For example, Ellen Feeney, a long-standing leader in socially responsible business, says, "For certain companies, branding or sponsoring an event that would fall into cause marketing wouldn't really do that much for them. If they are a business-to-business entity and it's a consumer event, it's not really a fit. But, if you've got a consumer packaged goods product and you're trying to raise awareness and this sponsorship offers you an opportunity to offer samples, go for it. Spend some real branding dollars on it—not just the philanthropic budget."

Charitable Dollars

Nonprofits frequently approach businesses asking for financial donations as a way to secure needed dollars to fund their services and cover their administrative costs. Dollars are sometimes the easiest "no-brainer" way for businesses to engage with nonprofits. Dollars combined with time, in-kind donations, or other resources can create a meaningful and impactful experience for both organizations. Nonetheless, contributing monetary resources alone to your nonprofit partners is a key way to show your support of their work and may work best for your company's needs as well.

Figure 6 shows the three primary sources of cash for charitable giving: company, customer, and employee dollars. Let's look at each in turn in the pages that follow.

Figure 6. Sources of Charitable Dollars

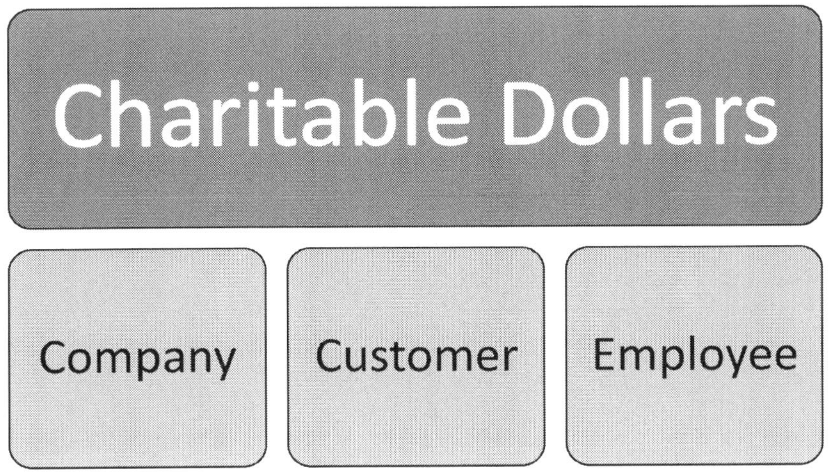

Company Dollars

Many companies operate annual giving programs to make charitable grants, funded as part of their annual operating budgets. A giving program has no independent endowment and its budget is typically administered by designated staff and directed by the CEO or an advisory committee. A giving program is not subject to the rules and regulations governing private corporate foundations.

As illustrated in Figure 7, there are seven main ways companies give back using company dollars. Each is described below with selected examples from companies that use each as part of their giving portfolio.

Figure 7. Ways to Give Company Dollars

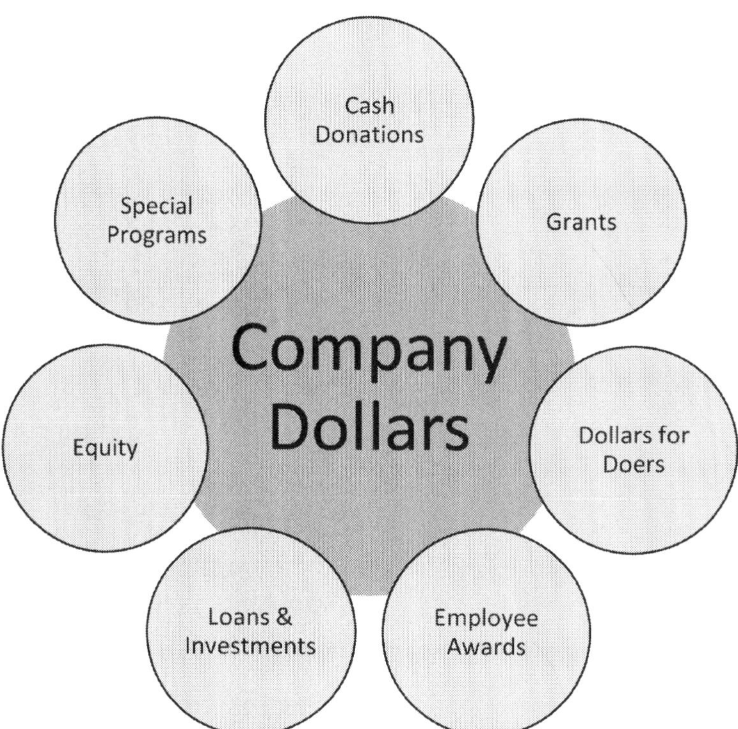

Cash Donations

Some companies, especially smaller ones, do not engage in formal grantmaking. Instead, they provide ad hoc and relatively small cash donations, often on a first-come, first-served basis to nonprofits that approach them. Small cash donations usually come with no strings attached—the company makes no request for reports on how the money was used or what results it helped the organization achieve. These are true gifts.

Tweezerman makes charitable donations but, according to company President Lisa Bowen, "We don't call it [a] grant, but in a way it is. We are deciding where to put the money. Some organizations, like Dress for Success, write to us and ask for a grant but mostly we view it is just charitable donations." She says that while they are informal in that they do not ask for reports back from nonprofits they give money to, they do check out the organization and make sure it is a 501(c)(3).[1]

BetterWorld Telecom donates a total of three percent of annual revenues to organizations that benefit children, education, fair trade, and the environment. Over the past five years, the company has contributed hundreds of thousands of dollars. Their goal is to donate $1 million per year by 2012.[2]

Tips

- *Avoid giving cash. Always make contributions by check and make your check payable to the nonprofit, not to the individual collecting the donation.*
- *Keep records of your donations (receipts, canceled checks, and bank statements) so you can document your charitable giving at tax time. Although the value of volunteer time is not deductible, out-of-pocket expenses (including transportation costs) directly related to volunteer service to a nonprofit are deductible.*
- *Realize that "tax exempt" doesn't always mean "tax deductible." "Tax exempt" simply means the organization does not have to pay*

taxes. "Tax deductible" means the donor can deduct contributions to the organization on his or her federal income tax return.

- *A payment to a charity qualifies as deductible only to the extent that it exceeds the fair market value of the privilege or benefit the donor receives in return. For example, if a charity charges $10 for a box of candy that normally sells for $8, only $2 can be claimed as a charitable contribution. The price of participating in a raffle or similar drawing cannot be deducted. Likewise, tickets to a fundraising dinner or other charity event are not fully deductible. Only the portion of the ticket price above the value of the meal or entertainment can be deducted. The same rule applies even if the donor donates her tickets to the disadvantaged. Finally, membership dues that merely cover the cost of privileges or benefits received by the "donor" are not deductible. However, dues for which the donor receives little or no benefit of monetary value in return are deductible.*
- *The Internal Revenue Code defines more than 20 different categories of tax-exempt organizations, but contributions to only a few of these are tax deductible.*
- *Consult your CPA or accounting department to determine if your donations are tax deductible and how best to utilize the tax benefits available to all companies.*

Grants

Mid-size and larger companies often engage in grantmaking as a way to support community organizations. Grants are awards of funds to a nonprofit organization to undertake charitable activities.

Grants generally are used by the nonprofit to cover program or direct service costs, organizational operating expenses, or a combination of both. Some businesses fund only programmatic expenses in the desire to reach those intended to benefit from the program. However, this programmatic bias can be problematic for nonprofits. All organizations have operating and administrative expenses, such as the critical role of the executive director. If a grant restricts spending to direct service costs, disallowing staffing and oversight, for example, service quality may suffer. Program-only grants can actually set nonprofits up for failure—the very opposite of what the donor intended! Consider being flexible in how your nonprofit partners may spend grant funds from your company.

Grant-making involves an application process and a competitive review to select the grant recipients. Potential grantees usually are asked to describe their organization, mission, and programming, and to explain how the funds would be used. Grant applications also typically ask for staff and board qualifications, specifics on the service delivery model, desired outcomes and how they will be measured, and budget information.

The process of reviewing and selecting grant applications ranges in complexity and level of scrutiny. Reviewers assess the applications based on how well they meet the predefined criteria, define their case, and show promise of positive impact. Grant reviews can be undertaken internally by a group of employees, by a team made up of both employees and outside community experts, or by an outside peer review process.

Establishing a grant review committee rather than a lone decision maker is a smart strategy. For starters, it takes you the owner or senior manager off the hook from having to personally say "no" to the flood of requests. When you're out in the community speaking at events or in meetings, you become a bright target for fundraising appeals. Having a committee enables you to graciously defer the decision making. This is especially helpful when you suspect a request is a poor fit for your company or your annual budget has been expended. What's more, offering others a chance to serve on the committee to review proposals and make funding decisions helps create buy-in and commitment from employees and/or community members.

Ted Rusinoff, Executive Director of **LifeQuest World Fund**, agrees. "When considering who will manage the grant award process, it may be beneficial to put these decisions in the hands of a committee of employees," he advises. "Depending on the size of the organization and the geographic disparity of the workforce, you may find that a board appointed committee of employees magnifies the perceived value of the program in the eyes of those who work for the organization. When a group of their peers evaluates the causes they are willing to support or, better put, 'reinforce' the efforts of their co-workers out in the community, a sense of control and accomplishment will accompany the dollars used to fund the programs and further supports a positive internal and external morale."

Grant programs can be run in-house, administered by the corporation's foundation, outsourced to a consulting business that will run the grants process for you, or set-up as a donor-advised fund through a local community foundation. Large companies often create their own private foundation to manage their community investment. Such foundations are funded through an annual percentage of company revenue or as an endowment from the "parent." Donor-advised funds are funds held and managed for the company for a small administrative fee. The donor, or a committee appointed by the donor, may recommend eligible charitable recipients for grants from the fund. There is usually a minimum contribution required to open an account. Donor-advised funds, especially for smaller companies, remove the day-to-day burden of managing a grants program in house.

Food for Thought

- What will be your company's funding priorities? What is the alignment with your overall community involvement strategy and business goals?

- Who will administer the company's grant programs? That is, who will be responsible for grant review, scoring, selection, and oversight? An internal department? The company or community foundation? Or independent consulting group?
- What will be your selection criteria? Who will choose?
- Are the grants one-time or is there a possibility of multiple-year funding? What will be the award amount? Is there a range?
- What will you fund? Program costs? Operating expenses?
- What is your funding cycle? When are the deadlines?
- What are the reporting requirements?
- How will you let potential applicants know of your grant opportunity? Through active outreach through a local nonprofit support agency? Sending an announcement to a mailing list of relevant current and former inquiries? On your website?

There are two main types of grants to consider: traditional and challenge, also called matching, grants. A description of both follows.

Traditional Grants

With traditional grants, the company runs a systematic process, often on an annual basis, to fund community action with an issue of concern to the company. For example, **Patagonia** commits a percentage of annual profits to grassroots environmental activism. Preference is given to innovative groups overlooked or rejected by other corporate donors—the company funds activists who take radical and strategic steps to protect habitat, wilderness, and biodiversity. Patagonia has given $38 million in grants and in-kind donations to more than a thousand organizations since the grants program began.[3]

Rock Bottom Foundation, the charitable arm of a parent company of restaurants and pubs, offers "Mini Miracles" to support community acts in their focus areas of hunger and homelessness. These grants assist their employees' volunteer efforts. An individual restaurant is free to determine how it wants to use the funds—either as a direct gift to a nonprofit or to underwrite the expense of running a fundraiser.[4]

New Belgium Brewing donates one dollar for every barrel of beer produced to its philanthropy program to fund activities in four areas.[5]

Zhena's Gypsy Tea's grants are designed "to teach a woman to fish." Explains Founder Zhena Muzyka, "We are not blindly putting money anywhere. We are making sure the money is going toward social programs that will help people's skills."[6]

Matching and Challenge Grants

In these grant programs, the company agrees to match a percentage of other resources raised by the nonprofit for a specific program or project—it might be an even one-to-one match or a generous four-to-one. 4:1. The grantor decides the ratio and agrees to contribute dollars provided the necessary other funding is secured, usually within a specified time period.

The major advantage of matching grants, as compared to outright grants, is that they permit nonprofit applicants to challenge other potential donors to contribute cash to worthwhile projects thus leveraging broader participation and support from multiple sources in the community.

Challenge grants are a special type of matching grant. The *challenge* refers to the actions or results the recipient must achieve before the money is released. This usually involves substantial effort, so that the recipients know they are helping themselves through their own hard work. Challenge grants often are given as the culmination of a larger capital campaign to renovate existing facilities, construct a new building, or purchase property or major equipment. Challenge grants provide credibility to leverage private dollars while helping nonprofits strengthen their long-term sustainability through brick-and-mortar projects.

For example, the **Kresge Foundation** awards challenge grants to help nonprofit organizations build their base of private financial support as they conduct capital campaigns to build or renovate facilities. Kresge makes these challenge grants to organizations that cater to the needs of the poor, disadvantaged, and disenfranchised in six program areas: health, the environment, arts and culture, education, human services, and community development, especially in Detroit. Most Kresge challenge grant awards are awarded to organizations undertaking exceptional projects that align with the strategic objectives of a given program that advances Kresge's values. Typically these grants range from $100,000 to $2.5 million, payable within 60 days of the date the grantee meets its campaign goal and other conditions outlined in the grant agreement.[7]

Special Programs

In addition to traditional and challenge grants, some companies run other special programs using company dollars. For example, each year **Annie's Homegrown** donates about two dozen $1,000 scholarships for undergraduate and graduate students studying environmental or health issues. Chelsea Simons, national cause and event marketing manager for Annie's Homegrown, explained that the environmental scholarship program "renews our faith in what we are trying to do as a company on a greater scale. As we read the application essays and students' life experiences that have led them to a really defined interest in environmental science, it keeps it real for us. Sometimes as you get deeper and deeper into the corporate world, you start to lose some of those initial passionate feelings about going out there and really changing things. So, the scholarship program is wonderful on both sides—the reward for us is as big as it is for the students."[8]

Dollars for Doers

A Dollars for Doers program is a company contributions program that donates cash grants to qualified nonprofit organizations at which the employees volunteer. The grants, which range typically from $500 and up, provide direct support to community organizations where employees volunteer time ranging from an hour a week to hundreds of hours per year.

When Dollars for Doers programs were first created, their purpose was twofold: to serve as an alternative to a company's matching gifts program for those employees who could donate time but not dollars and, second, to motivate employee participation in volunteer events and activities. In recent years, companies have implemented Dollars for Doers programs as a way to recognize employees for their community involvement as well as to stimulate civic participation from within the company.

Dollars for Doers is a growing phenomenon as companies seek ways to support their employees and the issues and organizations that are most meaningful to them and their communities. It is estimated that 60 percent of mid- and large-size businesses currently offer Dollars for Doers programs; the number is expected to reach 75 percent within a year or two. Studies report higher job satisfaction and employee retention in companies with organized employee volunteer programs, especially when coupled with Dollars for Doers programs.

Key benefits of Dollars for Doers programs include the following. They:

- Give employees choices on how to engage in the community
- Offer incentives for volunteerism
- Provide volunteer recognition

- Include a mechanism to better track employee volunteerism
- Combine well with other specific company-sponsored activities (e.g. science education)
- Give employees a way to contribute cash without taking it from their own pocket
- Offer flexibility in when volunteering takes place, since it rewards any volunteerism during work time or on employee's own time

Companies large and small offer Dollars for Doers programs. For example, the **Qwest Foundation** funds a matching program through which $500 donations are made to nonprofit organizations where employees volunteer at least 40 hours over a six-month period.[9] **Microsoft** matches volunteer time at $17 per hour through their program. Since 2005 in the United States alone, Microsoft employees have volunteered more than 1 million hours in their communities, generating $17 million in donations.[10] The **Public Service Enterprise Group** provides $250 grants to nonprofits on behalf of the first 200 PSEG volunteers that apply and are approved annually. Their policy on employee eligibility includes criteria that might help you develop your own. It states that employees:

- Must be a permanent full- or part-time PSEG employee with at least three months of continuous company service
- Volunteer activities must be in addition to and completely separate from job responsibilities
- Must be an established, active, non-compensated volunteer at the nonprofit organization
- Must provide a minimum of 50 hours of service per year to the nonprofit organization
- A maximum of two grants per employee will be awarded in a calendar year
- Volunteer activities that benefit the community including, but not limited to, board participation, committee work,

fundraising, tutoring, mentoring, or neighborhood revitalization, are generally eligible[11]

Awards and Incentives

There other ways you can offer employees fun and motivating ways to get involved in your company's community involvement. For example, Dave Ellis, author of *Falling Awake,* after a very profitable year, gave each of his employees $500 to donate to the nonprofit of their choice. **Cisco Systems** created a performance competition in which employees could nominate a peer for consideration as "Employee of the Year." The selected employee, instead of a personal bonus, was given $20,000 to allocate as they desired to local nonprofits and their programs. Instead of giving gifts to employees or customers for business or referrals, another option is to make a donation in their name to a nonprofit.

Loans and Investments

"Cash" doesn't always have to mean "donation." Some investors and businesses use their financial resources to provide loans to nonprofits to assist with special projects including capital investments. It's not a grant or a handout—the nonprofit is expected to pay the loan back with interest. In his book *Giving,* Bill Clinton states that "while government incentives and foundation efforts...are helpful, the truth is, there is money to be made by investing in underserved communities and groups."[12]

Karl Dakin, a Denver-based Business Consultant, further explained the concept to me. "One of the classical reasons investors make investments in businesses or new projects, whether professional angel investors or those who only occasionally invest, is to gain equity in that particular organization and participate in the profits that are earned over time," he said. "However, that avenue for access to capital is not open to nonprofits because by their very nature, they can't distribute profits or have people invest directly in the organization."[13]

Karl continued, "However, that doesn't mean that the nonprofit organization doesn't need the money for a particular activity. What they can do is take a loan from an investor, pay that investor an interest rate on the loan, or maybe even pay a royalty coming out of sales from a particular product or service resulting from that activity."[14] This approach gives an investor or business a chance to help the nonprofit get the capital it needs to carry out a particular program and, at the same time, avoid getting tied up in the limitations of an equity-style investment.

Karl gave an example of a nonprofit association he was working with that needed capital to produce an education curriculum concerning off-shore manufacturing for a business audience. Using this approach, the nonprofit secured loans from various businesses in order to fund their curriculum development project. They now sell the finished product for a fee and pay a royalty back to each of the business investors.

Give Something Back Office Supplies was approached by a nonprofit running a youth job development program in Oakland, California, seeking assistance to buy a building. They needed the money quickly and didn't have the time to do a capital campaign or find a bank and do all the due diligence required to get a loan. Founder Mike Hannigan shared, "We knew this organization and had a very long-term relationship with them. Frankly, we had the money in our account and credit lines. So, we lent them [the money] to place a down payment on the building."

The loan was guaranteed by the State of California which amortized the purchase of the building. "It was a no-risk loan on our part, but it was something that they couldn't have done without us stepping in and loaning them a half million dollars on a day's notice." Mike feels the loan was consistent with their business mission so there were no bureaucratic decisions to be made; it was "the right thing to do."

Give Something Back's unused asset catalyzed the growth of the facility into one of the most important community resources in Oakland for job development and training. The center now includes a charter school and foster care education. "Think of the business as a tool to enrich the community while maintaining your effectiveness as a business," Mike advises. "All kinds of things become possible and interesting to consider."[15]

Equity/Stock Donations

Companies can set aside a portion of their equity as a charitable contribution to a nonprofit. Start-up companies may elect to give founders shares of stock to a nonprofit that they support. Because the shares have no or minimal cash value, the allocation generally poses no negative cash consequence for the receiving nonprofit.

While a start-up's future is always uncertain, neither you nor the nonprofit can know what the true value of the company stock gift will be for the longer term. With a contribution of equity, a company creates a nest egg that can fund its future community investment without impacting future earnings or operating cash. Should your business become highly successful, it is "money in the bank" for the nonprofit. The earlier a company takes advantage of this unique financial vehicle, the greater the upside is for the company and for the community-at-large.

There are usually clauses written into company by-laws that stock given to nonprofits can't be sold without offering first right of refusal to the company and its shareholders. Companies may also offer stock options or allow employees to purchase stock for donation to nonprofits. If you decide to donate equity, make sure the nonprofit receiving a contribution of your equity checks with its lawyers and accountants to ensure that the gift is in fact beneficial for them and will not have negative tax consequences in the short term.

For example, when **Salesforce.com** launched, the company placed more than one percent of the new corporation's stock in the Salesforce.com Foundation.[16] The hope was that, as the company grew, the foundation would grow proportionately and be fully integrated into the company. Marc Benioff and Karen Southwick stated in their book, *Compassionate Capitalism*, "Our initial stock grant should be worth $25 to $30 million when we go public. Employees are also making donations of stock to the foundation. About 50 percent of employees made stock or cash contributions."[17]

You can donate equity directly to your own foundation, as Salesforce.com did, or to the nonprofit of your choice (consult a tax advisor or lawyer). However, using the services of a third party organization specializing in stock option donations, like the **Entrepreneurs Foundation of Central Texas** (EFCT), may be desirable. EFCT offers a financial vehicle for early stage companies to allocate inexpensive private equity to a donor-advised fund, creating a source of cash for community investments that doesn't impact future company earnings or operating cash. If a company donates shares of stock, it takes a tax deduction at the time of donation equivalent to the fair market value of the stock at that time. Traditionally, however, most of equity donations have been stock options or warrants due to the opportunity a company has to defer a charitable tax deduction until the shares are exercised.

EFCT provides its members the necessary documents and administrative support to set up the donation. They then liquidate the donated equity when it has cash value to create a donor-advised fund. The member company advises EFCT on which nonprofits to support with their 80 percent distribution of proceeds. The Foundation retains 20 percent to support their operations so that they can continue to coordinate and promote corporate giving and community involvement activities for participating companies that want assistance.

Since 1999, over 240 entrepreneurial companies in Central Texas have donated equity to the EFCT. To date, these donations of equity from predominantly venture capital-backed companies and monies have helped raise over $4 million in cash for nonprofits. EFCT's current portfolio contains equity from over 130 active companies.[18]

Webify Solutions, Inc. is one of the EFCT's success stories. Webify was formed in 2002 and acquired by IBM in 2006. Webify CEO Manoj Saxena said, "We care very much about the value we add to both our shareholders and the communities in which we operate. Our motto is to 'do well by doing good.'"[19] Webify has donated equity twice to EFCT to seed its charitable giving fund. So far, because of their equity donations, they have been able to contribute over $50,000 to community organizations.

Customer Dollars

There are several creative, easy ways your company can leverage financial support for nonprofits with dollars generated from your customers. All it takes is a little time, planning, and tracking. Providing vehicles for your customers to give can be a way for you to actively support a cause financially, even if your own company dollars set aside for donations are minimal or have been exhausted.

In addition to tapping "other people's money," involving customers in giving extends your nonprofit partner's reach into groups it might not otherwise come in contact with. This raises their visibility and credibility with new potential supporters. After all, you as one of their favorite businesses support them, right? So they must be worthy. This approach lets you visibly demonstrate your business values and at the same time invites customers to partner with your company to make a difference.

Figure 8. Ways to Leverage Customer Dollars

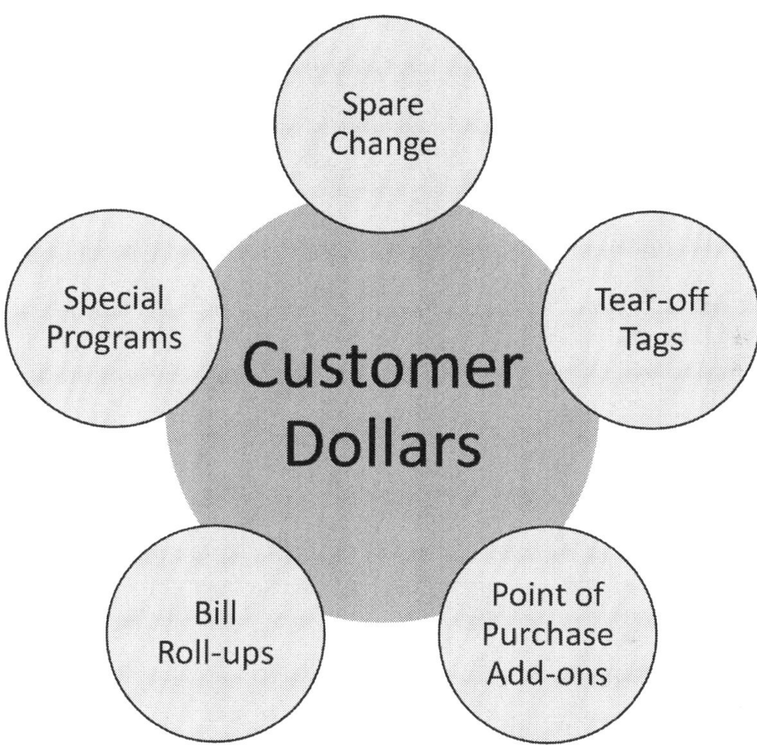

The relatively small amounts of money contributed will not be missed by most people. Customers are grateful you have given them an opportunity to "do good" that was really easy—similar to an impulse buy. Such point-of-purchase donations and customer billing add-ons can really add up. You provide the opportunity and the means to leverage support for your nonprofit partner(s) from a broader audience by tapping into your customer base.

Research has shown that about 80 percent of people step up to volunteer because they were asked. It is the same with giving money. You may be surprised at the response from your customers when you ask them to join forces with you to support the community by making a small donation. A little bit from many people adds up!

Spare Change

Retail stores and restaurants often place containers in the checkout area for customers to donate their pocket change to the featured nonprofit organization. This is a very low-effort activity and requires no receipts. **Panera Bread** has boxes for spare change at each register. Airlines often collect leftover foreign currency from their passengers on international flights and pool the money to give as a donation to a nonprofit.

A **7-Eleven** convenience store was approached for a donation by a senior services organization. The store had no funds available to fulfill the request. Instead, they offered to put a container in the register area labeled with the nonprofit's logo and program information so customers could choose to donate their spare change after making a purchase. In one month, the display raised over $3,000 in unrestricted funds for the nonprofit organization. That's a lot of dimes and quarters! The nonprofit was thrilled; this was a much greater sum than they had originally requested.

Checkout Tear-off Tags, Point of Purchase Add-ons, and Bill Roll-ups

Another way to invite your customers to contribute to your favorite causes is to place a special display of tear-off tags in various dollar amounts at the checkout area. The denomination the customer selects is added onto the bill with the other items being purchased. The customer gets an easy way to give, plus a written receipt for tax records, though on average the dollar values are small per sale. However, a modest amount from many customers can add up quickly into a significant donation for your favorite partners.

Whole Foods Markets often has a display at the cash registers with coupons in $1, $2, and $5 amounts. These donations fund the natural foods store's Whole Planet Foundation and its programs to help families escape poverty by securing access to capital to start their own small businesses. As a customer (like myself) waits in line, he or she sees the display of donation coupons in different denominations, along with informational brochures about the Foundation and its programs. I've "succumbed" many times to this approach.

PetSmart also offers customers the opportunity to donate during the checkout process to help homeless animals. The credit card processing machine automatically asks every customer to donate $1—no other amount is possible. The only options are "yes" or "no," making it easy to say "yes." I did, and following the asterisk next to the item, my receipt footnote states at the bottom: "PetSmart Charities is a 501(c)(3) nonprofit organization. Keep this receipt for tax purposes."

As another example, **Macy's** invites their customers to join the department store in "giving back" to causes that make a difference, both nationally and in local communities.[20] At the Cherry Creek Mall in Denver, Macy's posted a sign at the checkout in the women's clothing section inviting customers to donate $3 to benefit a program called Reading is Fundamental (RIF). Macy's offered a $10 savings pass for future purchases of $50 or more with every $3 donation. My donation was added on to the price of a jacket I had purchased. Being at the checkout, it was easy to make the donation, and on a $100 purchase it was a small add-on. Why not support the effort? The Macy's website reported that their fourth annual Book a Brighter Future campaign totaled a record-breaking $6.5 million to benefit RIF. Macy's and its customers have raised more than $13.5 million for RIF over six years.[21]

Another source of customer contributions is the bill roll-up. Some companies offer patrons the opportunity to round up the balance due on their bill; the difference is earmarked as a donation to a specific nonprofit or fundraising effort. Customers can choose whether to round up to the next dollar value or add more.

For example, after the 2004 tsunami, the restaurant at the **Willard Intercontinental Hotel** in Washington, D.C. added a second option to their customer bills after the tip write-in section allowing diners to add an additional dollar amount to support their tsunami relief fundraising.

Safeway Grocery Stores often ask for a purchase price roll-up as a donation to whatever nonprofit is featured at the time. I often roll up my purchases of groceries to the next nearest dollar amount for prostate cancer, breast cancer, animal care, or another cause.

Some local utility and phone companies allow customers to round up their electric, gas, or phone payments; the additional amount is earmarked for a fund to support low-income families or a nonprofit organization. When I used **Working Assets** (now **Credo**) as my cell phone service provider, their billing statements routinely stated, "round up your check to $xxx or more. The tax-deductible difference goes to nonprofit action groups."

Food for Thought

- Do you routinely mail or email statements to your customers? Could you offer the opportunity to round up payments as a contribution to one of your nonprofit partners?
- If you do not want to manage the additional donations generated by your customers directly, could you include a sentence on the bill about your support of a specific nonprofit and provide the link to make a donation directly?
- Are there other ways you can use your statements to report progress in raising funds so customers can see how their bit contributed to the initiative? This hopefully will encourage them to support your efforts in the future by giving again for the same or a different partner.

Special Customer Donation Programs

Other ways to tap customer dollars include asking for donations for free services you provide or running a raffle to benefit a nonprofit.

For example, **Trend Micro Incorporated** invites customers to participate in the company's community giving. Trend Micro offers network antivirus and internet content security software and services. One of their products, HouseCall, is a free online application to detect computer viruses, spyware, or other malware. The website reads, "After scanning for viruses and spyware, why not spend an extra two minutes to express your appreciation for HouseCall by a charitable donation to Schools Online?" When clicking the link to the donation page, customers see a screen with the following: "Pleased with HouseCall? Why not express your appreciation with a charity contribution! Trend Micro will contribute any amount that you volunteer to pay (minus transaction fee) to Schools Online, a division of Relief International, to help students gain access and use the internet for learning and cross-cultural dialogue. Since 1996, over 6,100 under-served schools in the U.S. and 35 other countries have received equipment and support necessary to get online through Schools Online." Customers are then able to click "yes" to make a voluntary payment for Trend Micro contribute to Schools Online. The minimum donation is $5, though customers can enter whatever amount they choose.[22]

In another innovative effort, **Willard Intercontinental Hotel** in Washington, D.C., hosted a raffle for tsunami relief. For a $100 donation, customers were entered in a drawing to win three nights in the hotel's Presidential Suite, airport pickup, a limousine tour of the city, dinner for two in the Willard Room, a cocktail party for 12 in the Presidential Suite, and other special amenities.

Before using a raffle to raise funds, be sure to check your local and state laws concerning raffles and door prizes. Your company might need to apply for a special permit or license to be able to do something like this.

Employee Dollars

Offering giving programs for your employees takes the burden off individuals to figure out which nonprofits to support. While some employees already know where they want to contribute financial resources, others just know they want to help but may not take the initiative on their own. When employees pool their resources, they can be part of a financial gift that is bigger than any of them are able to make alone. Figure 9 shows some of the ways to access employee dollars.

Employee Matching Grants

Instead of (or perhaps in addition to) making grants directly from the company, another way to leverage additional support for nonprofit partners is through employee matching grants. In employee matching grant programs, the company matches its employees' cash contributions to nonprofits. Nonprofit recipients can either be those preselected by the company or individually by the employee. Companies usually match employee gifts dollar-for-dollar. That means if an employee gives $500, the nonprofit actually receives $1,000. However, some companies will give double or even triple the amount of the original employee donation. Procedures and amounts vary with each company. Typically, employees must submit forms to their employers to either document their contributions or make a pledge. More information about employee matching grants (often considered an employee benefit) is often made available through the human resources department.

Figure 9. Ways to Leverage Employee Dollars

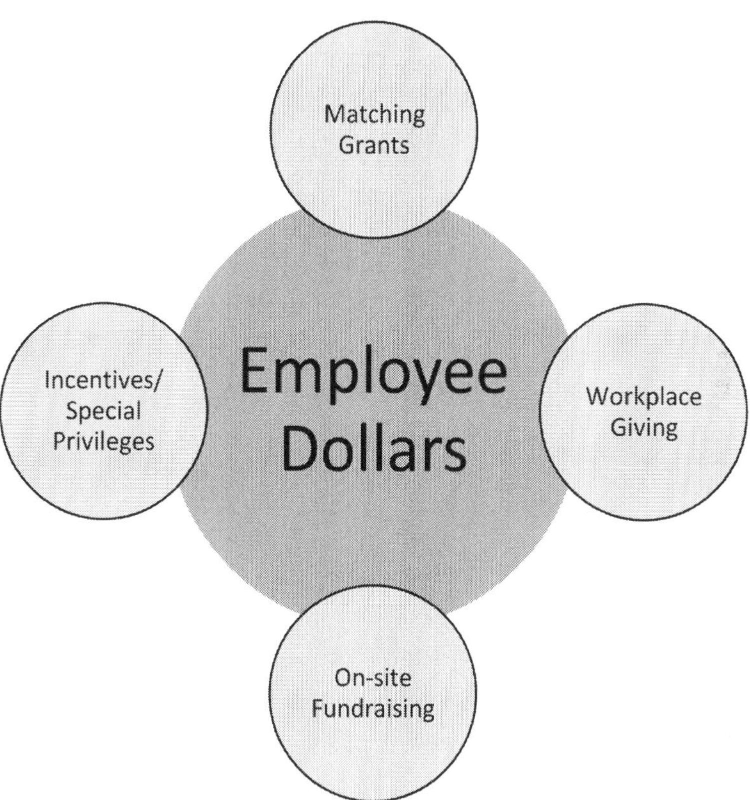

As an example, **Eileen Fisher**, a women's designer clothing company, established their employee matching gift program to enable the company to support nonprofits their employees cared about that fell outside the company's regular philanthropic focus on women-specific causes. After the program was launched and had been running for a few years, the company realized they needed to do more internal promotion of the program to increase employee participation, which they did.[23] So remember, just setting up such a program within your company is not enough. You must also make sure it is visible to your employees.

Tweezerman, maker of quality beauty tools, also has a matching program in which their employees can contribute financially to the nonprofit of their choice and the company will match donations up to $500 a year per employee. Tweezerman also matches other employee fundraising efforts. For example, after Katrina, employees launched a special campaign to raise money to support hurricane victims. These contributions also were matched by the company.[24]

Xcel Energy Company matches their employees' charitable contributions dollar-for-dollar through a matching gifts program. In 2009, corporate leadership approved a 50 percent increase in the annual matching dollar limit available to employees, from $500 to $750.[25] **Microsoft** offers a matching gifts program year round that matches U.S. employees' direct cash and software donations up to $12,000 annually to thousands of eligible 501(c)(3) and educational institutions.[26]

The largest of the **IBM**'s employee partnership programs is their matching grants program. This program enables employees and retirees to increase the value of their donations to educational institutions, hospitals, hospices, nursing homes, and cultural and environmental organizations with a matching gift from the company. The recipient organization can choose to receive their gift in the form of either cash or IBM equipment. If they choose to receive equipment, IBM will match an active employee contribution at two times the cash match. If the eligible institution chooses cash, the match is 1:1. For retirees, the match for equipment is 1:1 and cash is .5:1.[27]

Tip

- *To find out which companies match employees' gifts, consult the Foundation Center's Foundation Directory Online, a searchable database, or the National Directory of Corporate Giving, a print directory. These resources are often available at public city or university libraries.*

Workplace Giving Campaigns

For more than 50 years, U.S. companies have conducted workplace fundraising campaigns encouraging employees to contribute to nonprofits through their place of employment. While representing a small percentage of the total amount contributed by individuals, workplace giving is important in its support of charitable causes and as a reflection of business involvement in communities. Over the years, workplace giving has raised significant amounts of money for nonprofits. U.S. workplace campaigns generate more than $4 billion annually for nonprofits—approximately $2 billion from corporate donations and $2 billion from employee payroll deduction campaigns.[28]

Traditionally, workplace giving was associated with the United Way campaign or other federated giving programs, but that is no longer the exclusive model. More recently, companies have developed their own unique campaigns to appeal to employees thus increasing participation.

Federated giving programs are joint fundraising efforts usually administered by a nonprofit "umbrella" organization which in turn distributes contributed funds to other nonprofit agencies. United Way and community chests or funds, United Jewish Appeal and other religious appeals, the United Negro College Fund, and joint arts councils are examples of federated giving programs.

Workplace giving, whichever model is used, is an effective tactic because it reaches a large number of employees at the workplace with a single campaign, often supporting a wide-ranging group of nonprofits. The employer's commitment to support the campaign, coupled with the ease and convenience of payroll deduction, has been instrumental in raising nearly $100 billion for nonprofit organizations in the last 30 years.

Workplace giving campaigns are most effective when tailored to your organizational culture and other social impact initiatives. The most successful campaigns are supported by leadership, driven by staff, and have a specific fundraising goal over a given time period. Consider what might be popular times of the year to launch your campaigns and whether there are any well-established, recognized national events upon which you can piggyback your efforts. The key is to pick a goal and timeframe that works best for your company.

Tip

- *Conduct a thorough assessment of your workplace campaign to identify employee attitudes and perceptions about it. Then develop strategies and tactics to support a program focused on identified business and employees' nonprofit interests. As a result, you'll create a campaign that is more popular, effective, and financially successful.*

While workplace giving was designed to improve nonprofit efficiencies in generating charitable donations, benefits also exist for the company and employees. For companies, these programs boost visibility and reputation. For employees, they offer the convenience of automatic payroll deductions while retaining the tax benefits of charitable giving. Payroll deduction is convenient in that you do not need an acknowledgement from the nonprofit to claim your tax deduction.

There is, however, one exception to this rule. If you contribute $250 or more from a single paycheck, you must prove to the IRS that you made the donation and didn't receive anything in return for it. Simply keeping a copy of your pay stub fulfills the first requirement. To comply with the second, you'll need a pledge card or other documentation from the nonprofit stating you did not receive any goods or services in exchange for your gift.

According to *Changing Direction: Developing Employee-Friendly Workplace Campaigns with Technology and Best Practices,* future workplace giving campaigns will be built on three pillars. They will:

- Offer greater choices in giving, consistent with employees' diversity and varied giving interests;
- Use technology to facilitate ease of giving, the efficient operation of campaigns (so more of employees' donations go to the nonprofits of their choice), and expanded information content about participating nonprofits; and
- Develop a campaign that will engage employees and build value as one of the most effective ways to support the community through volunteerism and financial support."[29]

Other trends in workplace giving include allowing employee giving year round; offering multiple ways for employees to give; greater employer matching of employee payroll deduction gifts; establishing individual giving accounts so employees can decide both how much to give and to which organization(s); greater research on nonprofit effectiveness before giving; and requiring higher standards of accountability.[30]

For example, **Microsoft's** employee giving campaign is held each October for U.S.-based employees. In 2010, despite the current economic challenges, Microsoft employee giving raised more than $40.8 million dollars involving 34,500 employees for a total $84 million, including the corporate match.[31]

For **CH2MHILL**, a global full-service engineering, procurement, construction, and operations company, workplace giving is one component of the multipronged support it offers its nonprofit partner, Water For People, an organization helping the world's most impoverished people improve the quality of their lives by supporting locally sustainable drinking water, sanitation, and health/hygiene projects. CH2MHILL has supported Water For People since its founding in 1991. Its mission echoes CH2MHILL's commitment to building a better world. CH2MHILL has hosted a global online workplace giving campaign benefiting Water For

People since 2003, raising more than $647,000 to date. In 2009, employees from 110 offices worldwide contributed $229,000 to Water for People, making it the largest workplace giving campaign to date in the nonprofit's history.[32]

Food for Thought

- Can you create an interdepartmental competition to see who can raise the most dollars to support the company's fundraising campaign?
- How can you recognize employees for their efforts while making the campaign fun?
- Will you allow employees to opt in to the workplace giving campaign, or will it be a written or unwritten expectation for management and line staff?
- Does your approach allow employee contributors to know how their dollars are spent?

On-site Fundraising

Some businesses allow various nonprofits to set up manned or stand-alone displays, booths, or posters on their premises, such as in a staff room or lunch area, to educate employees about the nonprofits' services. "Lunch and Learn" presentations are a popular way for nonprofits to explain what they do and help generate employee motivation and interest in getting involved either financially or as volunteers.

For example, during a recent Toys for Tots campaign, in addition to partnering with local restaurants to generate funds for the holiday program, employees of the Iowa Department of Human Services held their own fundraiser. On a specific day, participating employees donated home-cooked soups that were sold to employees at lunch as a way to generate funds—largely by reallocating dollars that would have been spent on a meal anyway.

Food for Thought

- Is there a central area(s) at your business location(s) where employees gather, spend time, or pass through? Maybe a bulletin board, water fountain, or coffee machine, lunchroom, or employee lounge, where you can promote company giving campaigns?
- Could you allow employees to do on-site fundraising via special events, for example, using the old bake sale model or something more creative?
- Do you ever offer educational seminars for employees during or after the workday? Is there a way to link these efforts with your community involvement?

Employee Incentives and Special Privileges

Incentives can be connected to community giving in innovative ways that excite employees and benefit the community. Here's an idea: collect a $5 donation from employees in exchange for permission to wear jeans once a week. Use the funds to support the nonprofit of your choice. Another option could be to host a special event (e.g., a talent show, departmental skit competition, holiday decorating contest) and donate proceeds from ticket sales and auctions. The possibilities are endless. What perks could you offer employees that could translate into community investment?

To summarize this section, most nonprofits requesting support from the business community seek cold, hard cash. This section covered ways you can generate and donate funds from the company's coffers as well as from customers and employees. However, there are many other ways to give meaningfully to nonprofits that will benefit both the organization and your company. Let's turn to the next main category of business giving: in-kind contributions of products and services.

In-Kind Contributions

Donations of goods and services can be extremely valuable to nonprofit organizations and their programs. This type of charitable donation given by companies can range anywhere from paper clips to major equipment. For some businesses, providing in-kind donations to organizations doing good work is the easiest way to show support, especially if you are unable to provide financial donations. It may be easier and more possible to simply share resources you already have.

Figure 10 shows seven of the most common categories of in-kind contributions of businesses: products and services, equipment and vehicles, silent auction items, gift certificates, space, and other noncash donations. (Note: Provision of employee time for volunteering and pro bono services will be covered in the following section on contributions by people.)

Product and Service Donations

Current products and services that your company sells and would be willing to give as in-kind contributions are a common way to support nonprofits either for their internal use or as silent auction, door prize, or raffle items to raise funds. The typical types of product contributed include: current stock, excess stock, seconds, outdated product that is still usable, and new product for trial with target audience(s). Services could include anything from massages or spa services, to health club memberships and website development.

Samples of your current product or excess inventory can

make a contribution, be great marketing for your company, and get you tax benefits. **Dagoba Chocolate, Honest Tea,** and **Zhena's Gypsy Tea** all make product donations for various special events from athletic races to community festivals. They elect those organizations' events attended by their current and potential customers to promote customer loyalty and encourage future sales. Seth Goldman of Honest Tea reported that when their business was just getting to profitability, the company was unable to donate money. However, he was proud to say that instead, they gave away "tons of product" at road races and other community events because it was good marketing.[1]

Figure 10. Types of In-Kind Contributions

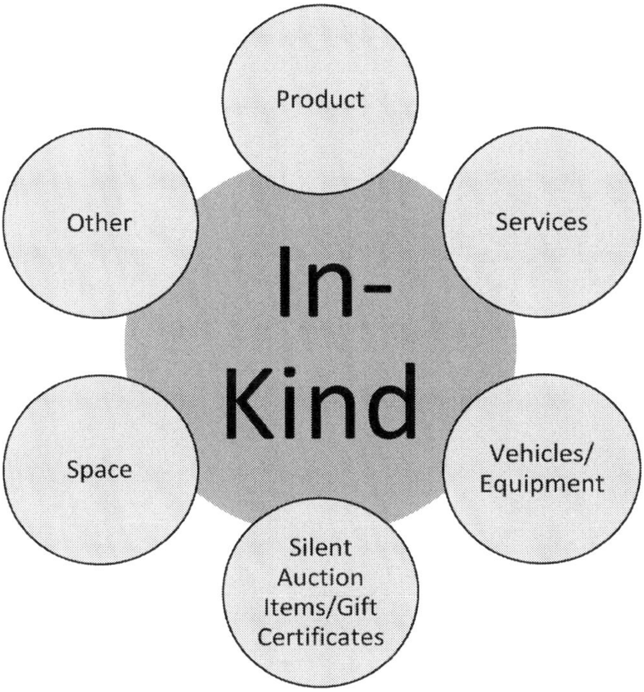

Product

Other

Services

In-Kind

Space

Vehicles/ Equipment

Silent Auction Items/Gift Certificates

Kimpton Hotels also donates "a tremendous amount of products for fundraising and silent auctions in the community for various causes." They provide certificates for weekend getaways at their various hotels and dinners for eight by a well-known chef in the home of the purchaser. They also donate leftover and unused food products to food banks.[2]

Aveda stores and salons are approached by event planners looking for volunteers to offer stress-relieving experiences such as chair massage to enhance their events and raise money. If the store is able, they will do that to help the local organization. For fundraisers, stress-relieving experiences such as back and hand massage are offered for $5 for five minutes. For Aveda, this is a way to showcase their salons and expertise in the community while offering support to a local nonprofit.[3]

Crocs, Inc. gave over 5,000 pairs of new second shoes to Katrina victims. Since 2007, the company has distributed more than 2.5 million pairs of shoes to people in impoverished areas and those affected by natural disasters in more than 40 countries. Most recently, Crocs donated more than 80,000 pairs of shoes to one of Haiti's largest medical providers, an organization dedicated to providing healthcare following the country's devastating earthquake.[4]

BitWise Solutions builds websites for nonprofits on a regular basis. Over the last five years, they have donated about $75,000 worth of IT services.

Food for Thought

- Do you have product you are looking to get out of your hair?
- Do you have outdated or closeout product that is still usable? Or leftover products that your company's sales manager wants to move?
- Do you have new product(s) ready for trial with target audience(s)? Need appropriate audiences for that testing and feedback?
- Do you have RMA's, x-outs, irregulars, misprints—factory

"seconds" of any type?

Instead of managing product and other in-kind donations directly, many companies now send their contributions to third-party organizations that make the match with nonprofits for a low administrative and/or shipping fee. For example, **Gifts In Kind International** works with companies to distribute each year nearly $900 million in new products donations to 150,000 community nonprofits throughout the U.S. and across the world serving over 13 million people in need. Today, nearly half of the Fortune 100 consumer product, retail and technology corporations rely on Gifts In Kind to place their product donations with their network of qualified nonprofits and to design and manage their product donation programs.[5] **Waste to Charity** specializes in all types of inventory donations: excess inventory, factory closeouts, and other types of product donations.[6]

Equipment and Vehicle Donations and Loans

Companies frequently donate outdated but functional equipment such as computer equipment, vehicles, tools, or office equipment such as fax machines or copiers to nonprofits. It helps the company by getting unused equipment out of your space and giving you a tax deduction. It helps nonprofits acquire needed equipment at low or no cost.

If you are unsure where to donate your equipment and your favorite nonprofit doesn't need it, check for a local organization similar to Denver's **Providers' Resource Clearinghouse** (PRC). PRC was created to bridge the gap between struggling human-service providers and businesses seeking to serve the community through in-kind giving. Since 1993, PRC has refurbished and redistributed more than $100 million worth of goods and supplies to thousands of community agencies throughout the Denver metro area.[7] PRC accepts donations from corporations (and individuals) of new and used office and household furnishings and supplies. For a small fee they find new life for the items by recycling or redistributing them to nonprofits through a local warehouse.

Silent Auction Items and Gift Certificates

Companies have traditionally given items or gift certificates for silent auctions and other nonprofit fundraisers. Such donations offer the nonprofit the opportunity to raise money from selling the product or certificate to the highest bidder. The winner is either a current customer or someone being exposed to a product or service they might not yet be familiar with—maybe they will become a customer in the future.

Sambuca Restaurants prefers product giveaways to purely cash donations as these bring people into the restaurant for a direct experience of the atmosphere, food, and service and can result in repeat visits and future sales. Sambuca supports nonprofits in several ways: catering special off-site events, offering gratis happy hours on site, and providing gifts certificates for dinner for two or happy hour for 10. In addition, each restaurant's catering and marketing manager is allocated 20 dinners for two to donate on a monthly basis.[8]

Tweezerman creates gift baskets of their products that they give for silent auctions or raffles. **Metafolics Salon** created gift baskets of hair care and other personal care and beauty products that they were no longer selling in the salon as a way to avoid re-stocking and shipping fees normally charged to return the products to the distributor.

Physical and Virtual Space

Sometimes businesses have an office or part of a suite they aren't actively using due to changes in employee numbers or slower than expected growth. Leases often make it almost impossible to fill the extra space until it is needed. So if you have no active use for the space, perhaps you could let a nonprofit use it for their office space temporarily. This works especially well for small or new nonprofits that have minimal staff.

For example, the **Dream Team**, an IT company in Denver, had an unused office in its suite. They donated use of that space for over a year to the Time Exchange Network (TEN), for which one of its staff members served as a board member. TEN is a local nonprofit that arranges neighbor-to-neighbor service exchanges using time dollars, a complementary currency. In addition to the office, TEN could sign up to use the conference room for board meetings, volunteer trainings, and other community meetings. **Western Resources**, a Topeka-based utilities company, provided free office space for three staff members of the Kansas Commission on National and Community Service for six years.

There are other ways to loan space to nonprofits that can be very helpful. Do you have a phone bank a nonprofit could use for a phonathon on a Saturday or a boardroom that is infrequently used by employees? When it was first founded, the National Center for Community Relations (NCCR), a Denver-based 501(c)(3), had various business members sponsor their monthly meetings, providing free space and snacks for the attendees. As a new organization, NCCR received benefits to make their meetings more attractive to current and potential members and the business sponsors got reputational value as well as had an opportunity to introduce people to their corporation and offices.

How about parking lots or warehouses or other space you could offer a nonprofit to use for a special event? **Virginia Village Texaco**, an auto repair and gas station that used to be in my neighborhood in Denver, allowed student groups from local schools to use their location for car washes to raise money for school teams and activities. Owner Ramon Elder believed strongly "that kind of community involvement does come back to bless you. Getting the students' moms and dads out is great exposure for our location and opens the eyes of people that really didn't know we were there. The kids also learn we're here and they can see we are an honest and clean organization. It's brought me a lot of customers."[9]

Chesapeake Energy, the second-largest producer of natural gas, a Top 20 producer of oil and natural gas liquids, and the most active driller of new wells in the U.S., is headquartered in Oklahoma City.[10] Chesapeake has a large campus in Oklahoma City and has been investing in various commercial real estate properties in the vicinity. After being approached by so many nonprofits requesting $1,500 to $3,000 grants, they decided to try something different as a way to support the local nonprofit community. The company converted a strip mall it owned into the Chesapeake Community Plaza offering discounted three- or five-year leases for office space to nonprofits serving Oklahoma at a rate one-third that of the going commercial rate.

After the first year at $6/square foot, lease rates will increase 50 cents a square foot per year over the term of the lease. The approximately 20 nonprofits that now office at the Community Plaza have free access to a common conference room with state-of-the-art audio-visual equipment. One of the tenants, Nancy Sharrock, Executive Director of the Oklahoma Community Service Commission, explained to me that co-locating with the other nonprofits has created many new opportunities for communication, mutual support, and collaboration. In their case, it has helped them grow their mission of providing AmeriCorps program resources to address local needs in the state. "It's been great for us!" Nancy said.[11]

Chesapeake's efforts to strengthen the local nonprofit community through their investment in the Community Plaza have been so successful, they are considering opening another one in another state where they actively work.

Other In-Kind Ideas

Supply Donations

Could your company order extra office or other supplies when placing orders? You may get a volume discount and could then donate the supplies to a nonprofit you are supporting. The relative additional cost to your company is minimal while the gift of free or deeply discounted necessary supplies is much appreciated by the nonprofit.

Open Training Slots

Sometimes you might offer a general skill building training to your employees that is not fully booked. To fill the empty seats, perhaps you could offer the appropriate staff from your favorite nonprofit to attend as your guest.

Collections from Customers

An executive search company moved to new office space in a high-rise building. They volunteered to be the collection point for a Thanksgiving food drive for a local food bank. As a result, not only did they support the community at the holidays, other businesses in the building came to their offices, registered their name, and learned about their services. It was a great way for the company to gain valuable exposure to potential clients.

Other examples include being a winter coat or holiday toy drop-off location. Sometimes, companies give customers a discount coupon to use on a new product if they bring in a used one that can be donated to people in need.

Creating Connections through Your Networks

One of the assets you bring to the table for your community work is your network of business contacts: your vendors, suppliers, distributors, and other companies. Mark Berzins,

Owner of the **Little Pub Company** based in Denver, feels there was a time when some of the vendors he works with "didn't realize they should be giving back to the community." He tells the story of reaching out to his insurance company to support a cause that meant a lot to him. They came back and said, "Sorry, we can't help out at this time." Mark's response was, "I'm very disappointed that you are not helping out because I do business with companies that have a philosophy consistent with ours around giving back. If you are not willing to give, I bet I can find an insurance company that will."

The insurance company did step up, and Mark is proud to report that more than 10 years later, everyone from the cleaning company to the food and beverage vendors who work with the Little Pub Company know they will "be hit up on a regular basis to help" whether by donating to a fundraiser or buying a sponsorship to an event. "Every single one of those companies at some point in the year gives something back to the community at our insistence…and that makes me feel good."[12]

Mike Hannigan of **Give Something Back Office Supplies** also leverages his business networks and relationships to benefit the community. For example, if a school is having difficulties, Give Something Back might approach one of the manufacturers of school supplies with whom they have a relationship and ask is they will sell the needed school supplies on a one-time basis at the manufacturer's cost. "We can facilitate that because we have the connections. We are not going to make or lose any money on the transaction," Mark explained. Some other office supply retailers wouldn't do that because they wouldn't want to eliminate the school as a potential customer by giving them something for free that they would otherwise have to buy. "It made perfect sense for us. It allowed us to use an asset we had built up over years for this community benefit that was in all of our interests."[13]

Food for Thought

- Do you have vendors, suppliers, or distributors you can approach to join forces with you to provide in-kind (or other resources) to your nonprofit partners?
- Do you know other businesses you could engage in your community efforts?
- How can you leverage your contacts and networks within your sphere of influence to provide additional support to your favorite causes?
- Could you leverage your database of clients or market prospects to join you in support of a cause?

People

"I know small business owners, including ourselves, are married to their business. We're here 60 to 70 hours per week—that's not uncommon. It's hard to give that extra time, but it's worth it in the long run. I just hope that people will find ways to either get their employees out there, get themselves out there, even if you just pick two or three things that are meaningful to you. You just have to do something. It is a responsibility of being in business. It is part of the package."

—John Joseph, Vice President, **Josephs Jewelers,** Des Moines, Iowa[1]

One of the most valuable resources to which has your company has access is the people who work for and with you. Your people can be an essential part of your giving portfolio by sharing their time and talents, and also bring vitality and new ideas that add immeasurable value to your nonprofit partners.

Giving of time and talents can be even more impactful than making a financial contribution. Volunteer programs in the workplace are most successful when they are based on integrating the priorities of the company, the interests of the employees, and the needs of the community. And your company benefits, too.

Companies can offer their employees as volunteers to engage in short-term or one-time service projects, ongoing service activities, or as professional volunteers to serve as board members or provide pro bono technical services to nonprofits.

Nita Winter, of **Nita Winter Photography**, photographs corporate employees going out in the community and doing work, so she has seen how much they get out of it. Volunteering "is really important not only for the company getting exposure but for having happy and more productive employees," said Nita. "Allowing them to get out and work with the community really feeds the heart and when the heart is fed, people can work better. They feel more proud of the company."[2]

Volunteering also opens employees' eyes to the community. In many cases people commute to work then get back in their cars and drive home. They may never have even seen any of the people who live in the area. Nita explained, "They may start to say, okay, I could sit in my car for two hours commuting during rush hour, or after work I can go spend 45 minutes tutoring a child, then get in my car and still get home at the same time because I am not sitting in traffic anymore."[3]

Looking for ideas? Many local communities have a corporate volunteer council (CVC). These are "local" networks that businesses join to share effective practices and address community needs through workplace volunteering. CVCs are typically affiliated with local community-based agencies such as HandsOn Affiliates and Volunteer Centers or United Way agencies. Some CVCs are incorporated as independent nonprofits. "CVC" is a general term that also refers to BVCs (business volunteer councils), corporate community relations councils, and workplace volunteer councils.[4]

General Volunteering versus Skilled or Pro Bono Services

"Extra-pair-of-hands" or general employee volunteering is a common practice among businesses. Employees give their time, sometimes as manual labor, to assist with projects and programs, often helping nonprofits serve more people or complete work that would otherwise not happen. Much employee volunteering falls under this category and includes such activities as building houses for low-income families, after-school tutoring, trash pickup, painting schools, building playgrounds or ramps to make buildings accessible, sorting clothes, and ladling soup.

As crucial as these tasks are, many companies are opting to leverage the specialized skills and talents of their employees through pro bono service. Pro bono is the donation of professional services that are included in an employees' job description and for which the recipient nonprofit would otherwise have to pay. Pro bono is a term traditionally associated with the legal field's practice of providing free legal services to persons or organizations in need. However, pro bono service has taken on a wider definition as more companies and individuals are volunteering professional skills to assist nonprofit organizations in creating or improving their business practices. As mentioned previously, the average value of pro bono service is $120 per hour, as opposed to $20.85 for general volunteering.

Pro bono service includes, but is not limited to, business services and skills in the following areas:[5]

- Strategic and business planning
- Fundraising and development
- Human capital and organizational development
- Marketing and communications
- Finance and accounting
- Information technology
- Logistics
- Product development

A Deloitte/Points of Light Volunteer IMPACT study found that 77 percent of nonprofit leaders believe that skilled volunteers could significantly improve their organization's business practices, yet only 12 percent of nonprofits actually put volunteers to work on such assignments. Furthermore, this study found that 40 percent of volunteers actively look for opportunities to apply their professional skills.[6] Research has found the retention rate is higher when people use their skills while volunteering compared to when they do not.[7] So the business gets more credit, makes more impact, and instills a higher level of motivation among employees. Other key research found that:

- Most volunteers do not perform service activities that relate to their professional or occupational skills;
- The legal profession is a leading example of a field where its professionals use their skills when performing their volunteer activities; and
- Many volunteers engage in fundraising, which although very important, may detract from opportunities to use their skills in other much-needed activities.[8]

Led by the Corporation for National and Community Service, ***A Billion + Change*** is a three-year campaign designed to increase the extent and effectiveness of pro bono service to help the nonprofit sector achieve greater scale, sustainability, and impact in meeting community needs. Since its launch in 2008, companies and organizations have committed more than $500 million of pro bono service—a powerful investment of human capital that is helping address tough community challenges. Selected participating companies include the following: **Allstate Insurance Company** will provide $45,000 worth of pro bono legal assistance to help domestic violence survivors build financial independence; **Capital One** will provide $2.4 million of professional services to help nonprofit organizations develop core business functions such as brand marketing, HR, IT, finance, and legal; and **UPS** will contribute a minimum of 100,000 pro bono hours valued at $15 million in efforts such as teaching safe driving techniques to teens; ensuring that supplies get delivered after natural disasters; and warehousing, supply chain management, technology, and other services.[9] What specialized business skills do you have to contribute?

Personal versus Company Time

Many companies encourage their employees and executives to be active in the community during personal, off-work time in the evening and on weekends. Such companies encourage volunteerism in general, leaving the selection of the nonprofit and role(s) to be played up to the employees' discretion. Others offer company-sponsored events in which employees and/or their families may participate if they choose during non-work hours. These companies offer participating employees no leave time or financial incentives though some actively track employees' volunteer time and activities in order to offer recognition for outstanding service through certificates and other small rewards.

As one example, employees of **Little Pub Company's** establishments are encouraged to get involved in their community on their own time. Owner Mark Berzins' philosophy is that he wants to foster "the spirit of volunteerism" among his employees. Therefore, it is important to him that they give of their own time. "It's something we pretty well insist on. It's not required for your job, but everyone is strongly encouraged to participate when we have volunteer bartending to be done, we're stuffing gift bags, or wrapping adoptive family presents."

Other companies have more formalized employee volunteer programs. These are planned, managed efforts that seek to motivate and enable employees to effectively volunteer under the leadership of the employer. Company support can include spending staff time to plan, promote, and/or manage employee volunteer activities, allocating financial or other resources or the volunteer activity, employee volunteer support (such as food, sunscreen, or transportation), employee recognition (such as t-shirts, cups, plaques, etc.)

Some allow employees to leave during the workday to participate in volunteer activities, either as a result of flextime policies or by requesting management approval. For example,

Janus Funds has entered into a partnership with Junior Achievement, a strategic selection of nonprofit partner, as Janus is about investment and wise use of financial resources and Junior Achievement uses hands-on experiences to help young people understand the economics of life. Janus allows their employees flextime to leave their job and go to a local school to present the Junior Achievement curriculum to the school children.

However, a growing number of companies are going the next step beyond negotiated flex-time to offer employees paid volunteer leave time, often four to six hours a month, as an employee benefit. Currently, according to the 2009 Community Involvement Index, 56.7 percent of the companies surveyed offer employees paid time off to volunteer in at least some of their locations.[10]

As an example, **Tweezerman** is very flexible on providing employees time to volunteer. Their employees get four hours a month they can use for volunteering and it counts as work time. If employees volunteer on the weekend, they can take a half-day off work during the week. "We feel that employees like to be acknowledged for the good work they are doing above and beyond their job, so we encourage that," says Jeannie Barnett, Director of Corporate Communications at Tweezerman.[11] For example, a team of a dozen employees got involved with a local boys' home—painted walls, planted gardens, and got the kids involved. "It was really rewarding. They did it because it felt great...but they also got the reward of half a day off work because they spent their whole Saturday doing that," said Jeannie. "I think that give and take is really important and to incentivize employees in a positive way gets them involved."[12]

Xcel Energy, Colorado's largest electric and gas utility company, launched a program in 2007 that allows all company employees to take 40 hours of paid leave per year to volunteer in the community. Full-time employees are eligible for volunteer paid time off (VPTO). Employees increased their use of VPTO by more than 70 percent in 2009 over the previous year's in number of hours served and by 84 percent in number of employees volunteering.[13]

BetterWorld Telecom, the only nationwide, full-service voice and data telecommunications carrier focused on serving businesses and organizations that support social justice and sustainability, implemented their corporate volunteer program in 2008. All employees volunteer at least 2.5 workdays per month to organizations in the communities they serve.[14] In addition, BetterWorld participates in various corporate volunteering programs and forums and helped to establish best practices in corporate volunteering at the Net Impact National Conference and the Points of Light Institute's National Conference on Volunteering and Service.[15]

Creating a policy to offer paid leave time to employees for volunteering may be something you want to consider. However, you also need to think about how to get the word out so that your people know to take advantage of the opportunity and will be supported by their managers if they choose to participate. For example, **Aveda** headquarters allows their employees up to eight hours of paid leave time to volunteer at local organizations—either as a one-shot deal such as working on a Habitat for Humanity house or spread out to two hours a month over four months. Mary T'Kach reported that "not a huge percentage participate. A lot of why they don't, we found out recently, is that they didn't know it existed." Since employees may not read the personnel policies closely, Aveda is planning to more actively promote the option to their employees in the future.[16] How will you ensure your employees know that they can volunteer on behalf of your company?

People to Involve

As a business, you have many types of people to enlist to support your community investment through volunteering and pro bono service. Figure 11 shows some of the options from within the company as well as from your business networks and relationships.

Figure 11. People for Volunteer Projects

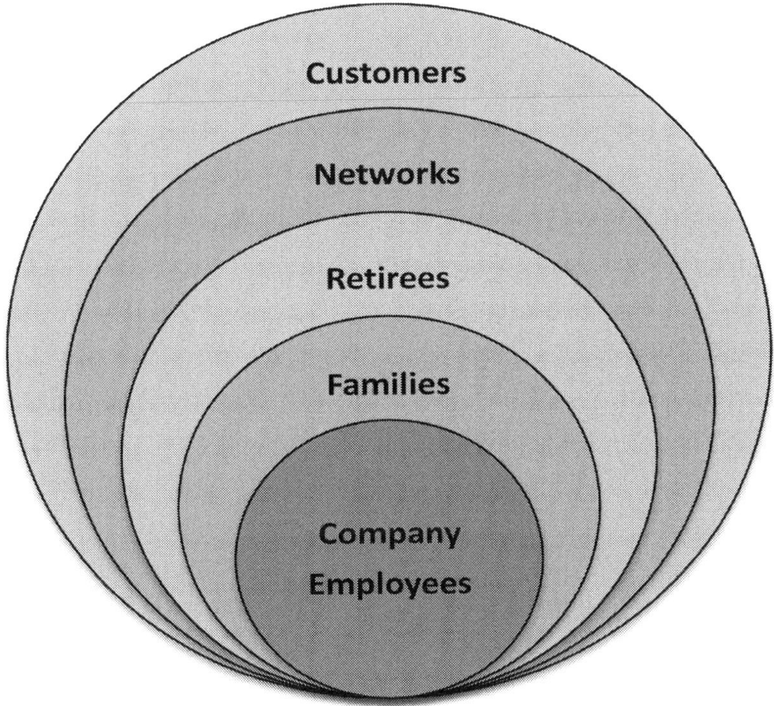

Employees are the most obvious and easiest source of time and talent to tap for service to the community. Beyond feeling good about giving back and making a difference, there are many benefits of employee volunteering, as discussed in Part I of this book. Remember that the loyalty and skill-building aspects of employee volunteering are powerful. You can encourage an employee to volunteer as a way to build skills when there is no money for a training program and no opportunity for on-the-job training at the company. Many more people would volunteer in this fashion if their boss encouraged it and it was a part of their normal workday.

In addition to building skills, an employee volunteer program can strengthen a company's stated values. Making community investment part of the recruitment and hiring process as well as senior managers' annual performance reviews is another way to highlight a company's commitment. Formally endorsing community investment as a corporate value and holding senior managers accountable for actively supporting and promoting that value helps heighten all employees' awareness and support for community investment programs.

Many companies design volunteer programs and activities on weekends so that employees may volunteer with their family and friends as a way of increasing participation and minimizing potential time conflicts during non-work hours. Participating together in community service enables parents and children to develop close relationships, learn together, and improve their neighborhoods.

Another great resource to tap for company volunteering is your retirees. In 2009, one in three companies looked beyond current employees to include retirees.[17] Though many of the formal retiree programs are run by larger companies, smaller companies can also find ways to involve retirees in special service projects, as well, with a little planning. Retirees often still feel a commitment to their former employers long after they no longer work for them. Many would enjoy staying involved with the company in some fashion, given the chance.

Offering retirees opportunities to volunteer on your behalf is a great way to retain the connection. Retirees, like other volunteers, get intense personal satisfaction from giving their time. Volunteering is fun and gives retirees a renewed sense of purpose, a way to get out, meet people and demonstrate that they are still productive and can fulfill real needs in the community. Your nonprofit partners win because they get needed service; your company wins because retirees can supplement your efforts "off the company clock" to strengthen the communities in which you operate and enhance your company's public image.

For example, **HP** has approximately 79,000 retirees, many of whom remain involved in HP's volunteer efforts. Their ranks of retirees grew by nearly one-third in 2009, with 19,000 new retirees joining Retiree Clubs worldwide. Every year HP retirees volunteer thousands of hours to support local nonprofits and schools around the world. Recognizing the potential of its retirees to make a difference, HP has launched a formal program to tap their expertise. In 2009, HP teamed with Civic Ventures to pilot the Encore Fellows program, which allows HP retirees to take the professional expertise they gained at HP into the nonprofit sector. Nine fellows were selected to receive a stipend of $25,000 each for a year of work. Encore Fellows put their talents toward projects ranging from after-school programs for low-income students to working for environmental organizations.[18]

Similarly, **Boeing** retirees' organization, the Bluebills, was created to provide opportunities for retirees to volunteer their time, energy, skills, knowledge, and experience to improve the quality of life in their respective communities, thereby enhancing their own lives, as well. In 2009, the Bluebills donated over 84,000 hours volunteering.[19]

Honeywell also has a retiree volunteer program (HRVP). In February 1979, they started with about 50 volunteers. Now, there are approximately 7,500 Honeywell retirees living in the Twin City area; more than 1,000 of them serve the community in every way imaginable one or two days a week. Since 1979, HRVP volunteers have donated 4 million hours, a contribution equivalent to more than $40 million.[20]

Tips

- *HR departments can be helpful in providing retiree contact information.*
- *Retirees are busy people. Many travel extensively. Many are able to volunteer only seasonally. Many are not willing to make long term volunteer commitments.*
- *Retirees may be sensitive to the location and safety of the volunteer work.*
- *Some may prefer to volunteer alone; others may enjoy working with a group of other volunteers.*
- *Some may prefer to volunteer with a group of friends from their previous job.*
- *It is important to know and understand the retirees health and family status*

Other people to tap for your company volunteering include customers, other local businesses with whom you share common interests, and your suppliers and vendors. In 2009, according to the Community Involvement Index, almost half of the surveyed companies invited customer participation in service projects at some locations.[21]

Food for Thought

- What is the primary motivation for having your employees serve as volunteers?
- Will your company have a formalized volunteer program? Will you give it a name? How will the program be administered? Paid staff, employee volunteer, employee committee?
- Which of the following will the company support: all company service days, special service events, ongoing

service, service during or after work hours?

- Does the nonprofit have the capacity to provide a quality volunteer experience that allows your employee volunteers to feel good about their contribution?
- How will the company promote service opportunities to your employees?
- Could a quality volunteer experience be the start of a relationship with a nonprofit that blossoms into other forms of support, such as cash grants?

Figure 12. Ways to Give Time

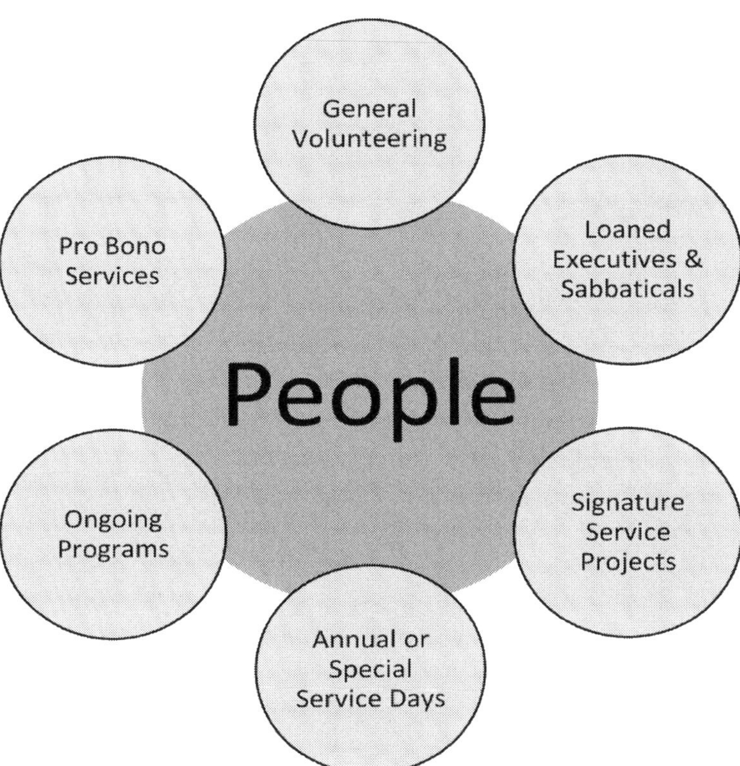

Ways to Give Time

There are many ways employees can be involved in the

community using their time and talents. Figure 12 shows some common ways employees volunteer on the company's behalf.

Company sponsored volunteer/service projects can take many forms including annual service days, signature service programs and events, ongoing programs, board service, and loaned executive or sabbatical programs. Each is described briefly below.

Annual service programs refer to those events and activities conducted every year on a company-wide basis where a significant portion of the workforce either volunteers or performs public service activities in the communities where they live and work. Annual service programs may take place over a day, a week, or even a month. Companies many choose to limit participation to employees only, while others may choose to open events up to retirees, families, friends, clients, customers, and business partners.

Such service projects may be done in conjunction with national or "global days of caring," such as the breast cancer awareness month in October, Martin Luther King, Jr. Day of Service in January, or USA Today's Make a Difference Day held the fourth Saturday of October. For most companies, such annual programs serve as a cornerstone to their community investment though they also offer other opportunities for involvement in volunteering throughout the year. For a few others, annual programs are the only company-sponsored events done during the year.

Signature Service Projects

A signature program, much like annual service, is a high-impact, highly visible company initiative that works to generate a considerable amount of exposure and goodwill for a company by including the following key characteristics: strategic in design, owned/branded by the company, and implemented/executed either annually or year-round. A classic example of a signature program is **McDonald's** Ronald McDonald House.

Another small business example is Beauty for a Cure, an annual signature event created by Denver's **Metafolics Salon** to raise money and awareness of melanoma. The signature service event was initially founded after a long-time salon client was diagnosed with stage four melanoma cancer. Salon staff learned that, with early diagnosis, melanoma is treatable. Salon staff volunteered on a Sunday for the "haircut-athon." For a $100 donation, people received one service in the salon as well as a full body skin cancer screening, donated by a local dermatologist.

Not only did the event raise money and awareness for melanoma research and treatment, 20 percent of the people screened at the event discovered they had a questionable mole they could then follow up on. It was also a great business opportunity as the stylists got many new clients after the event. "This was absolutely a win-win-win for everybody involved. Those are the types of events that really make me feel good at the end of the day," said Jason Linkow, the former owner of Metafolics.[22]

Board Service

Serving on a board is a great way for a business volunteer to participate in the vision and planning for a nonprofit organization. It's also a prime opportunity for leveraging professional skills and experiences for good. As a board member, people can have a direct and personal impact on causes they care about. While it is generally a greater time commitment (many boards seek a one year or more commitment), the actual time per month volunteered varies significantly.

Before joining a nonprofit board, you or your interested employees need to understand what you are signing up for so there are no surprises. Corporate boards are normally small and limited in scope. There are predetermined profiles usually consisting of senior business professionals that are normally well paid. Nonprofit boards, however, are typically large with working committees. Members have diverse profiles and roles, high turnover, convene board meetings after normal business hours, and are unpaid.

The eight basic responsibilities of all nonprofit boards are to:

1. Create and review mission/purpose statements and articulate the nonprofit's goals, means, and primary constituents served;
2. Select, support, and evaluate the executive director;
3. Actively participate in strategic and annual action planning and assist in implementing and monitoring achievement of the plans' goals;
4. Monitor and strengthen effectiveness of programs and services. Boards ensure programs are of high quality and consistent with the organization's mission so that "the tail does not wag the dog" by going after funding that does not directly support the mission;
5. Secure adequate resources for the nonprofit to fulfill its mission. Boards are also charged with protecting assets and providing financial oversight. This includes helping develop the annual budget and ensuring that proper financial controls are in place;
6. Build a competent board by identifying candidate qualifications, orienting new members, and periodically and comprehensively evaluating their own performance;
7. Ensure legal and ethical integrity; and
8. Enhance the organization's public standing through outreach and education to garner community support.

Many volunteer centers, United Ways, and nonprofit associations offer training for community members interested in board service. Board training usually has a minimal cost and includes an overview of the expectations and general policies of serving on a board of directors. During training volunteers can learn more about possible nonprofits to be paired with. Some organizations, like Denver's **Metro Volunteers**, require prospective board members to attend training before being given access to their "Board Bank." The Board Bank offers a way to connect nonprofit agencies experiencing vacancies on their board of directors and/or governance committee with trained, interested, and available professionals.

Even with training prior to joining a board, there is a period of transition while you or your employee learns the ropes of that organization. However, even when you are new, feel free to ask questions, and share your perspectives and ideas. In my board development work, I have seen too many people "check their business hat at the door" and refrain from offering their input. The social sector may be new to you, but your business experience can be very valuable to helping strengthen nonprofit capacity. Many board members default to fundraising as their primary role—remember you have so much more to offer.

Seth Goldman believes, "our employee involvement on nonprofit boards is really supporting the overall mission of **Honest Tea** so happens on company time."[23] **Microsoft's** board service programs encourage employees to take on leadership roles with nonprofit agencies and to provide high-value business and technology consulting to their communities.

Tips

- *Add an online application form nonprofits can complete to request an employee as a board member.*
- *Check your local volunteer center to see if they offer training for potential board members and/or host a board bank listing current nonprofit board openings.*

Food for Thought

Before joining the board of a nonprofit, there are a number of things to consider:

- Is the organization a registered not-for-profit?
- Can the organization provide you with the most current annual report, audited accounts, mission statement, and other relevant documentation?
- Does the organization have professional indemnity and liability insurance that covers board members?
- Is there a written position description for board members explaining the role expectations? Have you been fully briefed on the governance role of the board and the legal liabilities and requirements of a board member?
- Is the philosophy of the organization compatible with your company's values and beliefs? Is there a link with business (or personal) goals?

Loaned Executives and Sabbaticals

Many companies create loaned executive programs, often in partnership with their local United Way, to strengthen the nonprofit sector and support long-term sustainability. Such programs are often offered at no charge to the nonprofit, sometimes for as long as three years. Executive externships aren't new, but they've been on the rise in the post-Enron era, according to Steven May, a professor of business communication and ethics at the University of North Carolina at Chapel Hill. While there are no studies tracking the trend, firms are finding loaner programs to be a handy image-building tool.[24] Also, companies get a better employee back—a well-trained person who knows the needs of the community.

Loaned executive programs offer employees experience in such areas as strategic planning, setting and reaching goals, project management, sales and new business development, group facilitation and public speaking, working with diverse populations, team building, and problem solving.

For example, firms in Tulsa, Oklahoma, have been loaning executives to the United Way since 1984 in a kind of corporate giving that has grown in popularity. The companies pay their employees to work for local nonprofits for days, weeks, or months at a time.

Consulting firm **Accenture** has made its loan program an integral part of its business model. The program improves employee pride and morale, says Vernon Ellis, who heads the company's corporate citizenship initiatives. In order to fund it, Accenture charges the nonprofits about 15 percent of what it would generally charge consulting clients. The employees take a salary cut, though they still probably make more than they would at a nonprofit employer. At Accenture, executive loans are sometimes called "volunteerism on steroids."[25]

UVTV, a division of TV Guide, loaned their vice president of programming and marketing to the United Way in Tulsa for four months to help the agency during its annual fundraising campaign. UVTV paid the VP his full regular salary during the course of the "loan," but he worked solely for United Way during those four months, becoming the agency's lead person for contacting all the construction companies in Tulsa as part of the fundraising campaign.[26]

Deluxe Corporation's call-center operations manager was loaned to the Syracuse United Way as part of its loaned executive program. Designed to help the nonprofit organization during its busiest fundraising time, the program also offers businesspeople a chance to hone their skills and help the community at the same time.[27]

The annual United Way Loaned Executive Program helps businesses in the Puget Sound area of Washington develop and carry out their yearly giving campaigns. Through the program, **Microsoft** and other companies loan some of their best and brightest employees from August through November to help with fundraising in the local community. The Microsoft Loaned Executives also contribute their talents internally for the company's own giving campaign.

For employees interested in volunteering or public service for more than a couple hours at a time, many companies now allow employees to take extended leaves of absence, commonly referred to as *sabbaticals*. Ranging from three months up to two years, sabbaticals allow staff to work with such organizations as AmeriCorps and the Peace Corps. At the end of the sabbatical, employees' jobs are ready and waiting for them and employees are eager to have them back.

Sabbaticals are planned, strategic job pauses that allow an employee to volunteer and/or learn a new skill. The most meaningful sabbaticals have specific goals and objectives designed to benefit both the employee and the company. Sabbaticals give employees an opportunity to donate time to a nonprofit they and their companies believe in.

The number of companies offering paid sabbaticals is small but steadily rising—about five percent of corporate respondents according to a national survey by the Society for Human Resource Management (SHRM). Another 18 percent offer unpaid sabbaticals, an increasingly popular alternative to layoffs when demand slackens.[28] In all, about 23 percent of U.S. businesses offer either paid or unpaid sabbaticals, with unpaid being more common, according to SHRM.[29]

A business has to consider several criteria when developing a sabbatical program: the duration of the leave, which employees are eligible, the frequency, whether it's paid or unpaid, and extent of benefits if any during the leave. The parameters of the program are determined by each organization since no national standards exist.

The benefits of an extended leave program are many. Sabbaticals and loaned executives offer a way to retain valued employees, attract top talent, increase productivity, revitalize your work force, and enhance public relations. Sabbaticals are particularly valuable in high burnout industries. Employees are allowed time off to rejuvenate, and the employer saves money by retaining talent rather than spending funds to replace employees who get tired and quit. The cost to replace an employee is generally much higher—150 to 200 percent of the person's salary—than paid sabbatical costs.

Xerox offers employees a "Social Service Leave" to devote their full-time service to critical community projects. During their leaves, which range from six months to one year, the employees continue to receive full pay and benefits from Xerox. They apply their technical, business, and personal skills to help nonprofits address a range of social issues. Xerox has granted sabbaticals to more than 475 employees since the program began in 1971. One of few corporate sabbatical programs that provide paid opportunities for employees to volunteer full time, Xerox's Social Service Leave is believed to be the oldest of its kind in American business. [30]

Accenture offices in 16 countries participate in the Voluntary Service Overseas (VSO) Business Partnership program for one or two months. Employees have the opportunity to take a leave of absence to volunteer their time and skills to work, often at the grassroots level, as an employee of a development organization. For example, more than 450 employees participate in VSO "challenge events," such as treks to Mount Everest Base Camp. These efforts have raised more than $3 million for VSO initiatives around the world.[31]

Through the **Patagonia** Employee Internship Program, employees can leave their jobs to work for the environmental group of their choice. Patagonia continues to pay their salaries and benefits while they're gone, and environmental groups worldwide get them for free. To date, more than 750 employees have taken part in the program.[32]

Timberland created its service sabbatical program in 2001. Up to four employees each year are awarded three to six months of leave to work full time with a nonprofit organization of their choosing. The sabbatical comes with full pay and benefits and employees return to their same job after completing their assignment.[33]

Dow Chemical Company loaned one of their senior government relations managers to serve as the interim executive director of the Michigan Community Service Commission (MCSC). The manager was already a governor-appointed commissioner for the MCSC, and his leadership helped maintain the commission during the executive search process and following transition period. His service cost the organization nothing, as his salary was covered by Dow.

The Gap underwent massive renovations that required closing their retail stores while construction was under way. In Denver, Colorado, when the stores were closed, Gap employees were assigned to work with various local nonprofits on a range of activities. Gap partnered with the local volunteer center, Metro Volunteers, to identify and secure appropriate placements for teams of their employees.

Gap got great PR in the local media for this decision. After the stores reopened, employees I visited with shared that they had built stronger relationships with their fellow employees through the volunteer opportunity, and it had positively affected their impression of the company and their peers. They also felt good about actively contributing their time and skills with people less fortunate than themselves.

Tip

- *Your SABBATICAL partners with businesses to implement customized leave programs that attract, retain, and accelerate top talent through personal and professional enrichment.*

In addition to the contributions of money, in-kind resources, and employee time and talent we've just covered, many companies engage with nonprofit partners through joint commercial ventures designed to benefit both organizations. The next section explores this smart strategy.

Commerce Connections

To fulfill critical business functions, your company can partner with nonprofit partners as well as the commercial partners in your network. This type of strategic engagement in the community draws on resources allocated to *business* line items—such as marketing or shipping—not philanthropy or charitable donations. Figure 13 illustrates several ways business and nonprofit can engage commercially for mutual benefit. Each is described briefly below.

Figure 13. Ways to Partner with Nonprofits through Commerce

Cause Marketing

Cause marketing (also called cause-related marketing) refers to marketing that involves the cooperative efforts of a business and a nonprofit for mutual benefit. The term is sometimes used more generally to refer to any type of marketing effort for social and other charitable causes. In cause marketing, a portion of the sales from each identified product or service is given to the nonprofit partner by the company over a specified period of time.

Cause marketing is not funded from the community relations or company philanthropy budget (grants, donations, or in-kind support). Instead, it uses marketing budget dollars and is considered a direct business expense. It is a powerful marketing tool that businesses and their nonprofit partners are increasingly leveraging. According to the Cone Millennial Cause Study in 2006, 89 percent of Americans (aged 13 to 25) would switch from one brand to another brand of a comparable product (and price) if the latter brand is associated with "good cause".[1] Therefore, cause marketing is seen as a way to build brand loyalty and customer bonds.

Cause marketing was born more than 25 years ago. As an early example, **American Express** decided to donate a portion of their sales to help restore the Statue of Liberty. Over a three-month period, they committed to donating one penny for each purchase made with the American Express card, $1 for each new card application, and a percentage of travel packages and travelers checks sold. The results of the campaign made marketing history. Card use rose 27 percent, new card applications rose 45 percent, and the campaign raised $1.7 million in three months for the Statue of Liberty.[2]

Another great example is of a domestic violence shelter for women and children in rural Iowa that needed a washer and dryer. A shelter representative contacted **Amana**, maker of appliances, to ask for a donation and was turned down because

Amana policy did not allow for equipment donations. However, after discussion, the company agreed to give the shelter a percentage of sales of Amana appliances over a given period of time through one of their retailers. The shelter could then use their percentage to buy the appliances they needed.

It was win-win and a creative way around company policy; the cause marketing campaign increased appliance sales and provided a direct benefit to the community. In the end, the percentage of sales raised by Amana for the shelter allowed them to buy not only the washer and dryer originally requested but other needed appliances as well.

Zhena's Gypsy Tea offered the "Tea for a Cause" series of specialty teas that funded specific nonprofit organizations. Zhena Muzyka explained, "Every tea from Gypsy Tea is going to give back to a cause, but Teas for a Cause are a little different in that they are created *for* the cause. They have a lot more educational material on the tins making the tea an educational tool you can imbibe."[3]

Tweezerman picked breast cancer as the one issue for which they do cause marketing. They started by putting the pink ribbon on a limited edition of tweezers and donated 50 cents per unit sold. They initially committed to making at least a $50,000 donation so that meant selling 100,000 tweezers. Due to a fantastic response from big accounts like CVS and Walgreens, the company increased their target to $75,000 in 2005.

Leslie Sheridan, Owner of The **Added Edge**, a conscious, international business consulting firm, personally chooses a number of local nonprofits to support based on her interests in and knowledge of current community needs. These community investments receive five percent of the total consulting contract fee paid by her clients. Each client selects the nonprofit to receive their five percent from The Added Edge's list of favorites. After receiving payment, the company sends a check in the client's name to that organization. Once Leslie selects her list of nonprofits to support for the year, she sends a letter letting them know they have been chosen. In the letter, she asks that they send a thank you for any funds generated directly to The Added Edge's client. She also mentions that, should they wish to obtain even more donations, "feel free to tell your friends and members about my business and its investment in community programs. Feel free to offer my brochures in your lobby, and let your patrons know that they can choose, as a recipient of any work I do for them, to give back to your organization. Additionally you may wish to challenge other local businesses to do the same."[4]

Retail venues often invite customers, the general public, or supporters of a nonprofit into their store for special sales events offering to donate a percentage of sales as an incentive. For example, **Beau Jo's Pizza** in Colorado hosts on-site fundraisers for Clear Creek County nonprofits. Organizations arrange to hold their special event at the restaurant and the company donates 15 to 20 percent of every dollar spent by the fundraiser attendees.[5]

Twice a year, in the spring and fall, **Eileen Fisher** stores hold special shopping days. These in-store promotional events often coincide with the launch of the designer's newly released seasonal line of clothing. Each store designates a nonprofit partner for such events, usually an organization based in the community near the store. A percentage of sales for the event goes to the nonprofit. The organization establishes a presence in the store for the day so it can interact with Eileen Fisher customers. Amy Hall, Social Consciousness Director for the company, told me, "it is a win-win for both the charity and our stores. I think this is a pretty interesting way for the stores to get involved, the store customers to get involved, and for us to add a little bit of value to the nonprofits. Plus, we receive more customers because the charity's supporters may come to the event."[6]

Every April, **Aveda** sponsors Earth Month, involving their customers and network of salons, spas, and stores. This cause marketing and philanthropy "combo" program is designed both to raise awareness of global water, endangered species, and other environmental concerns. In 2010, Aveda exceeded their goal by raising $3.7 million dollars for global and local water projects from the sales of designated products and customer donations. Since the program began, Aveda has raised a cumulative total of $18 million. In 2005, they also collected over 220,000 signatures globally to help protect threatened and endangered species.[7]

Macy's raised nearly $6 million in one day through their annual Shop For A Cause national shopping day to benefit local, regional, and national nonprofit organizations. Shop For A Cause has raised approximately $34 million in the four years the event has been held.[8]

In Des Moines, Iowa, **Quiznos** and the **Olive Garden** restaurants partnered with Toys for Tots during the 2007 holiday season offering special promotions in the workplace to generate donations for the program. The Iowa Department of Human Services (DHS) was engaged as a partner as well. Quiznos and Olive Garden were assigned special days to set up and sell lunch in the building to state government employees for just $6. Olive Garden's offering included lasagna, salad, and a breadstick. Quiznos served up a submarine sandwich, chips, and a cookie, also for $6. Half of the money from either special offer was donated to Toys for Tots. **Krispy Crème** offered a similar promotion for DHS employees through on-site donut sales.

AIDE, Inc., a now-defunct for-profit company, was ahead of its time in offering win-win online cause-marketing campaigns for companies and their nonprofit partners. Their model had many interesting features for consideration in your own efforts. Here's how it worked in a nutshell. A nonprofit would partner with a business sponsor whose products were relevant to their supporters. For the expected exposure, the business sponsor agreed to pay a program fee to AIDE, plus a per-click fee to the nonprofit. The nonprofit would send an email to its supporters asking them to click on a link. After clicking the link, supporters were connected to a webpage containing information about the nonprofit and its program(s), as well as a small advertisement for the business product. Supporters received a daily email until the target fundraising goal was reached and were encouraged to forward the email to their personal networks, thus increasing exposure for the business and raising dollars for the nonprofit.

Beau Perry, Co-Founder of AIDE, Inc. reported that the response rate to their daily emails during any given campaign was about 75 percent per day, indicating that people enjoyed participating in the process and were responding positively to it. One of their most significant campaigns (that I participated in myself) was designed to support a small nonprofit, the Turtle Conservation Project, located in the coastal region of Sri Lanka damaged by the 2004 tsunami. AIDE, Inc. helped them raised over $20,000 and attracted thousands of people to participate in the campaign.

Consider also the example of **Barefoot Wine**. When Co-Founders Michael Houlihan and Bonnie Harvey launched the company 25 years ago, they were broke—they started the business in the laundry room using a door for a desk. They couldn't afford print, radio, or television advertising, but they had to figure out a way to promote and sell their product. Driven by necessity to be creative, the owners decided the best way to market their wine was through "worthy cause marketing," a term they coined in the 1980s.

First, they identified small local nonprofits that resonated with their values then selected specific ones working on the causes that mattered most to them. Next they offered donated wine for fundraisers or special events with the stipulation that the nonprofit help promote the wine to their members and donors.

The nonprofit partner agreed to include the Barefoot logo on all event materials, display the bottles with labels clearly visible and hang the company banner at the event, hand out printed material on why the company supported the nonprofit and where the wine was sold locally, and publicly thank Barefoot in the organization's newsletter. Both parties greatly benefited from the collaboration.

Michael and Bonnie also used worthy cause marketing as a way to leverage shelf space in stores. "I don't care whether it's a widget, a flashlight, or a bottle of wine, you're facing the distribution of that product," Michael explained. "If there is a store in a neighborhood that's going to carry your product then you are either going to hope that they can sell it or you're going to have to sell it for them in their store."

The owners found the best and fastest way to get their wine into a store was to tell local merchants they'd be donating product to a nonprofit fundraiser and would like to direct attendees to the local stores that carried the wine. The magic words "we'd like to put your store on the list" quickly opened doors and turned the conversation into "where shall we put the stack?"

Barefoot Wine recently was sold to E & J Gallo, which continues to successfully market the brand through worthy cause promotions. In 2009, over 10 million cases of the wine were sold. Michael and Bonnie's approach was so successful they are writing a book, *The Barefoot Spirit,* to share their story and worthy-cause marketing principles with other start-up businesses and nonprofits.

Event Sponsorships

Corporations have a long history of sponsoring symphony concerts, public television, art exhibitions, and special events with nonprofits such as fundraisers, sports races, concerts, and walkathons. Many nonprofits mistakenly label any support from a business as a sponsorship. This is incorrect. Sponsorships are considered part of a company's marketing expenses and are tied to a specific activity or event. With sponsorships, the nonprofit usually offers a range of support levels from which potential business sponsors can choose. Each level comes with specific benefits and ways to make the company's support visible; the highest level provides the greatest benefits and requires the largest contribution.

Sponsorships are well suited to a variety of corporate goals. For example:

- Marketing goals can be met by designing an event to appeal to a target market.
- Community affairs goals can be met by designing an event that responds to the needs in the community and includes the community in its implementation.
- Employee relations goals can be met by building in staff participation. Events can build pride and provide perks for employees.
- Philanthropic goals can be met by picking an event that falls within your corporate giving policy.
- Public relations goals can be met by designing an event that is unusual and therefore of interest to the media.

However, before engaging in a sponsorship, be sure to think through the actual benefit you expect to accrue. If you plan to support a gala, know that donor, sponsor, and attendee fatigue can impact your return. If you are not careful about your involvement, you could be disappointed.

Discounted and Regular Sales

If you are unable to donate products or services that your nonprofit partners need, you may be able to negotiate and offer them a discounted sales price. For example, Serve Idaho used to receive free photocopying from **Office Depot** in Boise. When the store could no longer provide free services, it nevertheless was able to offer a deep discount on regular consumer prices, saving the organization dollars.

Energy Products, a Minnesota heating and cooling company, offered Habitat for Humanity furnaces at cost plus a small administrative fee, which saved Habitat dollars that could be spent for other needed materials.[9] Owner John Curtis explained, "We try not to just give a financial donation. We try to get involved with the group we are working with in the design and decision of what product is the best choice for them. We get involved beyond selling to providing labor to install as well."[10]

Other companies offer products tailored for the nonprofit market, such as the **Social Enterprise Reporter** or my company, **CORE THOUGHT.** The Social Enterprise Reporter is an online site designed to be a community-building and -networking tool for North American social enterprise practitioners, funders, consultants, academics, and those interested in knowing more about the realities of social entrepreneurship. My company offers consulting, training, and educational products on a variety of topics including strategic partnerships with businesses, program evaluation and performance measurement, and strategic planning for the nonprofit market.

Consider the example of **Nita Winter**, a photographer based in Marin, California, nationally acclaimed for her work with children and diversity. Nita explained to me that one of her challenges is being approached by many nonprofits looking for free services. "I tell them a large part of my income comes from working with nonprofits and I can't give it away to one organization and not to another. I need to educate them as to the value of photographs—in many cases they are more important than words. It gets people to stop and read the words."[11]

For selected projects she finds especially intriguing, Nita helps the nonprofit locate funding sources that they can use to purchase her services. Because of her community connections, she was able to point out grants for which the nonprofit could apply. Also, her reputation and inclusion as a partner in the grant application, helped several projects get funding.

Nita also shared the example of her work with Bread and Roses, an organization bringing music to retirement and convalescent homes, juvenile halls, prisons, and schools for troubled youth. "They came to me and really liked my work. I brainstormed with them [how to generate the needed funds.] I suggested maybe they could find a board member or volunteer who would underwrite the photography and in return, they will get a family portrait," Nita said. "So we worked that into their budget, a board member underwrote it, and we were able to do the project...Instead of my saying, 'okay, I will do it for nothing because you don't have the money,' we came up with a creative way to find the money."[12]

Nonprofit Fundraising and Affiliate Sales Programs

Instead of providing cash or gratis product donations to nonprofits, you might consider developing fundraising programs for nonprofit and community organizations to purchase your products at a reduced rate. The organization's members or volunteers then sell your products to their networks. The difference between the cost of the product and the sales price is kept by the nonprofit for use in its programs or operations.

Some fundraising programs require no upfront purchase of products to sell by the nonprofit. In this model, business motivation to develop a formal fundraising program is not only to help nonprofits raise money for their cause but also to expand distribution channels and pools of customers. Many nonprofits have large networks of loyal supporters that, when tapped, can yield large numbers of sales. Such an arrangement can be mutually beneficial: the nonprofit earns a percentage of the sales to its network, and the company makes a profit through the overall increase in sales volume. Some companies have designed such an approach as a core component of their overall distribution strategy.

Business Consultant Karl Dakin explained the approach this way. "As a new business is starting, one of the things you are trying to figure out is how to get your product in front of your targeted audience. With particular products, your audience may be the same audience that sits in church every week or happens to support a particular nonprofit. If that is correct, then there is an opportunity for the business to grow by using nonprofits and churches as retail outlets and at the same time to set up a program that would be a benefit or a fundraiser for the nonprofit or the church," said Karl. "For example, ordinarily if I sold a particular product through a retail outlet, I'm going to expect to discount my price anywhere from 20 to 60 percent off the retail price in order to get somebody to put it on their store shelf and sell it to a customer. If I work with a church or a nonprofit and they essentially fulfill the same purpose, which is to take that product and sell it directly to the customer, that money could go to the church or nonprofit instead of to another business or retail outlet."[13]

During his work developing the marketing and distribution strategy for a new gluten-free bakery, Karl Dakin worked with the owners to establish a partnership with a local nonprofit addressing the concerns of people suffering from celiac disease. As part of expanding its services and value to its members, the nonprofit agreed to promote the bakery's products, taking orders from its members and delivering the products directly to their homes. The nonprofit received a percentage of sales to their customers and the bakery gained more people as customers—a win-win proposition for both organizations.

For local nonprofits and faith-based organizations, **Beau**

Jo's Pizza offers discounted (and sometimes free) pizzas. The organization can then sell the pizzas to raise money. Beau Jo's also offers a 10 percent discount card for local residents. For every discount card purchase in the restaurant, Beau Jo's gives the customer's favorite local Clear Creek County nonprofit five percent of the food total.[14]

Shaman Chocolates, makers of fair trade, organic, gourmet chocolate bars, helps schools and other organizations raise money for their group. In addition, profit generated is used by the company to help support the Huichol Indians, early makers of chocolate for ceremonial purposes, and their way of life. The Huichol live in Mexico's Sierra Madre Mountains and are perhaps the last tribe in North America to have retained their pre-Columbian traditions. Local nonprofits and clubs sell Shaman Chocolate bars for $3 each, earning $1 per bar for their organization.

King Soopers grocery hosts a fundraising program in which the nonprofit buys gift certificates redeemable for a set dollar value at a reduced rate. They sell the certificates to their constituencies at full face value, earning the difference between their price and the sales prices. Parent company, Kroger, states on its website, "More than 25,000 schools, clubs churches, synagogues and other nonprofit organizations earned funds through the discounted gift certificate and rebate programs in all retail divisions. This fundraising program is Kroger's largest community activity, resulting in contributions of more than $36 million in 2009."[15]

BetterWorld Telecom offers an affiliate program in which they work in concert with nonprofits to market their services to the organizations' members and stakeholders. Matt Bauer, the president and co-founder of BetterWorld Telecom, explained, "On a monthly basis we donate a percentage back to those organizations for every member that signed up with us."[16]

For example, BetterWorld Telecom has developed an affiliate partnership with Goodwill Industries International. According to the website, "BetterWorld is now featured within the Goodwill ecosystem and offers to all Goodwill members in the U.S. our discounted services, as well as a donation from all bills directed back to Goodwill International."[17]

Start-up ink company **OnPoint Direct** designed their multi-level marketing program with nonprofit sales as a cornerstone of their planned roll out. They developed a fundraising program to be offered by their affiliate sales reps to nonprofits, initially at no charge. As part of the program, the nonprofit affiliate received a website portal customized with their logo and name. The assumption was that since most U.S. homes now have at least one printer, there would be a high demand for quality, reduced rate ink and toner cartridges. Since nonprofits tend to have extensive networks in communities, tapping the reputation and reach of those nonprofits was one way the company planned to rapidly expand its sales.

The nonprofit essentially became an affiliate, directly marketing OnPoint products (at the regular below-retail price) to their networks via their usual communication channels such as emails and newsletters, as well as using targeted campaigns. OnPoint Direct developed template materials and toolkits to help the nonprofits maximize their sales. Supporters would be asked not only to buy their ink from OnPoint but to use viral marketing and pass along the word to their personal networks as well, thus further expanding the pool of potential customers for ink and a revenue stream for the nonprofit. Supporters were provided the link to the nonprofit's web portal to buy ink directly from the company, making it easy for the nonprofit as no stock or money handling were required—OnPoint handled it all. For each purchase made, the nonprofit earned a percentage direct deposited into their bank account monthly. Once an ink customer created their account via the nonprofit portal, all their future sales also would be credited to the nonprofit.

Food for Thought

- Will you sell your product at a reduced or wholesale rate to a nonprofit? Will you fix the price the organization will sell it for?
- What is the cost structure?
- Will the nonprofit take orders or sell products without an upfront investment on their part? How often will you send them their "commission"? Check by mail or direct deposit? What paperwork will they need to fill out to be eligible?

For-Benefit Products

A "for-benefit" product is one that is developed purposely to generate dollars to support a cause. A percentage of every sale of the product is allocated to tackle the identified social issue. For-benefit products are a great way to enlist consumer support and buying power to raise dollars. Such offerings definitely influence my purchasing decisions as a consumer—I love opportunities to "do double duty" with what I buy. For example, M•A•C cosmetics company launched the VIVA GLAM lipstick/lipgloss line. Every cent of the selling price of VIVA GLAM is donated to the M•A•C AIDS Fund to support men, women, and children living with HIV and AIDS.[18]

(RED) is a for-benefit product initiative created by Bono and Bobby Shriver to raise awareness and money for The Global Fund by teaming up with the world's most iconic brands to produce (RED) branded products. A percentage of each (RED) product sold is given to The Global Fund to help women and children affected by HIV/AIDS in Africa. (RED) is not considered a charity or "campaign." It is an economic initiative that aims to deliver a sustainable flow of private sector money. Current (RED) partners include Converse, Gap, Motorola, Emporio Armani, Apple, Hallmark, and American Express. To date, (PRODUCT) RED generated contributions have reached over $150 million.[19]

Licensing (Nonprofit Logo) and Endorsements

Licensing is an agreement in which you pay to attach a nonprofit's name to your product(s). Typically, a nonprofit licenses a company to develop, produce, market and/or distribute a mission-related product that is promoted either with the organization's brand name or co-branded with both the company's and nonprofit's names. Another kind of licensing partnership occurs when a nonprofit grants use of its information or knowledge. With licensing, a business pays to use the nonprofit organization's name, logo, and images to enhance their marketing activities and the nonprofit's visibility and finances.

An endorsement is express approval or support of a company's product or service, typically conveyed through advertising or a statement of endorsement on the product packaging. The Federal Trade Commission (FTC) guidelines for use of endorsements and testimonials in advertising define an endorsement as any advertising message that consumers are likely to believe reflects the opinion, belief, findings, or experience of a party other than the sponsoring advertiser. According to the FTC this includes any verbal statements, demonstrations, or depictions of the name, signature, or seal of an organization. Further, the FTC identifies "expert endorsements" as those which must be supported by an evaluation or testing of the endorsed product.

Endorsements can be controversial. For example, Anya Kamenetz reported in *Fast Company* (September 2008) about Sierra Club's endorsement of Clorox's line of environmentally friendly products called Green Works for "an undisclosed fee." Evidently, Clorox was thrilled though many in the rank and file of the Sierra Club found the endorsement contentious.[20]

Many nonprofits have long-standing policies against endorsing any company, product, or service, but still may license use of their logo to a company in exchange for payment or a portion of the sales when there is a benefit to their stakeholders or cause. Sometimes this arrangement includes the opportunity to distribute educational information along with the product. The issue of what constitutes an endorsement continues to be discussed and debated by the IRS, state attorneys general, and the nonprofit community. Be sure you check with your legal team before proceeding.

Vendor Contracts

Many products and services needed by businesses currently purchased from for-profit vendors also can be purchased from nonprofits either through long-term arrangements or short-term contracts. Two common areas of vending from nonprofits are purchases of technical consulting or specialized services, and premiums/business gifts. Nonprofit enterprises that can be beneficial vendors are mission-driven organizations that apply market-based strategies to achieve their social purpose. Such social enterprises actively earn income to fund their programming to avoid dependency on government and foundation grants and donations. Unfortunately, figuring out which nonprofits have products or services that might be of interest to your company requires some digging and inquiry.

The benefits of this arrangement to nonprofits include income and exposure from selling their products and services to assist in achieving their mission. The benefits to your business from using nonprofit vendors are several. First, nonprofit vendors can be less expensive than for-profit equivalents, because they may have different cost structures. Second, a nonprofit's offerings come loaded with goodwill, which positively affects your company. Third, you can purchase products and services tailored to your specific needs. Finally, you can gain access to experts in their field.

For example, John Sullivan, Co-Founder and Creative Director of **BTS Communication,** won the Los Angeles Social Innovation Fast Pitch in 2010. This is an event sponsored by Social Venture Partners Los Angeles, the University of Southern California, and the Academies for Social Entrepreneurship. BTS Communication is the only advertising and social media agency housed within a drug treatment center, dedicated to helping their residents recover by providing professional career training in the advertising and marketing fields. When you choose to work with BTS Communications, you not only get top-quality creative work, you also participate in the development of highly talented creative people who are unleashing their passion for advertising, graphic design, copywriting and marketing. BTS handpicks their team who, under close supervision, works together to craft effective materials on your behalf. They offer marketing and creative services, without the large agency price tag to help small and medium size nonprofits and businesses achieve their marketing objectives.[21]

The **American Red Cross** sells first aid and disaster training and emergency preparedness kits. Businesses wanting unusual yet useful holiday, thank you, or recognition gifts for employees or customers can buy training or kits directly from ARC to give out. Such purchases provide revenue for the agency and promotional items for the company.

The **Women's Bean Project** in Denver is a nonprofit dedicated to helping women break the cycle of poverty and unemployment. The agency teaches workplace competencies for entry-level jobs through employment and job-readiness training in their gourmet food production business. They sell attractive prepackaged clear tubes of "make it yourself" soup using various colorful beans and spices—a perfect product to give as holiday gifts to clients.

Women's Bean also runs a catering business. Companies in the market for box lunches for meetings or special events can buy them from Women's Bean. In doing so, they purchase a product they would buy anyway, provide income for an organization that empowers women, and give the women served by the agency opportunities to practice their job skills.

Businesses needing bulk mailing services can purchase assistance from an Easter Seals organization or other nonprofit group providing job skills training for the developmentally disabled. Their patronage provides revenue to support organizational programs, as well as work for clients of the organization. At the same time, the company fills a necessary business function, perhaps even saving some money while doing good.

A premium is a gift or special offer given by a company to its customers or employees as added value. Typical examples include company logo mugs, calendars, prizes in cereal boxes, and other goods (free or purchased) for proof of purchase seals from a product.

Many nonprofits produce educational or other products that you could purchase as thank-you or incentive gifts for customers. Purchasing premiums from nonprofits is highly beneficial for companies. Not only do you get a unique product that stands out from the generic issue of supply houses, you also associate your brand with a credible, worthy cause, strengthening your company image.

Benefits to selling premiums for nonprofits include reaching a larger audience with their message than they could on their own; unrestricted operating cash; and support for what they do best—create educational products that carry out their mission.

Examples of premiums from nonprofits abound. **Meredith Corporation**, for example, bought American Red Cross first aid kits and life-saving classes to give as gifts to their employees.

Georgia Pacific's MD toilet tissues offered World Wildlife Fund stuffed animals for $1 plus two proof of purchase seals.

Texize Division of Dow Brands, manufacturer of home cleaning products, teamed with the National Crime Prevention Council to provide McGruff posters, puppets, audiotapes, and other items to retailers to increase sales. Puppets and audiotapes were available to parents for $4.99 and one proof of purchase seal from any Texize product. During the campaign, Texize saw its best quarter of sales ever.

A Tulsa, Oklahoma, convenience store chain gave away disaster preparedness booklets prepared by and purchased from **Tulsa's Citizen Corps**.

Food for Thought

- What nonprofits might be logical suppliers of the kinds of products or services you need for employee or customer gifts?
- Can the nonprofit's level of production handle additional demand?
- Is there any seasonal connection to your premium?
- Instead of giving gifts to customers for business or referrals, could you make a donation in their name to a nonprofit?

Product and Ingredient Sourcing

Companies can source products and ingredients from community organizations as a way to purchase things they need and do good at the same time. One well-known example comes from **Ben and Jerry's,** who buys chocolate fudge brownies for its ice cream from Greyston Bakery in New York.[22] The bakery is run by the Greyston Foundation, a nonprofit providing employment, training, and child care for homeless and low-income people. Greyston Bakery, a for-profit business, has a double bottom line. "We don't hire people to make brownies, we make brownies in order to hire people," the company philosophy states. Those hired at the bakery are considered to be "hard to employ."[23] Each year Ben and Jerry's buys millions of dollars' worth of brownies from Greyston.

Aveda connects its mission to "care for the world we live in, from the products we make to the ways in which we give back to society" with product development by sourcing ingredients from traditional communities around the world. For Aveda, one type of strategic partnership involves local NGOs in areas where the company purchases source products. For example, Aveda sources urukum, an orange-red colorant from the Yawanawa people in Brazil, through a purchasing agreement. In 1992, Aveda Founder Horst Rechelbacher and Anthropologist May Waddington started a partnership to create a urukum tree plantation that would help the Yawanawa to sustain themselves. Aveda's research chemists discovered that the urukum pigment harvested by the Yawanawa was ideal for creating superior lip color. The partnership with Aveda has since evolved into a sustainable business model, helping to prevent the breakdown of the Yawanawa community. It continues to create jobs and a means of cultural survival for the community, while preserving the pristine beauty of the Yawanawa's land from the threat of loggers and rubber-tappers.[24]

In addition, Aveda supports social development projects to increase community capacity to continue supplying the desired product using sustainable practices. These include using solar energy for drying facilities and boats and motors to get the product to market. Mary T'Kach, Executive Director of Environmental Sustainability, emphasizes that "the actual purchasing of the colorant is vital to our business, but these social projects are really vital to the community so it's a win-win situation."[25]

Dagoba Organic Chocolate also actively supports developing country communities where their product ingredients originate through their buying practices. Says Founder Frederick Schilling, "The money we pay for our cacao goes to help build infrastructure and to further the growth of local communities."[26]

World of Good was founded upon a theory of change about how best to alleviate poverty in developing countries. The company focuses on product sourcing and tapping into the U.S. consumer market. Co-Founder Priya Haji explained, "Through our purchasing, World of Good is helping shape the world in a more humanitarian fashion by practicing ethical or fair-trade sourcing. The things that we're consuming are actually made in ways that empower the communities where they come from."[27] World of Good specializes in fair-trade handicrafts mostly made by women in poor communities. They saw the opportunity to build a bigger market for fair-trade handicrafts which would at the same time empower women to create intergenerational change and long-term impact on quality of life.

The **Boeing Company** purchases sheet metal supplies from Pioneer Human Services, a nonprofit organization that trains and employs ex-offenders and former substance abusers. The Boeing Company helped Pioneer Human Services launch Pioneer Industries in 1966 and became a steadfast customer, accounting for between 55 and 70 percent of its annual sales. Boeing receives top-quality supplies for its planes along with an enhanced corporate community involvement, and Pioneer Human Services harnesses employment opportunities for its workforce and earns revenue from this sustainable social enterprise.[28]

Other Ways to Support Nonprofits

An easy way to help organizations or any other cause you care about is through a new Yahoo!-powered search engine and online shopping mall called GoodSearch.com. **GoodSearch** will make a donation to your favorite nonprofit or school every time you search the internet and every time you purchase something at one of their partner merchants—including Target, Gap, eBay, Macy's, Best Buy, Barnes & Noble and hundreds more! It doesn't cost you a thing. The money comes from the advertisers and the stores. The more people use the site, the more money goes to nonprofits serving their communities.

What do you love to do whether it relates directly to your company products or services or not? John Harris of Denver's **Belcaro Paint and Decorating Center** and his wife are strong supporters of children's education and health. One of John's favorite ways to give back and get their retail store's name out in the community is to donate himself. "I am a Scottish bagpiper so for silent auctions, I donate an hour of my piping time. I get all dressed up in the full class A Highland attire and perform at a mutually agreeable time and place. If you get a bunch of Celtic people at these functions, they can get into a bidding frenzy and they end up paying a lot more than I am worth! If it helps the cause, they don't care."[29] In addition, Belcaro Paint gives away paint mismatches to nonprofits and heavily discounts or donates paint for selected special projects.

One of the principal things **State Farm Insurance** focuses on is auto safety. Clayton Adams, Executive Vice President of Community Development, states, "Because we are the number one auto insurer in the U.S., it is incumbent upon us to create a very high profile on auto safety."[30] To this end, they have partnered with organizations who share their concern. For example, State Farm partners with the Children's Hospital of Philadelphia on a research study concerning child passenger safety. State Farm has allowed them to use State Farm's national accident data to look at such things as safety and booster seat use, where a child should be located in the car, how they should be strapped in, and under what conditions.

Minneapolis-based **Peace Coffee** offers an interesting example for to consider. It is a for-profit subsidiary owned by the Institute of Agricultural and Trade policy (IATP), a nonprofit organization. Peace Coffee was founded as a way for IATP to support small family farms in coffee-growing regions of developing countries and support sustainable environmental practices. While IATP receives a percentage of Peace Coffee sales to use for their programs, this was not a primary motivation for incubating the coffee company, according to Andy Lambert. Instead, IATP was more interested in establishing an effective business model to show how a company in a capitalist economy could use consumer purchases to drive sustainable practices.[31] Coffee deliveries in the Twin Cities were even made by bicycle!

Here is an action I personally take every time I travel. Any company that has employee travel can do it, too—all it takes is a little time and a bit more room in a suitcase. As you know, hotels provide personal product amenities in the guest rooms. If you use them one day, housekeeping leaves a new set for the next day. If you are like me, you don't actually use all of those bottles of lotions and potions, or maybe you take your own along. So, every day, take the bottles you haven't opened (you've already paid for them...) and put them in your suitcase. Use the plastic laundry bag from the closet hanger to prevent leaks during the trip home. The cleaning folks will give you a new set each day of your stay. Back at the office, set up a collection point where everyone who travels deposits their extra toiletries. Periodically deliver all the collected items to a shelter for the homeless or domestic violence survivors. The donation doesn't cost your company a dime and can be a much appreciated gift for a worthy organization trying to make ends meet. Remember this on your next trip!

I received a Ticketmaster email announcing upcoming concert tickets for sale. I noticed a link that said, "Charity Auctions. Bid on side-stage seating, front row, VIP, and more! " Upon clicking, I was taken to the Ticketmaster website and learned that, for the past three years, the band Big Head Todd and the Monsters (BHTM) have used their annual Red Rocks show in Denver as a vehicle to benefit causes. BHTM partnered with footwear maker Crocs' Soles United to help meet a goal to donate over one million pairs of shoes to those in need. The shoes are shipped worldwide to orphanages, humanitarian relief efforts, village support groups and other nonprofit organizations.

The Ticketmaster website is used as a communication mechanism to promote nonprofit auctions put together by event organizers. For this nonprofit auction, the site states, "To demonstrate their appreciation and support of BHTM, Soles United will donate a pair of shoes for every ticket purchased to a BHTM show in 2008. BHTM fans can be assured that their presence at a BHTM concert will make a real difference in the life of a child or adult living in poverty. Shoes help prevent injury and disease. Shoes allow children to go to school. Shoes allow parents to work. Shoes are a first step to making one's life better." Online nonprofit auction packages offered by BHTM for the Red Rocks concert included reserved, side stage, and VIP seating tickets, CD/DVD Collections, and a sound check and photo-op.[32]

Zhena's Gypsy Tea holds sweepstakes to give away in-home Gypsy Tea Parties. The parties not only offer an opportunity for the company to market their teas but are also about women's empowerment, teaching women "how to have fun, release fears, bond with one another, drink a bunch of tea, learn how to belly dance, laugh, talk about their lives and passions." The Tea Parties are designed to teach attendees about being powerful women, the benefits of fair trade and organic products, as well as how to choose the best things for themselves and their children. Zhena says, "We've got a lot of fingers in a lot of pieces…and I love it!"[33]

Funding Factory offers fundraising opportunities for collecting and recycling old cell phones, ink cartridges, and toner cartridges. They send you the boxes and the UPS labels to send what your company collected in to them (paid by them). Funding Factory also provides Adobe PDF files of already made flyers and letters for participating nonprofits to download and use to inform their supporters of the fundraising program they are doing and why. The credit you accumulate by donating empty printer cartridges and used cell phones will be directly deposited into the account of the nonprofit of your choice.[34]

Call to Action

"Just do the right thing, and the right thing will happen to your company."

—Gary Erickson, Founder, **Clif Bar & Company**, Emeryville, California[1]

Did you pick up this book because you want to do good in the community as a business owner or executive? Most business owners are motivated by more than just profit; we want to be valued members of our community. Or perhaps you were looking for guidance on how to deal with an endless flood of charitable requests. Maybe your constituents have called for more corporate responsibility, transparency, or philanthropy from your company. Or perhaps your business has given generously for a long time, but with little return or visible impact. You wonder if there's a more effective way to use your hard-earned resources to create real change.

Whatever your original reason for reading this book, I hope you've found what you were looking for. Just as important, I hope you've gained a new understanding of the power of strategic business giving. As these pages have shown, business philanthropy is not just for the Fortune 500; it's for all of us. Every company can do something to support the people and communities in which we operate. All it takes is some planning and a little effort to reap huge benefits—everything from attracting a slew of new customers and boosting sales, enhancing your reputation, keeping and motivating great employees, and feeling deep satisfaction over your company's part in making a difference where you live.

With Strategy for Good as your guide, you can take your business giving to the next level for even greater benefit and impact. If you already sponsor an annual fundraising event, consider deepening your relationship with that nonprofit. Keeping in mind the four main ways to contribute—dollars, in-kind, people, and commerce—what next step could you take to benefit both organizations? Maybe next year you could leverage your networks to boost attendance at the event—or knock their socks off with a bold, innovative idea. Whatever you do, remember to share your story with us. People want to know what works!

In our fast-paced world, business giving strategies, trends, and best practices evolve quickly. For that reason I am already compiling material for a revised edition of this book. Help me make it a vital resource for business givers like you by sharing your experiences. Please visit my website, *www.StrategyforGood.com* to ask questions, share success stories and lessons learned, and learn about other companies' community involvement programs. (If you're a nonprofit, the website offers resources for you, too. Check out the information-packed workbook on maximizing partnerships with businesses.)

As Patricia Aburdene notes in the foreword to this book, we live in uncertain, challenging times. Small business can be a potent force for positive change. After all, small business drives the U.S. economy, accounting for half of GDP and more than half of all jobs, according to Business.gov. Small to mid-size companies are critical anchors in each of our communities, providing employment, needed goods and services, economic vitality, stability, and growth. We can harness our power for even more good through strategic partnership with the nonprofit sector, blending our mutual expertise and resources to benefit the entire community. As Gary Hirshberg, Stonyfield Farm CE-Yo, puts it: "Whether you are active as a for-profit or a nonprofit, we all have to be active. No one has more or better credibility than anyone else. Everybody has got to grab an oar. The world is in too much trouble."[2]

Remember: We are ALL part of the solution.

Appendix A: Resources

American Association of State Service Commissions

www.asc-online.org

The American Association of State Service Commissions (also known as America's Service Commissions-ASC) is a peer network of governor-appointed commissioners, along with staff from the state commissions. State service commissions are governor-appointed public agencies or nonprofit organizations made up of more than 1,110 commissioners - private citizens leading the nation's philanthropic movement. The nation's 52 state service commissions operate at the state and local level granting more than $215 million from federal national service funds while matching these federal dollars with over $28 million from state and local sources to support citizen service and volunteerism in America. These funds support more than 650 AmeriCorps programs and 33,000 AmeriCorps members.

B Corporation

www.bcorporation.net

Certified B Corporations are a new type of corporation that uses the power of business to solve social and environmental problems. B Corps are unlike traditional businesses because they: meet comprehensive and transparent social and environmental performance standards; meet higher legal accountability standards; and build business constituency for good business.

BALLE – Business Alliance for Living Local Economies

www.livingeconomies.org

BALLE's mission is to catalyze, strengthen and connect networks of locally owned independent businesses dedicated to building strong Local Living Economies. Currently BALLE's network of socially responsible businesses, comprises over 80 community networks in 30 U.S. states and Canadian provinces representing over 22,000 independent business members across the U.S. and Canada.

Boston College Center for Corporate Citizenship

www.bcccc.net

The Boston College Center for Corporate Citizenship is a membership-based research organization associated with the Carroll School of Management. They work with global corporations to help them define, plan and operationalize their corporate citizenship. Through research, executive education and the insights of their 350 corporate members, they create knowledge, value and demand for corporate citizenship. Membership with the Center offers many benefits, including the education programs and webinars. Dues start at $2000/year. Excellent source for research reports, many of which can be accessed free.

Business for Social Responsibility

www.bsr.org

BSR, based in San Francisco, works with its global network of more than 250 member companies to develop sustainable business strategies and solutions through consulting, research, and cross-sector collaboration. With offices in Asia, Europe, and North America, BSR uses its expertise in the environment, human rights, economic development, and governance and accountability to guide global companies toward creating a just and sustainable world. Any company committed to improving its sustainability performance is eligible to join BSR. Membership dues are based on annual gross revenues; dues start at $2,500/year. Members are generally larger companies.

Cause Marketing Forum

www.causemarketingforum.com

Helping businesses and nonprofits succeed together with practical information, connections, and recognition

Committee Encouraging Corporate Philanthropy
www.corporatephilanthropy.org
A national forum of business CEOs that includes information, resources and seminars.

Cone, Inc.
www.coneinc.com
Provides a variety of studies on community relations, cause marketing and corporate social responsibility.

Corporation for National and Community Service
www.nationalservice.gov
The Corporation for National and Community Service is the federal agency that engages more than five million Americans in service through Senior Corps, AmeriCorps, VISTA, and Learn and Serve America, and leads the national call to service initiative, United We Serve. National service programs are a great way to get involved in local communities. The CNCS website provides program information searchable by state.

Corporate Responsibility Newswire
www.csrwire.com
A searchable site that includes up-to-date press releases and information from throughout the world.

Giving USA
www.givingusa.org
The Giving USA Foundation publishes data and trends about charitable giving through its seminal publication, Giving USA, and quarterly newsletters on topics related to philanthropy.

Green America

www.greenamerica.org

Green America promotes socially and environmentally responsible business, publishes the National Green Pages, and promotes socially responsible investing.

Green Business Network

www.greenamerica.org/greenbusiness/network.cfm

The Green Business Network of Green America provides the networks, resources, and technical assistance needed for socially and environmentally responsible businesses to emerge and thrive in communities across the US. To become a member of the Green Business Network™, businesses submit an application and undergo screening to determine the company's familiarity with and commitment to social and environmental responsibility, and significant action in terms of this commitment.

Hands On Network

www.handsonnetwork.org

HandsOn Network is the go-to destination for companies of all sizes looking to improve their community service initiatives.

ImagineNations Network

www.imagine-network.org/about

Helps educate, mentor and empower young entrepreneurs (ages 15-29), linking them to local and global organizations and connecting them with each other to develop friendships, provide encouragement, share ideas, develop business plans and learn from other young people whose ideas have become a reality.

Independent Sector

www.independentsector.org

Independent Sector is the leadership forum for charities, foundations, and corporate giving programs committed to advancing the common good in

America and around the world.

LOHAS

www.LOHAS.org

LOHAS is an acronym for Lifestyles of Health and Sustainability, a market segment focused on health and fitness, the environment, personal development, sustainable living, and social justice. LOHAS is not a membership organization and has no member fees. Their goal is to foster LOHAS oriented community development and facilitate interaction and idea exchange among decision-makers.

MicroMentor

www.micromentor.org

MicroMentor is a free online service that connects small business owners with business mentors. MicroMentor puts experience to work by offering business professionals meaningful volunteer opportunities and by offering entrepreneurs one-on-one advice to help build successful businesses.

NetImpact

www.netimpact.org

Net Impact is an international nonprofit organization with a mission to inspire, educate, and equip individuals to use the power of business to create a more socially and environmentally sustainable world. Net Impact is a 501c3 nonprofit with a central office in San Francisco. Their more than 260 professional and student chapters represent 200 campuses and cities in 23 countries around the world.

1% for the Planet

www.onepercentfortheplanet.org

1% for the Planet is a global movement of companies donating at least 1% of their annual net revenues to environmental organizations worldwide. Membership consists of more than 1,400 businesses in 38 countries, together giving over $15 million annually to over 2,000 environmental groups worldwide. To date, 1% for the Planet has initiated over $50 million in environmental giving.

Serve.gov

www.serve.gov

Serve.gov is an online resource for not only finding volunteer opportunities in communities, but also for creating your own.

Social Venture Network

www.svn.org

Social Venture Network (SVN) is a peer-to-peer network that addresses the unique challenges facing entrepreneurs and investors who want to leverage business for a more just and sustainable world. Membership in SVN is based on an applicant's commitment and capacity to effect positive change through business. Applications are evaluated on four key factors: alignment with SVN's mission, level of impact, diversity of experience, and finances (revenue/budget/assets).

Social Venture Partners International

www.svpi.org

SVPi is an international network of 26 Social Venture Partner organizations with 2,000+ Partners in the USA, Canada and Japan, who have contributed $36 million in grants and countless hours of strategic volunteering to more than 397 nonprofit organizations. All SVPs share the dual mission of seeking to catalyze significant, long-term positive social change in their communities through philanthropy development and capacity building.

United Nations Volunteering

www.unv.org/en.html

The United Nations Online Volunteering service offers a database of online volunteering opportunities submitted by development organizations worldwide. Interested individuals identify opportunities that match their interests, expertise and skills, and submit their applications directly to the organizations, which select the volunteers they would like to engage in their activities.

United Way Worldwide

www.worldwide.unitedway.org

Partnering with United Way provides companies a way to invest strategically in their communities and advance the common good by creating lasting, sustainable changes that lead to better, stronger places to live and work.

Volunteering in America

www.volunteeringinamerica.gov

VolunteeringInAmerica.gov hosts the most comprehensive collection of data on volunteering and civic engagement ever assembled, including data for every state and nearly 200 cities.

VolunteerMatch

www.volunteermatch.org

VolunteerMatch offers a variety of online services to support a community of nonprofit, volunteer and business leaders committed to civic engagement.

Appendix B: Suggested Reading

Aburdene, Patricia. 2005. *Megatrends 2010: The Rise of Conscious Capitalism.* Charlottesville, VA: Hampton Roads Publishing Company.

Albion, Marc. 2006. *True to Yourself: Leading a Values-based Business.* Social Venture Network Series. San Francisco, CA: Berrett-Koehler Publishers, Inc.

Andresen, Katya. 2006. *Robin Hood Marketing: Stealing Corporate Savvy to Sell Just Causes.* San Francisco, CA: Jossey-Bass.

Andriof, Jorg and Malcolm McIntosh. 2001. *Perspectives on Corporate Citizenship.* Austin, TX: Greenleaf Publishing.

Arena, Christine. 2004. *Cause and Success: 10 Companies that Put Profits Second and Came in First (How Solving the World's Problems Improves Corporate Health, Growth and Competitive Edge).* New World Library.

Arena, Christine. 2007. *The High-Purpose Company: The TRULY Responsible (and Highly Profitable) Firms That Are Changing Business Now.* HarperCollins Publishers.

Austin, James E. 2000. *The Collaboration Challenge: How Nonprofits and Businesses Succeed Through Strategic Alliances.* San Francisco, CA: Jossey-Bass.

Batstone, David. 2003. *Saving the Corporate Soul & (Who Knows) Maybe Your Own.* San Francisco, CA: Jossey-Bass.

Benioff, Marc and Karen Southwick. 2004. *Compassionate Capitalism: How Corporations Can Make Doing Good an Integral Part of Doing Well.* Career Press.

Benioff, Marc and Carly Adler. 2007. *The Business of Changing the World: Twenty Great Leaders on Strategic Corporate Philanthropy.* McGraw-Hill.

Berkley, Bert and Peter Economy. 2008. *Giving Back: Connecting You, Business, and Community.* Hoboken, NJ: John Wiley & Sons, Inc.

Bernholz, Lucy. 2004. *Creating Philanthropic Markets: The Deliberate Evolution.* Hoboken, NJ: John Wiles & Sons, Inc.

Besser, Terry L. 2002. *The Conscience of Capitalism: Business Social Responsibility to Communities.* Westport, CT: Praeger Publishers.

Bishop, Matthew and Michael Green. 2008. *Philanthrocapitalism: How the Rich Can Save the World.* NY: Bloomsbury Press.

Boles, Nicole Bouchard. 2009. *How to Be an Everyday Philanthropist: 300 Ways to Make Difference in Your Home, Community and World – At No Cost.* New York: Workman Publishing.

Bornstein, David. 2004. *How to Change the World: Social Entrepreneurs and the Power of New Ideas.* NY: Oxford University Press.

Brest, Paul and Hal Harvey. 2008. *Money Well Spent: A Strategic Plan for Smart Philanthropy.* New York: Bloomberg Press.

Bronfman, Charles and Jeffrey Solomon. 2010. T*he Art of Giving: Where the Soul Meets a Business Plan.* San Francisco, CA: Jossey-Bass.

Bruce, Peter. 2000. *Better Business for a Better World: Connecting Principle and*

Profit to Build Socially Responsible Business. Tucson, AZ: Hats Off Books.

Burg, Bob and John David Mann. 2007. *The Go-Giver: A Little Story about a Powerful Business Idea.* London: The Penguin Group.

Burlingame, Dwight F. and Dennis R. Young (ed.)1996. *Corporate Philanthropy at the Crossroads.* Bloomington: Indiana University Press.

Chappell, Tom. 1994. *The Soul of a Business: Managing Profit and the Common Good.* NY: Bantam Books.

Clinton, Bill. 2007. *Giving: How Each of Us Can Change the World.* NY: Alfred A. Knopf.

Cohen, Ben and Jerry Greenfield. 1998. *Ben & Jerry's Double Dip: How to Run a Values-led Business and Make Money, Too.* NY: Fireside.

Cohen, Ben and Mal Warwick. 2006. *Values-driven Business: How to Change the World, Make Money, and Have Fun.* Social Venture Network Series. San Francisco, CA: Berrett-Koehler Publishers, Inc.

Conley, Chip and Eric Friedenwald-Fishman. 2006. *Marketing the Matters: 10 Practices to Profit Your Business and Change the World.* Social Venture Network Series. San Francisco, CA: Berrett-Koehler Publishing, Inc.

Crutchfield, Leslie R. and Heather McLeaod Grant. 2008. *Forces for Good: The Six Practices of High-Impact Nonprofits.* San Francisco, CA: Jossey-Bass.

Daley-Harris, Shannon and Jeffrey Keenan with Karen Speerstra. 2007. *Our Day to End Poverty: 24 Ways You Can Make a Difference.* San Francisco: Berrett -Koehler Publishing, Inc.

DeBold, Elizabeth. 2005. "The Business of Saving the World" in*: What is*

Enlightenment. Issue 28, March-May 2005. Pp.60-93.

DeThomas, Louis and Neal St. Anthony. 2006. *Doing Right in a Shrinking World: How Corporate America Can Balance Ethics & Profit in a Changing Economy.* Austin, TX: Greenleaf Book Group Press.

Duncan Clark and Richie Unterberger. 2007. *The Rough Guide to Shopping with a Conscience.* London: Rough Guides.

Elkington, John. 1998. *Cannibals With Forks: The Triple Bottom Line of 21st Century Business (Conscientious Commerce).* New Society Publishers.

Erickson, Gary. 2004. *Raising the Bar: Integrity and Passion in Life and in Business.* NY: Jossey-Bass.

Fogarty, Michael and Ian Christie. 1990. *Companies & Communities: Promoting Business Involvement in the Community.* London, England: Policy Studies Institute.

Garfield, Charles et al. 1997. *The Soul of Business.* Carlsbad, CA: Hay House.

Gary, Tracy and Nancy Adess. 2008. *Inspired Philanthropy: Your Step-by-Step Guide to Creating a Giving Plan and Leaving a Legacy.* San Francisco, CA: Jossey-Bass.

Gibb, Blair; and Schwartz, P. 1999. *When Good Companies Do Bad Things: Responsibility and Risk in an Age of Globalization.* Hoboken, NJ: John Wiley & Sons, Inc.

Grace, Kay Sprinkel and Alan L. Wendroff. 2001. *High Impact Philanthropy: How Donors, Boards, and Nonprofit Organizations Can Transform Communities.* NY: John Wiley & Sons, Inc.

Gunther, Marc. 2004. *Faith and Fortune: How Compassionate Capitalism is Transforming American Business.* NY: Three Rivers Press.

Hammel, Laury and Gun Denhart. 2007. *Growing Local Value: How to Build Business Partnerships that Strengthen Your Community.* Social Venture Networks Series. San Francisco, CA: Berrett-Koehler Publishers, Inc.

Hilton, Steve and Giles Gibbons. 2004. *Good Business: Your World Needs You.* Mason, OH: TEXERE.

Himmelstein, Jerome L. 1997. *Looking Good & Doing Good: Corporate Philanthropy and Corporate Power.* Bloomington: Indiana University Press.

Hodges, Adrian and David Grayson. 2002. *Everybody's Business.* BK Publishing.

Hollender, Jeffrey and Linda Catling. 1995. *How to Make the World a Better Place: 116 Ways You Can Make a Difference.* NY: W. W. Norton & Company.

Hollender, Jeffrey and Stephen Fenichell. 2004. *What Matters Most: How a Small Group of Pioneers is Teaching Social Responsibility to Big Business, and Why Big Business is Listening.* Basic Books.

Izzo, John and Pam Withers. 2001. *Values Shift: The New Work Ethic and What it Means for Business.* Fairwinds Press.

Jackson, Ira. And Jane Nelson. 2004. *Profits with Principles: Seven Strategies for Delivering Value with Values.* NY: Currency Book by Doubleday.

Jamal, Azim and Harvey McKinnon. 2009. *The Power of Giving: How Giving Back Enriches Us All.* New York: Jeremy P. Tarcher/Penguin.

Jones, Ellis, Ross Haenfler, Brett Johnson and Brian Kloche. 2001. *The Better*

World Handbook: From Good Intentions to Everyday Actions. New Society Publishers.

Kloser, Christine. 2008. *The Freedom Formula: Put Soul in Your Business and Money in Your Bank.* Love Your Life Publishing.

Kofman, Fred. 2006. *Conscious Business: How To Build Value Through Values.* Boulder, CO: Sounds True.

Korngold, Alice. 2005. *Leveraging Good Will: Strengthening Nonprofits by Engaging Businesses.* San Francisco, CA: Jossey-Bass.

Kotler, Philip and Nancy Lee. 2005. *Corporate Social Responsibility: Doing the Most Good for Your Company and Your Cause.* Hoboken, NJ: John Wiley & Sons, Inc.

Lager, Fred "Chico." 1994. *Ben & Jerry's: The Inside Scoop: How Two Real Guys Built a Business with a Social Conscience and a Sense of Humor.* NY: Three Rivers Press.

Lendrum, Tony. 2003. *The Strategic Partnership Handbook: The Practitioners' Gide to Creating Partnerships and Alliances.* 4th edition. NY: McGraw-Hill.

Levy, Reynold. 1999. *Give and Take: A Candid Account of Corporate Philanthropy.* Harvard Business School Press.

Logan, David. 2002. *Employees in the Community: A Global Force for Good.* London: The Corporate Citizenship Company.

Makower, Joel. 1994. *Beyond the Bottom Line: Putting Social Responsibility to Work for Your Business and the World.* Simon & Schuster.

Mcintosh, Malcolm, Deborah Leipziger, Keith Jones, and Gill Coleman.

1998. *Corporate Citizenship: Successful Strategies for Responsible Companies.* Financial Times/Pitman Publishing.

Nelson, Jane. 2002. *Building Partnerships.* New York: United Nations Department of Public Information.

Newman, Paul and A.E. Hitchner. 2003. *In Pursuit of the Common Good: Twenty-five Years of Improving the World, One Bottle of Salad Dressing at a Time.* NY: Broadway Books.

Oster, Merrill J. and Mike Hamel. 2003. *Giving Back: Using Your Influence to Create Social Change.* Colorado Springs, CO: NavPress.

Paulson, Daryl S. 2002. *Competitive Business Caring Business: An Integral Business Perspective for the 21st Century.*

Pelosi, Peggy. 2007. *Corporate Karma: How Business Can Move Forward By Giving Back.* Toronto, Canada: Orenda Press.

Peter F. Drucker Foundation for Nonprofit Management. 2002. *Meeting the Collaboration Challenge Workbook: Developing Strategic Alliances Between Nonprofit Organizations and Businesses.* San Francisco, CA: Jossey-Bass.

Rochlin, Steven and Janet Boguslaw. 2001. *Business and Community Development.* The Center for Corporate Citizenship at Boston College.

Rochlin, Steven and Brenda Christoffer. 2000. *Making the Business Case: Determining the Value of Corporate Community Involvement.* Boston College Center for Corporate Community Relations.

Rochlin, Steven, Platon Coutsoukis, and Leslie Carbone. 2001. *Measurement Demystified.* The Center for Corporate Citizenship at Boston College.

Roddick, Anita. 1991. *Body and Soul: Profits with Principles – the Amazing Success Story of Anita Roddick and the Body Shop.* NY: Crown Publishers, Inc.

Roddick, Anita. 2000. *Business as Unusual.* London: Thorsons.

Rothman, Howard and Mary Scott. 2003. *Companies with a Conscience: Intimate Portraits of Twelve Firms that Make a Difference (3rd Edition).* Myers Templeton Book Published by the Publishing Cooperative.

Roy, Delwin, Laurie Regelbrugge, and David Logan. 1997. *Global Corporate Citizenship: Rational and Strategies.* Washington DC: Hitachi Foundation.

Rubenstein, Doris. *The Good Corporate Citizen.* 2004. Hoboken, NJ: John Wiley & Sons, Inc.

Sagawa, Shirley and Eli Segal. 2000. *Common Interest Common Good: Creating Value through Business and Social Sector Partnerships.* Harvard Business School Press.

Sanders, Dan J. 2008. *Built to Serve: How to Drive the Bottom Line with People-First Principles.* NY: McGraw-Hill.

Savitz, Andrew W. and Karl Weber. 2006. *The Triple Bottom Line: How Today's Best-Run Companies are Achieving Economic, Social, and Environmental Success – and How You Can Too.* San Francisco, CA: Jossey-Bass.

Schultz, Howard and Doris Jones Yang. 1997. *Pour Your Heart Into It: How Starbucks Built a Compnay One Cup at a Time.* NY: Hyperion.

Schwerin, David A. 1998. *Conscious Capitalism: Principles for Prosperity.* Boston, MA: Butterworth Heinemann.

Shore, Bill. 1999. *The Cathedral Within: Transform Your Life by Giving*

Something Back. NY: Random House.

Skog, Susan. 2009. *The Give-Back Solution: Create a Better World With Your Time, Talents, and Travel.* Naperville, IL: Sourcebooks, Inc.

Sosodia, Raj, Jag Sheth and David B. Wolfe. 2007. *Firms of Endearment: How World-Class Companies Profit from Passion and Purpose.* Upper Saddle River, NY: Wharton School Publishing.

Steckel, Richard, Robin Simons, Jeffrey Simons, and Norman Tanen. 1999. *Making Money While Making a Difference: How to Profit with a Nonprofit Partner.* High Tide Press.

Sullivan, Jeremiah. 2002. *The Future of Corporate Globalization: From the Extended Order to the Global Village.* Quorum Books.

Tabb, William K. 2002. *Unequal Partners: A Primer on Globalization.* New Press.

Temple, Nick (ed.) 2005. *500 Ways to Change the World.* Global Ideas Bank. NY: HarperCollins Publishers.

Thompson, Nadine A. and Angela E. Soper. 2007. *Values that Sell: Transforming Purpose into Profit Through Creative Sales and Distribution Strategies.* Social Venture Network Series. San Framcisco, CA: Berrett-Koehler Publishers, Inc.

Tichy, Noel, Andrew McGil and Lynda St. Clair. 1998. *Corporate Global Citizenship.* Lexington Books.

Twist, Lynne. 2003. *The Soul of Money.* NY: W. W. Norton & Company.

Waddock, Sandra A. 2001. *Leading Corporate Citizens.* Irwin / McGraw Hill.

Watson, Tom. 2009. *CauseWired: Plugging In, Getting Involved, and Changing the World.* Hoboken, NJ: John Wiley & Sons, Inc.

Weeden, Curt. 1998. *Corporate Social Investing: The Breakthrough Strategy for Giving and Getting Corporate Contributions.* San Francisco: Berrett-Koehler Publishers, Inc.

Wilson, Ian. 2000. *The New Rules of Corporate Conduct: Rewriting the Social Charter.* Westport, CT: Quorum Books.

Wymer, Walter M. Jr. and Sridhar Samu (ed.) 2003. *Nonprofit and Business Sector Collaboration: Social Enterprises, Cause-Related Marketing, Sponsorships, and Other Corporate-Nonprofit Dealings.* NY: Best Business Books.

Zadek, Simon, Niels Hojensgard, and Peter Raynard. 2001. *Perspectives on the New Economy of Corporate Citizenship.* Copenhagen: The Copenhagen Center.

Zadek, Simon and John Weiser. 2000. *Conversations with Disbelievers.* The Ford Foundation.

Appendix C: Glossary

SELECTED NONPROFIT TERMS

501(c)(3): Section of the Internal Revenue Code that designates an organization as charitable and tax-exempt. Organizations qualifying under this section include religious, educational, charitable, amateur athletic, scientific or literary groups, organizations testing for public safety or organizations involved in prevention of cruelty to children or animals.

509(a): Section of the tax code that defines public charities (as opposed to private foundations). A 501(c)(3) organization also must have a 509(a) designation to further define the agency as a public chari¬ty. (See Public Support Test)

Advisory Board: A group of individuals, who offer advice, inform or notify. An advisory board differs from an elected board in that they do not have any oversight responsibilities.

Altruism: Altruism, like passion, is the key intent that philanthropy expresses; a concern for the welfare of others; selflessness.

Annual Report: A voluntary report published by a foundation or corporation describing its grant activities.

Assets: Cash, stocks, bonds, real estate or other holdings of a foundation. Generally, assets are invested and the income is used to make grants. (See Payout Requirement)

Bequest: A bequest can be a legacy; a sum of money committed to an organization and donated upon the donor's death.

Board of Directors: An organized body of advisors with oversight responsibility.

Challenge Grant: A grant that is made on the condition that other funding is secured, either on a matching basis or some other formula, usually within a specified period of time, with the objective of encouraging expanded fundraising from additional sources.

Charitable Giving Plan: A plan that best reflects one's life experiences, values, goals and passions that structures giving to a charitable organization(s).

Charitable Lead Trust: A legal device used to set aside money or property of one person for the benefit of one or more persons or organizations. Specifically, this type of trust allows for a regular, fixed amount to go to a charity for a specific number of years. At the end of that time, the remainder of the trust passes to one's heirs.

Charitable Remainder Trust: A legal device used to set aside money or property of one person for the benefit of one or more persons or organizations. Specifically, this type of trust allows one to take a deduction for a gift to the trust in the year in which the trust is formed. One receives income from this type of trust for life and after one's death, the assets pass to the charity you designated.

Charity: In its traditional legal meaning, the word "charity" encompasses religion, education, and assistance to the government, promotion of health, relief of poverty or distress and other purposes that benefit the community. Nonprofit organizations that are organized and operated to further one of these purposes generally will be recognized as exempt from federal income tax under Section 501(c)(3) of the Internal Revenue Code (See 501(c)(3)) and will be eligible to receive tax-deductible charitable gifts.

Community Foundation: A community foundation is a tax-exempt, nonprofit, autonomous, publicly supported, philanthropic institution composed primarily of permanent funds established by many separate donors for the long-term diverse, charitable benefit of the residents of a defined geographic area. Typically, a community foundation serves an area no larger than a state. Community foundations provide an array of services to donors who wish to establish endowed and non-endowed funds without incurring the administrative and legal costs of starting independent foundations.

Corporate Foundation: A corporate (company-sponsored) foundation is a private foundation that derives its grantmaking funds primarily from the contribu¬tions of a profit-making business. The company-sponsored foundation often maintains close ties with the donor company, but it is a separate, legal organization, sometimes with its own endowment, and is subject to the same rules and regulations as other private foundations.

Corporate Giving Program: A corporate giving (direct giving) program is a grantmaking program established and administered within a profit-making company. Gifts or grants go directly to charitable organizations from the corporation. Corporate foundations/giving programs do not have a separate endowment; their expense is planned as part of the company's annual budgeting process and usually is funded with pre¬tax income.

Designated Funds: A type of restricted fund in which the fund beneficiaries are specified by the grantors.

Discretionary Funds: Grant funds distributed at the discretion of one or more trustees, which usually do not require prior approval by the full board of directors. The governing board can delegate discretionary authority to staff.

Donee: The receiving organization of a donor's resources. (See Grantee)

Donor: A donor is anyone who gives resources - financial, social, intellectual and time - to a nonprofit organization, public charity or fund. A donor is committed to making a difference in society. (See Grantor)

Donor Advised Fund: A fund held by a community foundation or other public charity, where the donor, or a committee appointed by the donor, may recom¬mend eligible charitable recipients for grants from the fund. The public charity's governing body must be free to accept or reject the recommendations.

Donor Designated Fund: A fund held by a community foundation where the donor has specified that the fund's income or assets be used for the benefit of one or more specific public charities. These funds are sometimes established by a transfer of assets by a public charity to a fund designated for its own benefit, in which case they may be known as grantee endowments. The community foundation's governing body must have the power to redirect resources in the fund if it determines that the donor's restriction is unnecessary, incapable of fulfillment or inconsistent with the charitable needs of the community or area served.

Endowment: The principal amount of gifts and bequests that are accepted subject to a requirement that the principal be maintained intact and invested to create a source of income for a foundation. Donors may require that the principal remain intact in perpetuity, or for a defined period of time or until sufficient assets have been accumulated to achieve a designated purpose.

Family Foundation: "Family foundation" is not a legal term, and therefore, it has no precise definition. Yet, approximately two-thirds of the estimated 44,000 private foundations in this country are believed to be family managed. The Council on Foundations defines a family founda¬tion as a foundation whose funds are derived from members of a single family. At least one family member must continue to serve as an officer or board member of the foundation, they or their relatives play a significant role in governing and/or managing the foundation throughout its life. Most family foundations are run by family members who serve as trustees or directors on a voluntary basis, receiving no compensation; in many cases, second- and third-generation descendants of the original donors manage the foundation. Most family foundations concentrate their giving locally, in their communities.

Federated Fund: A centralized campaign whereby one organization raises money for its member agencies. These annual workplace giving campaigns raise millions of dollars for distribution to local, state, and national nonprofit organizations. The United Way campaign and Community Works are examples.

Field of Interest Fund: A fund held by a community foundation that is used for a specific charitable purpose such as education or health research.

Giving Pattern: The overall picture of the types of projects and programs that a donor has supported historically. The past record may include areas of interest, geographic locations, dollar amount of funding or kinds of organizations supported.

Going to Scale: Reaching larger numbers of a target audience in a broader geographic area by institutionalizing effective programs. Taking a model that works well in one community and trying it out in another. Interventions that go to scale can benefit from being part of a larger network where they can share resources and operating procedures. This larger network can often allow an intervention to produce bigger outcomes and at a faster pace than each individual site would be able to do on its own.

Grant: An award of funds to an organization or individual to undertake charitable activities.

Grant Monitoring: The ongoing assessment of the progress of the activities funded by a donor, with the objective of determining if the terms and con¬ditions of the grant are being met and if the goal of the grant is likely to be achieved.

Grantee: The individual or organization that receives a grant. Grantor: The individual or organization that makes a grant.

In-Kind Contribution: A donation of goods or services rather than cash or appreciated property.

Independent Foundation: An individual usually founds these private foundations, often by bequest. They are occasionally termed "non-operating" because they do not run their own programs. Sometimes individuals or groups of people, such as family members, form a foundation while the donors are still living. Many large independent foundations, such as the Ford Foundation, are no longer governed by members of the original donor's family but are run by boards made up of community, business and academic leaders. Private foundations make grants to other tax-exempt organizations to carry out their charitable purposes. Private foundations must make charitable expendi¬tures of approximately 5% of the market value of their assets each year. Although exempt from federal income tax, private founda¬tions must pay a yearly excise tax of 1%-2% of their net investment income. The Ford Foundation and the John D. and Catherine T. MacArthur Foundation are two examples of well-known "independent" private foundations.

Legacy: The gift that an individual leaves, both in the details of their will and in the tradition of giving they shared with their descendents. (See Bequest)

Leverage: A method of grantmaking practiced by some foundations and individual donors. Leverage occurs when a small amount of money is given with the express purpose of attracting funding from other sources or of providing the organization with the tools it needs to raise other kinds of funds; sometimes known as the "multiplier effect."

Matching Gifts Program: A grant or contributions program that will match employees' or directors' gifts made to qualifying educational, arts and cultural, health or other organizations. Specific guidelines are established by each employer or foundation. (Some foundations also use this program for their trustees.)

Matching Grant: A grant or gift made with the specification that the amount donated must be matched on a one-for-one basis or according to some other prescribed formula.

Memorialize: To commemorate; to present a memorial to; to honor the memory of an individual or group by donating resources or establishing a fund that reflects the gifts, values or concerns of the individual or group.

Nonprofit Organization: A term describing the Internal Revenue Service's designation of an organization whose income is not used for the benefit or private gain of stockholders, directors, or any other persons with an interest in the company. A nonprofit organization's income must be used solely to support its operations and stated purpose.

Operating Foundation: Also called private operating foundations, operating foundations are private foundations that use the bulk of their income to provide charitable services or to run charitable programs of their own. They make few, if any, grants to outside organizations. To qualify as an operating foundation, specific rules, in addition to the applicable rules for private foundations, must be followed. The Carnegie Endowment for International Peace and the Getty Trust are examples of operating foundations.

Operating Support: A contribution given to cover an organization's day-to-day, ongoing expenses, such as salaries, utilities or office supplies.

Parity: Equality, as in amount, status, or value. Parity in philanthropy is the equal participation by spouses or other family members in the allocation of charitable dollars and in receiving the satisfaction and recognition of their contributions.

Passion: Boundless enthusiasm; deep and positive emotion; fervent expression of hope; belief in the essential connection of individual and community; and love of humanity. Passion, like altruism, is essential to the action of giving and the purpose of philanthropy.

Payout Requirement: The minimum amount that a private foundation is required to expend for charitable purposes (includes grants and necessary and reasonable administrative expenses). In general, a private foundation must pay out annually approximately 5% of the average mar¬ket value of its assets.

Philanthropist: A person who loves humanity, is committed deeply to making society a better place, who believes that each individual, each dollar and each action makes a difference.

Philanthropy: Philanthropy is defined in different ways. The origin of the word philanthropy is Greek and means love for mankind. Today, philan¬thropy includes the concept of voluntary giving by an individual or group to promote the common good. Philanthropy also commonly refers to grants of money given by foundations to nonprofit organizations. Philanthropy addresses the contribution of an individual or group to other organizations that in turn work for the causes of poverty or social problems, improving the quality of life for all citizens. Philanthropic giving supports a variety of activities, including research, health, education, arts and culture, as well as alleviating poverty.

Pledge: A promise to make future contributions to an organization. For example, some donors make multiyear pledges promising to grant a specific amount of money each year.

Private Foundation: A nongovernmental, nonprofit organization with funds (usually from a single source, such as an individual, family or corporation) and program managed by its own trustees or directors, established to maintain or aid social, educational, religious or other charitable activities serving the common welfare, primarily through grantmaking. U.S. private foundations are tax-exempt under Section 501(c)(3) of the Internal Revenue Code and are classified by the IRS as a private foundation as defined in the code.

Professional Advisor: Individuals who assist in planning and executing charitable giving through providing information on giving options according to one's specific financial situation. Types of professional advisors include: attorney, accountant, estate planner, financial planner, stockbro¬ker, insurance broker, planned giving officer, philanthropy consultant.

Public Charity: A nonprofit organization that is exempt from federal income tax under Section 501(c)(3) of the Internal Revenue Code and that receives its financial support from a broad segment of the general public. Religious, educational and medical institutions are deemed to be public charities. Other organizations exempt under Section 501(c)(3) must pass a public support test (See Public Support Test) to be considered public charities, or must be formed to benefit an organization that is a public charity (see Supporting Organizations). Charitable organizations that are not public charities are private foundations and are subject to more stringent regu-latory and reporting requirements (See Private Foundations).

Public Foundation: Public foundations are nonprofit organizations that receive at least one-third of their income from the general public. Public founda¬tions may make grants or engage in charitable activities. The IRS recognizes public foundations, along with community foundations, as public charities. Religious, educational and medical institutions are deemed to be public charities.

Restricted Funds: Assets or income that is restricted in its use, in the types of organizations that may receive grants from it or in the procedures used to make grants from such funds.

Seed Money: A grant or contribution used to start a new project or organization.

Social Enterprises: An organization or venture that advances its social mission through entrepreneurial, earned income strategies. Organizations which focus on innovations that blend methods from the worlds of business and philanthropy, creating sustainable social value with the potential for large-scale impact.

Social Investing: Also referred to as ethical investing and socially responsible investing, this is the practice of aligning a foundation's investment poli¬cies with its mission. This may include making program-related investments and refraining from investing in corporations with prod¬ucts or policies inconsistent with the foundation's values.

Strategic Giving: Engaging in philanthropy in a strategic manner to make a major philanthropic impact through making better choices surrounding how much one spends, invests and gives back to society.

Supporting Organization: A supporting organization is a charity that is not required to meet the public support test because it supports a public charity. To be a supporting organization, a charity must meet one of three complex legal tests that assure, at a minimum, that the organization being supported has some influence over the actions of the supporting organization. Although a supporting organization may be formed to benefit any type of public charity, the use of this form is particularly common in connection with community foundations. Supporting organizations are distinguishable from donor-advised funds because they are distinct legal entities.

Sustainability: In the business world, sustainability refers to the production of goods and services in ways that do not endanger the environment or people involved. In the nonprofit world, sustainability refers to the range of actions taken to insure that the organization and/or its critical services can be maintained over time.

Tax-Exempt Organizations: Organizations that do not have to pay state and/or federal income taxes. Organizations other than churches seeking recognition of their status as exempt under Section 501(c)(3) of the Internal Revenue Code must apply to the Internal Revenue Service. Charities may also be exempt from state income, sales and local property tax.

Technical Assistance: Operational or management assistance given to a nonprofit organization. It can include fundraising assistance, budgeting and finan¬cial planning, program planning, legal advice, marketing and other aids to management. Assistance may be offered directly by a foundation or corporate staff member or in the form of a grant to pay for the services of an outside consultant. (See In-Kind Contribution)

Tithing: A belief, found in many faiths, of giving 10% - the first and best part - back to the place of worship.

Trust: A legal device used to set aside money or property of one person for the benefit of one or more persons or organizations.

Trustee: The person(s) or institutions responsible for the administration of a trust.

Unrestricted Funds: Normally found at community foundations, an unrestricted fund is one that is not specifically designated to particular uses by the donor, or for which restrictions have expired or been removed.

Venture Philanthropy: A philanthropy that borrows some of the best practices of the venture capital world to invest deeply in nonprofits to build their capacity effectively. Venture philanthropists value their donor dollars in terms of the social return of investment.

Volunteerism: Performing an act of kindness, freely giving of your talent, time, and effort for the simple fulfillment of community expectations.

Women's Giving: Considered by some to be the next frontier of the women's movement, women's giving builds on the tradition of volunteerism and is empowered with women's financial resources.

Appendix D: Companies Interviewed

The Added Edge

www.theaddededge.com

Industry: Management Consulting

Headquarters: Clearlake, CA

Founder: Leslie Sheridan

Founded: 1995

Number of Employees: 1

Markets: Nationwide

The Added Edge is engaged in human resources, marketing, and sales consulting, as well as catalytic coaching, an innovative twist on performance evaluation. The firm's unique win-win consulting services are derived from more than 25 years of combined experience in communications, human resources, marketing, sales, and coaching.

Working to make a difference for businesses in various stages of growth, the firm has successfully delivered solutions and services to a variety of industries nationwide. The company's experience includes consulting at numerous large companies as well as many mid-sized and small organizations.

The founder's "Investment in Community" program is based on the philosophy that "we all have to take responsibility for giving back to our communities," explains Leslie Sheridan. The program was set up to support local nonprofits selected based on local needs and their continued commitment to their stated missions. As part of each new client contract, The Added Edge asks the client to select an approved nonprofit to receive 5 percent of the company's fee. For instance, if an organization hires The

Added Edge for $20,000, the selected nonprofit gets $1,000. The donation is given on behalf of the organization that hired The Added Edge in their name, on letterhead from The Added Edge. To be considered for participation in this innovative give-back program, a nonprofit must agree to recognize each client donor with a thank-you note. Nonprofits that fail to meet this condition are removed from future consideration for support from The Added Edge's client pool.

Nonprofits are also encouraged to support The Added Edge by spreading the word to their constituents/supporters, knowing that if they use The Added Edge, the non-profit they support will benefit. The biggest benefits of community involvement for The Added Edge have been the intrinsic reward which comes from giving, the satisfaction in making a difference in one's community, and building the firm's reputation in the community.

Annie's Homegrown
www.annies.com
Industry: Food products
Headquarters: Napa, CA
Co-Founder: Annie Withey
Founded: 1989
Number of Employees: 70
Markets: Nationwide
Interviewed: Chelsea Simmons, National Cause and Event Marketing Manager, 2005 and Kathryn Keslosky, Cause Marketing Assistant, 2005

Annie's Homegrown makes natural and organic pasta meals, cereals, and snacks. The company is perhaps best known for its macaroni and cheese product line, which was developed by co-founder Annie Withey as a healthy, all-natural alternative to the mac and cheese products available at the time. Annie's Homegrown recognizes that as family mealtime becomes more fragmented by life's fast pace, there is a growing need for convenience food that is healthy. Giving customers confidence in the convenience foods they feed their families allows them to take the time to share a sit-down meal and reinforces family as a safe place for children to grow and develop.

Annie's Homegrown is passionate about three things: food, people, and the planet. The firm pays special attention to all of the Earth's inhabitants, not only by supplying natural and organic comfort foods, but also through various programs that give back to communities on a local and global scale. The company's community involvement philosophy is based on Annie's personal belief that positive social and environmental change can come about by changing the way people live their everyday lives. Annie's Homegrown enables its customers to integrate doing good in communities into their everyday lives through the purchase and use of Annie's products.

Aveda
www.aveda.com
Industry: Professional hair care, personal care
Headquarters: Blaine, MN
Founder: Horst Rechelbacher
Founded: 1978
Number of Employees: 3,000
Markets: Global
Interviewed: Mary T'Kach, Executive Director of Environmental Sustainability

The worldwide leader in botanical hair and personal care products, Aveda was founded in 1978 with the goal of providing beauty industry professionals with high performance, plant-based products better for them, their guests, and the planet. The brand's roots are planted in Ayurveda, the ancient east-Indian art of healing, which takes a holistic approach to life and wellness, with a focus on cultivating balance. More than 30 years later the company is still at the industry's cutting edge—innovating in botanical technologies and wellness rituals that promote beauty and balance, while pursuing an ambitious social and environmental agenda.

Aveda's pure flower- and plant-based products are sold in more than 7,000 salons, spas, and Experience Center retail locations in more than 30 countries, including the U.S., Canada, United Kingdom, Italy, Germany, Korea, Taiwan, Hong Kong, Russia, Australia, and Singapore.

Empowered by its unique mission, Aveda seeks to set a new business standard in environmental sustainability and corporate responsibility. To Aveda, beauty is not only a product result but also the process followed in pursuing that result. From ingredient sourcing and product manufacture to transport and business operations, Aveda conducts its business in a manner that is kind to the Earth and her inhabitants.

Beau Jo's Colorado Style Pizza

www.beaujos.com

Fundraising: http://www.beaujos.com/fundraising.cfm

Industry: Food service

Headquarters: Idaho Springs, CO

Founder: Chip Bair

Founded: 1973

Number of Employees: 330

Markets: Colorado, South Dakota

Interviewed: Chip Bair, Founder

Beau Jo's is a Colorado-based company that owns a chain of pizza restaurants. The company is an institution in Denver, both for the thick pizzas and for the way you finish them off: with a bottle of honey in which to dip the remaining crust ("built-in dessert"). There are two types of pizzas at Beau Jo's: the original Mountain Pies with rolled crust at the end and Prairie Pies without the roll but a thinner layer of toppings. They come with a variety of sauce options and the usual pizza toppings along with a couple of unusual signature toppings such as tofu. The restaurant allows patrons to leave their mark at each casually decorated, mining antiques-filled site by drawing on a napkin and hanging it on the wall. *Denver Westword* named Beau Jo's the

"Best Pizza" readers' choice winner in 2006. The restaurant strives to use healthy fixings in its pizzas, including whole wheat and gluten-free crust, and natural ingredients and toppings whenever possible.

Idaho Springs, where Beau Jo's began, is a small community. The company's giving philosophy has to do with the reality that the business can only grow so much within a small community without being involved. Originally the firm began its involvement to make the community in which it operates a better place to live for the residents and a better place for the company to do business. One of the ways the firm supports the community is by establishing dates sponsored by community organizations, where 20 percent of the pre-taxed revenues are donated to the sponsoring organization.

Belcaro Paint and Home Decorating

www.belcaro.com

Industry: Home improvement wholesale

Headquarters: Denver, CO

Founders: Cindy and John Harris

Founded: 1986

Number of Employees: 11

Markets: Denver Metro Area

Interviewed: John Harris, Owner

Belcaro Paint and Decorating Center is a wholesale paint and decorating retail store in Denver. The company's diverse client base consists of two types of customer. The first is the do-it-yourselfer—people wanting to fix up their own homes. Belcaro also sells to other businesses, including retail outlets and painting contractors. Products offered include wall coverings, solvents, painting tools and supplies, patching and texture materials, and abrasives. Paint brands include Benjamin Moore, Pratt Lambert, and C2.

As with that of many small, family-owned companies, the community involvement of Belcaro Paint and Decorating Center reflects the owner's deeply held values. The Harrises believe in supporting children's health and education and, as such, the business is involved in the community supporting these causes.

BetterWorld Telecom
www.betterworldtelecom.com

BitWise Solutions
www.bitwisesolutions.com
Community Involvement: http://www.bitwisesolutions.com/about_involvement.asp
Industry: Website services
Headquarters: Indianapolis, IN
Co-Founders: Ron Brumbarger and Scott Workman
Founded: 1991
Number of Employees: 16
Markets: Central Indiana and the Great Lakes Region
Interviewed: Ron Brumbarger, President and CEO

BitWise Solutions is a web design and development company with a history of partnering with clients to provide measurable results through internet-based technology. The firm provides a myriad of professional services including web design, web application development, website management, web hosting, and web analytics. The company also offers web-based software solutions to common problems encountered when working with customers. These include software solutions for team collaboration, online event management, and collections management. In addition to website services and software, BitWise also offers workshops such as Web Camp and a content development seminar. The guiding philosophy at BitWise is based on continuous improvement, positive relationships, and a focus on results.

BitWise Solutions believes that giving back to the community in which it operates is the only way to manage a successful business. BitWise uses its involvement in the community, with the CEO serving on nonprofit boards such as United Way, as a way to grow the firm's client base through building relationships with other business owners and organizations in the community.

Clif Bar & Company
www.clifbar.com
Industry: Energy food and healthy snacks
Headquarters: Emeryville, CA
Founder: Gary Erickson
Founded: 1992
Number of Employees: 246
Markets: U.S., UK, Canada
Interviewed: Gary Erickson, Founder and co-CEO

Clif Bar & Company began as Kali's Sweets & Savories, founded by Gary Erickson and named after his grandmother. An avid cyclist, Gary realized on a long biking trip that the energy bars he had brought along were insufficient and that he could make something better himself. Thus, the first CLIF® BAR was born. Products increased to include energy drinks and gels, LUNA® bars, CLIF MOJO® bars, CLIF Builder's® bars, CLIF Kid Organic ZBaRs, and CLIF Kid Organic Twisted Fruit®. The company's Five Aspirations are sustaining its company, its brands, its people, its community, and the planet. Clif builds these values into its products and programs.

At Clif Bar & Company, being a good corporate citizen is being a good community member. The firm is honest about what it does and good to its local neighbors, as in the communities where it does business. The firm also prioritizes how it treats the community of people who work for the company, both indirectly and directly. Finally, the company is devoted to doing the right thing for the planet with a serious effort to reduce its ecological footprint in everything the firm does, from the field to the final product. The firm devotes company time to volunteerism and environmental work; the company pays employees more than 2,000 hours a year to do community service.

Colorado State Bank and Trust

www.csbt.com or *www.bokf.com*

Industry: Financial Services

Headquarters: Denver, CO

Founded: 1908

Markets: Metro Denver and Colorado communities

Number of Employees: 250

Interviewed: Aaron Azari, Vice-Chairman and Executive Vice President

Colorado State Bank and Trust (CSBT) has a history of providing financial services to Colorado communities dating back to 1908. The bank offers commercial and consumer banking, investment and trust services, and mortgage origination and servicing.

With 13 Front Range locations including a branch in Boulder, CSBT has $1 billion in bank assets and over $3 billion in trust and investment assets under administration.

Serving and supporting the community is an important part of CSBT's culture. Not only does the bank provide financial and in-kind contributions to local nonprofit organizations but employees also honor the sense of community caring by volunteering hundreds of hours annually to a wide spectrum of nonprofit, community and civic organizations. A large part of that volunteer activity includes teaching financial education and financial responsibilities to clients, families and individuals.

CSBT is a division of BOK Financial, a regional financial services company based in Tulsa, Oklahoma, (NASDAQ: BOKF). BOK Financial Holdings include BOKF, N.A., BOSC, Inc., Cavanal Hill Investment Management, Inc., and Southwest Trust Company, N.A. Operating divisions of BOKF, NA include Bank of Albuquerque, Bank of Arizona, Bank of Arkansas, Bank of

Oklahoma, Bank of Texas, Colorado State Bank and Trust, Bank of Kansas City, and the TransFund electronic funds network. Shares of BOK Financial are traded on the NASDAQ under the symbol BOKF.

Corona Insights

www.coronainsights.com
Industry: Business services
Headquarters: Denver, CO
Founder: Kevin Raines
Founded: 1999
Number of Employees: 11
Markets: Nationwide private, nonprofit, and government clients
Interviewed: Karla Raines, Principal (and current CEO)

Corona Insights serves as a partner to clients needing to make decisions on a wide variety of topics. Based in Denver, Corona helps clients uncover the right answers to the questions most important to them, and then guide them on how those answers inform their decisions and plans. The firm's mission is to provide accurate and unbiased information and counsel to decision makers. Corona works in all sectors of the community, including nonprofit organizations, private businesses, higher education institutions, and public/governmental entities. In order to meet each client group's unique needs, Corona provides a valuable blend of research and consulting. Corona's services range from primary and secondary market research, data analytics, and strategic planning.

Inherently, Corona's work benefits the community. Much of their work involves helping nonprofit and governmental agencies understand the needs and desires of their clients and constituencies, and how best to implement programs and services. The community outreach philosophy of Corona Insights is based on building mutually beneficial and long-term relationships with local organizations. In this way, community involvement facilitates the firm to play an active part in their community and to promote and drive results.

Dagoba Chocolate

www.dagobachocolate.com

Full Circle Sustainability: http://www.dagobachocolate.com/fullcirclesustainability.html

Industry: Chocolate

Headquarters: Ashland, OR

Founder: Fredrick Schilling

Founded: 2001

Markets: Nationwide

Interviewed: Frederick Schilling, Founder

Dagoba is an organic brand of high-quality chocolate, founded by Frederick Schilling in Boulder, Colorado, and now based in Ashland, Oregon. The firm's commitment to creating deeply satisfying, sustainable chocolate grew out of Frederick's realization that cacao production is all too often associated with rainforest destruction, loss of heirloom varietals, and producer poverty. Frederick regularly travels to producing countries to locate high-quality sources, establish direct partnerships, collaborate on post-harvest processing, and learn how equitable cacao trading supports communities and the environment. This intensive process is rare across the industry, but it is essential in fulfilling the firm's mission to offer the best of all worlds. The company makes premium organic chocolate, with many selections enhanced by infused exotic oils, fruits, and nuts from around the world. Dagoba Chocolate has received high awards, such as *Food & Wine*'s 2005 "Tastemaker Award," "World's Best Chocolate" from CNN/Money, and "Best Dark Chocolate" from the *San Francisco Chronicle.*

Dagoba, now owned by Hershey, is dedicated to the art of chocolate through Full Circle Sustainability, blending equity, quality, ecology, and community. The company seeks out fine flavors, sustainable and certified organic cacao through direct, equitable partnerships, and manufactures in small batches with great care. It is the goal of Dagoba to be involved in improving communities, not just where their products are sold but also at the source of its chocolate products, helping to improve the developing communities there.

The Denver Post
www.denverpost.com
www.denverpostcommunity.com
Industry: News publication
Headquarters: Denver, CO
Founded: 2001
Number of Employees: 1,000
Market: Colorado
Interviewed: Tracy Ulmer, Director of Promotions and Community Relations

The Denver Post is Colorado's first, most trusted source of information and market reach. Customers of the publication receive top-quality service and the best information, education and entertainment content in Colorado and the region. *The Post* is committed to producing an array of high quality, profitable core and niche products and services and providing the highest value to its readers, advertisers, and employees.

The Denver Post is focused on touching thousands of lives in Denver and Colorado through community service with confidence and optimism. The company has a long-standing tradition and legacy of giving back to the community. Community involvement has always been important to the newspaper as a media outlet and as a concerned corporate citizen. Through its community giving program, Denver Post Community, over $6.5 million annually is distributed to charitable agencies in the Denver metro area.

Eileen Fisher
www.eileenfisher.com

Industry: Women's clothing and accessories
Headquarters: Irvington, NY
Founder: Eileen Fisher
Founded: 1984
Number of Employee: 900
Annual Sales: $300 million
Markets: U.S. and Canada
Interviewed: Amy Hall, Director of Social Consciousness

Eileen Fisher is a designer, manufacturer, and retailer of women's clothing that has been in business for over 25 years. Headquartered north of New York City, the firm has 50 of its own stores and four showrooms. In 2004 the firm had revenues of about $177 million. The company's clothing is known for simplicity, durability, and comfortable, loose-fitting pieces that suit women at midlife. The company makes clothing for customers who do not correspond to the fashion world's ideal of youthful, slender bodies. To reinforce the "real woman" image of its clothing, Eileen Fisher uses non-traditional models in print advertisements, including employees of the company.

As a clothing company, Eileen Fisher is about helping women simplify their lives and feel more comfortable in their own skin and going through their day. The firm's approach to community involvement emanates from that philosophy. The firm supports broad categories of women's issues: initiatives that address women's well-being, that help women gain access to income-generating solutions, and that address or prevent violence against women and girls.

Endangered Species Chocolate
www.chocolatebar.com
Industry: Chocolate
Headquarters: Indianapolis, IN
Founded: 1993
Number of Employees: 50

Markets: Nationwide
Interviewed: Jennifer Stander, Director of Marketing

Endangered Species Chocolate was founded in a small town in Oregon with the mission to increase awareness of endangered animals and their habitats and the social responsibility that humans have for one another. The company uses their product, chocolate, to achieve this mission and has been very successful in doing so—it is one of the top chocolate companies in the natural food product category.

The firm endeavors to inspire proactive conservation of animals confronting struggles such as habitat encroachment, poaching, and pollution. The company confirms that all beans used in its products are purchased from family-owned properties where the income benefits the community. The firm has been successful in terms of business results and in spreading its mission because of the many consumers who are aware about the products they are purchasing: not only what they are putting in their bodies but the impact of the product on the environment and humanity. The company's business model is driven by the purchase of ethically traded chocolate and the donation of 10 percent of the profit to help support species, habitat, and humanity.

Energy Products (Hydro-Smart, Inc.)
www.hydro-smart.com
Industry: Energy products
Headquarters: Elk River, MN
Founder: John Curtis
Founded: 1990
Number of Employees: 14
Interviewed: John Curtis, Founder and Owner

Energy Products is a national distributor of radiant heating and other high efficiency energy products for residential, commercial, and industrial customers. Some of the products offered include outdoor snow and ice melting solutions, hydronic and solar energy products, and other environmentally friendly, high efficiency energy solutions.

Energy Products supports Habitat for Humanity and other nonprofit organizations that can best benefit from the heating solutions the company provides. In this way, the company is able to use its core competencies to help organizations that support the less fortunate.

Equal Exchange
www.equalexchange.coop
Industry: Organic, fair trade foods and beverages
Headquarters: West Bridgewater, MA
Founders: Rink Dickinson, Jonathan Rosenthal, and Michael Rozyne
Founded: 1986
Number of Employees: 115
Annual Revenue: $36 million
Markets: Nationwide, Taiwan, Saudi Arabia
Interviewed: Rodney North, employee-owner and "The Answer Man"

Equal Exchange was founded in 1986 to create a new approach to trade, one that informed consumers and created honest and fair trade relationships and cooperative principles. Equal Exchange's mission is "to build long-term trade partnerships that are economically just and environmentally sound, to foster mutually beneficial relations between farmers and consumers, and to demonstrate through our success, the viability of worker cooperatives and Fair Trade." All of its products are Fair Trade certified and include coffee, tea, cocoa, chocolate, sugar, bananas, almonds, and cranberries. In 2009, despite the recession, Equal Exchange successfully grew by 4 percent to $35.8 million, with profits of $774,000, and with 95 worker-owners in their cooperative.

At the time of the firm's founding in 1986, there were three kinds of communities directly related to the business that the company wanted to support. First was the community of small farmers with whom the firm would trade. Second, the firm desired to consider the environment and the global community. Third was the community of employee worker-owners and the co-op. This is an approach that resonates with the firm's target market and has brought it success through customer loyalty.

Give Something Back Office Supplies

www.givesomethingback.com

Community Giving: http://www.givesomethingback.com/community.html

Industry: Office products

Headquarters: Oakland, CA

Founders: Mike Hannigan and Sean Marx

Founded: 1991

Markets: Nationwide

Number of Employees: 90

Annual Revenue: $30 million

Interviewed: Mike Hannigan, Founder

Give Something Back is a business products firm selling office supplies, furniture, and printing to businesses, nonprofits, and governmental agencies. The company started with a basic idea: to sell business products for less and donate the profits back to the community. The model is based on the for-benefit business model utilized by Newman's Own. Essentially, the company operates a conventional business model in a competitive marketplace to produce a profit that is donated back to the community. The nonprofit organizations supported are chosen democratically by customers and employees. GSB has been widely recognized for its success as a business and for its philanthropic mission. Out of a field of more than 400 companies, Paul Newman, Marian Wright Edelman, John Kennedy, General Norman Schwartzkopf, and other national luminaries voted the firm one of the 10 most generous companies in America—and the most generous one in California. *Inc.* named GSB one of the 50 fastest-growing city-based companies in the nation in 1999, 2000, and 2001. That same magazine named the firm one of the fastest-growing privately held companies in America.

Give Something Back Office Supplies is unique because its community outreach is built directly into its business model and mission. The founders started the company so that they could use their business skills on behalf of their community work.

Honest Tea
www.honesttea.com
Industry: Organic beverages
Headquarters: Bethesda, MD
Founders: Seth Goldman and Berry Nalebuff
Founded: 1998
Annual Revenue: $50 million
Markets: Nationwide
Interviewed: Seth Goldman, Founder and TeaEO

Honest Tea was started in Seth Goldman's kitchen, in the pursuit of a less sweet, but flavorful, beverage. More than 10 years later, the company is the best-selling brand of organic bottled tea in the country. Seth Goldman met co-founder Barry Nalebuff in graduate school, where Barry was the professor of one of Seth's classes. Barry's research into the tea industry uncovered that tea purchased for bottling by American companies was the lower quality dust and fannings left after quality tea had been produced. Seth and his professor decided to start a company that sold "Honest Tea," made with real tea leaves. Organic certification, the uniqueness of the product offerings, and the firm's fair trade philosophy have facilitated the company's rapid growth and great success.

Community involvement at Honest Tea is driven by the realization that while tea is consumed by the wealthiest countries in the world, it is produced by the poorest. Honest Tea strives to improve these communities however possible when doing business there. When presented with a purchasing decision between two financially comparable alternatives, the company attempts to choose the option that better addresses the needs of economically disadvantaged communities. In 2010 the company made a commitment to making all of its teas Fair Trade certified.

Josephs Jewelers
www.josephsjewelers.com
Industry: Jewelry
Headquarters: Des Moines, IA
Founder: Solomon Joseph
Founded: 1871
Number of Employees: 76
Markets: Primary Des Moines Area, Iowa; do business in virtually every state in U.S.
Interviewed: John Joseph, Vice President

Josephs Jewelers consists of three family-owned and -operated jewelry stores in Iowa. The family has owned the company for 140 years, since Solomon Joseph started S. Joseph and Sons in the Kirkwood Hotel in Des Moines in 1871. From calibrating the watches of railroad men to selling license plates and eyeglasses, the firm has always focused on the needs of its customers. Today, Toby and John Joseph, as well as the dedicated employees, continue to ensure the satisfaction of every Josephs patron by providing quality merchandise at competitive prices and unmatched personal service. A full-service jeweler, Josephs has 19 registered jewelers and certified gemologists, the most American Gem Society Certified employees on staff in an independent jeweler in the U.S. The company offers expert jewelry and watch repair, as well as a unique design center. Voted "Best Jeweler in Des Moines" each of the last 14 years by the readers of the *Business Record*, Josephs Jewelers takes pride in offering unsurpassed service quality.

At Josephs Jewelers, they believe that it is the firm and the owners' corporate and personal responsibility to be involved in the community that has supported the business and helped it to be successful. The firm does not have an overriding philosophy about the types of causes with which it gets involved; instead, whenever management sees an opportunity they think is worthwhile, they do what they can to help support it.

Kimpton Hotels & Restaurants
www.kimptonhotels.com

Landscapes Within, Inc.
www.landscapeswithin.com
Industry: Greeting cards
Headquarters: Boulder, CO
Founder: Judith O'Neill
Markets: Nationwide, Canada
Interviewed: Judith O'Neill, Owner

Landscapes Within grew out of Judith O'Neill's photography talent, love of nature, and grief over her father's struggle with Alzheimer's. After his death, Judith left her work as a hospice social worker to follow her passion of taking beautiful pictures of nature. She began to sell her images on a small scale at the Boulder Farmer's Market Fine Art and Craft Fair, then steadily larger fairs until becoming one of the Boulder's Open Studios and joining the fine art realm. With the company, she fulfilled her vision of printing greeting cards and floral bouquet cards and selling them nationally. By growing her company and increasing profits, Judith found a way not only for herself and her employees to thrive, but also a way to facilitate the ability to donate frequently to organizations supporting research on Alzheimer's disease.

The community involvement of Landscapes Within is driven by the owner's strong connection to her family legacy of service. Judith O'Neill sees the business success of Landscapes Within as an outlet to support a cause in which she strongly believes.

Little Pub Company

www.littlepubco.com

Industry: Food service

Headquarters: Denver, CO

Founder: Mark Berzins

Founded: 1994

Number of Employees: 350

Markets: Denver Metro Area, CO

Interviewed: Mark Berzins, Founder

Little Pub Company is a group of neighborhood bars in Denver loosely collected under that company name. Each pub is a distinct neighborhood place for patrons to hang out and be social with their neighbors and other members of the community. The firm has grown over the past 13 years to have about 350 employees and 19 different pubs. The company's business model is to provide an evening alternative to the morning coffee shop, a place where people can routinely go to end their day with folks in their community. Some of the company's restaurants include Don's Club Tavern, Salty Rita, Three Dogs Tavern, Spot Bar & Grill, and Irish Hound.

Little Pub Company's community involvement began as a way to reach their desired target market of locals, neighbors, and pedestrian traffic. In order to build relationships and reputation among their desired clientele, the company devoted its marketing budget toward getting involved with various nonprofit and community organizations.

Maggie's Functional Organics

www.organicclothes.com

Beyond Organics: Social Aspects: http://www.organicclothes.com/social.asp

Industry: Clothing and accessories

Headquarters: Ypsilanti, MI

Founder: Benà Burda

Founded: 1992

Number of Employees: 13

Markets: Nationwide
Interviewed: Benà Burda, Founder

Maggie's has been in business since 1992 providing affordable, comfy, durable clothing and accessories, all the while supporting the founders' beliefs and values in integrity, social responsibility, humility, sustainability, and fun. The company began when the founder was marketing organic blue corn tortilla chips. One of the farmers growing the corn added organic cotton to the crop rotation to help the quality of the blue corn, then asked the founder to see the new organic cotton. After doing some research about cotton growing techniques and discovering the harsh facts of conventional cotton cultivation and garment manufacturing, the firm began making garments a different way, using the farmer's organic cotton. The firm began with a line of organic cotton socks and today sells a comprehensive line of organic cotton and organic wool clothing and accessories, including baby clothing. Being the first company to utilize organic materials in non-food products, Maggie's and founder Benà Burda are considered pioneers in the organic product industry. Large companies such as WalMart and Nike now sell products utilizing organic cotton.

The community involvement philosophy of Maggie's Organics is that there is no environmental sustainability without social responsibility. The firm practices social responsibility by using environmentally sustainable methods and materials in production as well as in all aspects of business, and by adhering to fair labor standards. The company's apparel line recently became one of the first apparel lines to be Fair Trade certified by FairTradeUSA™ under a new pilot program designed to raise standards for apparel workers around the world.

Metafolics Salon

Jason Linkow, former owner, is now with Salon on the Boulevard, Denver, Colorado.

Nestlé Dreyer's Grand Ice Cream

www.dreyersinc.com

Industry: Food products

Headquarters: Oakland, CA

Founder: William Dreyer and Joseph Edy

Founded: 1928

Number of Employees: 4,000+

Markets: Nationwide

Interviewed: Diane McIntyre, President of Dreyer's Foundation

Nestlé Dreyer's Ice Cream has been in business since 1928, founded by William Dreyer and Joseph Edy who partnered to start a small ice cream factory on Grand Avenue in Oakland. The company is credited with inventing, in 1929, the well-known Rocky Road ice cream flavor. Nestlé Dreyer's became a division of Nestlé in 2006 and is currently the leading ice cream company in the country with more than 4,000 employees.

New Belgium Brewing

www.newbelgium.com

Industry: Beer brewing

Headquarters: Fort Collins, CO

Founders: Jeff Lebesch and Kim Jordan

Founded: 1991

Number of Employees: 375

Markets: 26 U.S. states

Interviewed: Bryan Simpson, Media Relations

New Belgium Brewing is an employee-owned brewery in Colorado. The company's best-selling brand is Fat Tire Amber Ale, named for the founder's bike trip through Belgium that inspired him to start the company. New Belgium brews Belgian-style beers, which tend to be more heavily spiced and use more fruit, including exotic fruit strains. The Belgian brewing process used by New Belgium is arguably a more creative process than English or

German styles.

New Belgium has a unique culture that comes to life through its passion for sustainability, philanthropy—and folly. New Belgium is a strong advocate of bicycling and awards all co-workers a new bike after one year of employment. As a result, most days the bike racks at New Belgium get more use than the parking lots, with many people commuting to work on a bicycle year round.

New Belgium strives to be a good corporate citizen through its community involvement. Since New Belgium established its philanthropy program in 1993, the company has donated one dollar for every barrel produced. Funds from this program are given to four different causes, including environmental, social, cultural, and drug and alcohol awareness. The funds are distributed regionally based on sales, with one dollar donated to every state for each barrel of beer sold in that state. New Belgium is also a member of 1% For The Planet, with one percent of its annual net revenue going to environmental organizations worldwide.

Nita Winter Photography
www.nitawinter.com
Industry: Photography services
Headquarters: Sausalito, CA
Founder: Nita Winter
Founded: 1982
Number of Employees: 1
Markets: San Francisco Bay Area
Interviewed: Nita Winter, Owner

Nita Winter has been in business for 25 years as a professional photographer. Before becoming a photographer, Nita worked for two and a half years scheduling events at the Women's Building in San Francisco, which sparked her passion for working with nonprofit organizations. In this position, Nita had extensive exposure to the diverse projects of Bay Area nonprofits. When she established her freelance photography work, her first clients were mostly nonprofits due to her existing connections in the community. Over the next 25 years, Nita Winter Photography has continued to work with nonprofits. Nita's photographic specialty is people; she has become nationally known for the work she does with children and diversity.

Nita works mostly with nonprofit and philanthropic causes because it is the work she finds most fulfilling. It is her community involvement philosophy that if people had a stronger sense of community there would be less conflict and healthier children, and that a healthier sense of self-worth contributes to a stronger community. Early in her career, Nita realized the power of the photograph as a universal visual language and how she could harness that power to create stronger communities and to communicate the essence of a community with those outside of and different from it.

In 1985 she illustrated the book *The Children of the Tenderloin,* which garnered national recognition. This led to an invitation to illustrate six Children's Defense Fund calendars over the following years. Nita's most visible projects were her "Faces of Marin City, Vallejo, Novato and the Canal" series. Hundreds of larger-than-life images celebrating the Bay Area's diversity were printed on seven-foot vinyl banners and hung in the streets of these communities.

Nita's award-winning fine art images (black and white, color, and hand colored) have been purchased by hospitals, corporations, and foundations and are found in private collections nationally. They also have appeared in fine art galleries and corporate and public exhibitions.

Nita lives in Marin City, near Sausalito, California, with photographer Rob Badger. Their collaboration on photographing wildflowers began seven years ago. They are currently working on their first joint book, *Impressions of Spring: Wildflowers of the West on Our Public Lands.*

Peace Coffee

www.peacecoffee.com, www.mapmybeans.com, www.peacecoffeeshop.com, www.iatp.org

Fair Trade: *http://www.peacecoffee.com/fairtrade.htm*

Industry: Coffee

Headquarters: Minneapolis, MN

Founder: Institute for Agriculture and Trade Policy (IATP)

Founded: 1996

Number of Employees: 28

Annual Income: Optional

Markets: Midwest U.S.

Interviewed: Andy Lambert, Sales Manager

Peace Coffee is a 100 percent fair trade organic shade-grown coffee company that was started in 1996. The firm buys coffee directly from farmer-owned and -operated coffee cooperatives from 13 different countries: Guatemala, Mexico, Colombia, Nicaragua, Bolivia, Brazil, Peru, Dominican Republic, Uganda, Tanzania, Ethiopia, East Timor, and Sumatra. The coffee is delivered locally in the Minneapolis area by bike year round. To deliver to suburban accounts, the firm uses a van that runs a blend of bio-diesel and conventional diesel. The company's commitment to fair trade and organic farms goes well beyond buying coffee; the firm also practices social and environmental responsibility by offering employees living wages, health benefits, and a retirement savings plan. The main office and roastery portion of the business are located in a green, energy-efficient, mixed-use office building about a mile away from their retail coffee shop in the Longfellow neighborhood of south Minneapolis. Peace Coffee is a for-profit subsidiary of a nonprofit organization. The nonprofit organization that owns Peace Coffee is the Institute for Agricultural and Trade Policy (IATP).

The community involvement philosophy of Peace Coffee revolves around the firm's total devotion to the idea of a fairly traded, farmer-friendly product and the wonders of a great cup of coffee. The fair trade principles the firm uses to buy its coffee helps the farmers and their communities thrive in a sustainable way, giving them the capacity to improve their quality of life along with the quality of the coffee they grow. The firm also believes it is important for small business to support the local community, whether in supporting the arts, education, or other small businesses, working and making connections to help their own business thrive.

PeaceKeeper Cause-Metics
www.iamapeacekeeper.com

Pura Vida Create Good
www.puravidacoffee.com
Industry: Coffee, wine, and chocolate
Headquarters: Seattle, WA
Founders: Jeff Hussey
Founded: 1998
Markets: Nationwide
Interviewed: John Sage, Chairman of the Board and Co-Founder

Pura Vida gives proceeds to its charitable partner, the Create Good Foundation. CGF is committed to creating good in the lives of poor people who live and work in coffee-growing regions. CGF's work is focused on water and economic infrastructure projects with current projects in Mexico, Guatemala, and Nicaragua. CGF continues to support funding work in Costa Rica.

Pura Vida was founded in 1998 with the clear notion that business could be used to help those in need. As an early leader in fair trade and organic coffee, Pura Vida set a new standard for how business is done. Pura Vida sells the highest quality coffee and other products and uses the proceeds to fund infrastructure projects in coffee-growing regions around the world through CGF. In 2009 the Foundation deployed over $290,000 to projects in these regions.

Rock Bottom Foundation

www.rockbottomrestaurantsinc.com

Industry: Food service, beer brewery

Headquarters: Louisville, CO

Founded: 2000

Number of Employees: 2

Annual Income: $900,000

Markets: Selected states, nationwide

Interviewed: Jessica Newman

Rock Bottom Foundation is the corporate giving arm for Rock Bottom Restaurants, Inc., which includes Rock Bottom Restaurants and Brewery, Old Chicago Restaurants, The Chop House and Brewery brands, Sing Sing, Walnut Brewery, and Boulder Beer Company.

Rock Bottom Restaurants' mission statement is "to run great restaurants for the benefit of our guests, our communities, and ourselves." To that end, the firm started the Foundation, which became the engine for all company-wide volunteer projects and business giving. Dedicated to combating hunger in the communities in which the company operates, the Foundation provides support through the restaurants to organizations and programs that address this social issue. Additionally, the Foundation provides grants for employee-driven volunteer efforts and administers a fund to benefit teammates who experience an unforeseen crisis. All of the restaurants are casual dining establishments featuring friendly, attentive service, high-quality, moderately priced food, and a distinctive selection of microbrewed and specialty beer served in a comfortable and entertaining atmosphere.

Sambuca Restaurants

www.sambucarestaurant.com

Seventh Generation

www.seventhgeneration.com

Making a Difference: http://www.seventhgeneration.com/making_difference/
Industry: Cleaning products
Headquarters: Burlington, VT
Founder: Jeffrey Hollender
Founded: 1987
Markets: Nationwide
Interviewed: Gregor Barnum, Director of Corporate Consciousness

Seventh Generation is a producer and seller of over 52 different environmentally friendly cleaning products, including soaps and paper products. It is the number one producer of non-toxic, environmentally safe household cleaning products in the country. The name refers to seven-generation sustainability, the idea that decisions should be considered for their impact on the seventh generation to come, inspired by the laws of the Iroquois. The business began as a catalog company and has, over the years, evolved to retail distribution in thousands of natural product and grocery stores nationwide.

The community involvement philosophy of Seventh Generation is closely related to the philosophy that gave the company its name—the idea of doing business in a way that improves the plant and communities for future generations. As a small company starting out, Seventh Generation did not have a lot of money to throw at the problem of improving the community. Instead, the company looks for proactive ways to solve community and environmental problems. The business tries to be a satisfying company to work for and do business with; a major part of that effort is having a well-developed vision of what it means to be a responsible business and a good corporate citizen.

Signature Accents
www.cityscarves.com
Industry: Accessories

Headquarters: Scottsdale, AZ
Founder: Maria Simone
Founded: 1998
Markets: Nationwide
Interviewed: Maria Simone, Co-Founder and CEO

Combining fashion, culture, and the allure of travel, Signature Accents helps its customers salute their hometown or pay tribute to a great city they've visited. The firm's collectible line of opulent silk accessories commemorates some of the country's favorite travel destinations. The whole concept behind Signature Accents is to create unique silk scarves and other accessories that celebrate the cities. In 1998, the first City Scarf was designed by a creative team for the San Francisco Mayor's Office of Protocol. Mayor Willie Brown gave the elegant scarf, printed with cherished landmarks of the city, such as cable cars, the Golden Gate Bridge and Victorian row houses, to visiting celebrities, dignitaries, and VIPs. Sophia Loren, Hillary Clinton, and Mrs. Anwar Sadat were among the recipients. The founders of Signature Accents wanted to create new symbols of urban national pride, colorful, artistic, unique souvenirs that would excite customers to wear them and celebrate a city they care about.

Signature Accents grows its business by giving back to organizations in the community. As the company makes a scarf to celebrate a specific city, it identifies local nonprofit organizations to receive proceeds from sales of the scarf. The company's charitable giving is built into its business model: it donates products at cost for nonprofit fundraising efforts and times product releases to coincide with nonprofit events. Also, CEO does personal work with national nonprofits such as the American Cancer Society and the Arthritis Association.

State Farm Insurance
www.statefarm.com
Industry: Insurance services

Headquarters: Bloomington, IL
Founder: George J. Mecherle
Founded: 1922
Number of Employees: 66,500
Markets: Nationwide, Canada
Interviewed: Clayton Adams, Vice President Community Development; Tony Waller, Assistant Director of Public Affairs; Mike Williams, Manager of Media Relations

State Farm was founded by George J Mecherle in 1922. In nearly 90 years, State Farm has grown from a small auto insurer based in a farming community to one of the world's largest financial institutions. Despite this tremendous growth, the founder's original philosophy of insurance coverage at a fair price, coupled with fair claim settlement, has remained the cornerstone of the firm's success. Today, State Farm Insurance Companies is one of the 35 largest corporations on the Fortune 500. State Farm's 18,000 agents and 66,500 employees serve over 79 million auto, fire, life, and health policies in the U.S. and Canada, and more than two million bank accounts.

State Farm has been involved with the community since its inception. Community involvement is crucial to the company's brand and slogan "like a good neighbor, State Farm is there®." The firm puts its motto into practice through community-based grants and employee community service. The company's agents and employees are involved in the community, trying to become good neighbors. The firm's mission is to help people manage the risk of everyday life, recover from the unexpected, and realize their dreams. Community involvement contributes to the company's fulfillment of this mission.

Stonyfield Farm
www.stonyfield.com
Industry: Dairy products
Headquarters: Londonderry, NH

Founder: Samuel Kaymen and Gary Hirshberg
Founded: 1983
Number of Employees: 467
Annual Revenue: $360 million
Markets: U.S., Canada, UK, France
Interviewed: Gary Hirshberg, President and CE-Yo

Stonyfield Farm produces and sells certified organic dairy products. The company is the world's leading organic yogurt producer, and number-three overall yogurt brand in the U.S. The firm's founders set out to prove that a business could make the environment and family farmers a priority and still succeed; they have proven that bottom line orientation is not a prerequisite for business success. Stonyfield Farm is committed to keeping artificial ingredients out of food. To that end, the firm uses only pure all-natural and organic ingredients, with no preservatives or artificial flavors, colors, or sweeteners. Stonyfield uses premium certified organic milk from farmers who use no antibiotics, synthetic bovine growth hormone (rBGH), or toxic, persistent pesticides and chemical fertilizers.

Stonyfield Farm's community involvement is based on the philosophy that business should be part of the solution to environmental, social, and community problems. The mission is to show consumers that they can relate to commerce in a different way, beyond just the exchange of money and products. Stonyfield wants to change the way consumers view business from a way to profit some at the expense of others, to a force for genuine good in communities and the world.

Tweezerman
www.Tweezerman.com

White Dog Cafe
www.whitedog.com
Social Action: http://www.whitedog.com/action.html

Industry: Food service
Headquarters: Philadelphia, PA
Founder: Judy Wicks
Founded: 1983
Market: Philadelphia, PA
Interviewed: Judy Wicks, Founder

The White Dog Cafe is located in three adjacent Victorian brownstones in the University City section of Philadelphia. Known for its unusual blend of award-winning cuisine and social activism, the café presents numerous events throughout the year which please palates while raising consciousness. The café's cuisine is contemporary American and incorporates many other culinary influences from Native American to Southeast Asian. It emphasizes high quality, farm-fresh ingredients purchased from local sustainable farmers whenever possible. The menu balances the familiar with the new, presenting dishes with flair, originality, and outstanding flavor and freshness. The White Dog Cafe's support of sustainable agriculture is driven by both taste and food politics. Seasonal, local, and organically grown ingredients taste better. Humane and sustainable agriculture produces safe, wholesome food in a manner that is ecologically sound, economically viable, equitable, and humane.

At White Dog Cafe they use good food to lure customers into social activism. The firm's goal is to be in service in four areas: serving customers, serving community, serving each other as fellow employees, and serving nature. Through extensive programming and a newsletter, White Dog Cafe gets its loyal customers involved in its many social action issues. The topics in which the café is engaged include economic justice and fair trade, environmental sustainability, socially responsible business, criminal justice reform, peace and nonviolence, children, seniors, diversity, and social change through the arts.

World of Good

www.worldofgood.ebay.com

Zhena's Gypsy Tea

www.gypsytea.com
Industry: Beverage
Headquarters: Ojai, CA
Founder: Zhena Muzyka
Founded: 2001
Number of Employees: 15
Markets: U.S., Canada, Japan, Korea, Australia, Iceland
Interviewed: Zhena Muzyka, Founder and CEO

Zhena's Gypsy Tea formulates and sells a variety of bagged teas. All of Zhena's tea blends are sourced from fair trade, organic gardens in Sri Lanka, India, and China. The company has direct relationships with its tea growers, the tea pluckers, and the families who depend on the income from its fair trade purchases. Zhena guarantees only the finest, highest grade essential oils of fruits and flowers used in its hand-blended teas, and only natural flavorings of liqueurs and spices are used. The natural flavors are derived from organic fruits, spices, and spices. They are certified GMO and allergen free and are 100 percent natural.

The goal of Zhena's Gypsy Tea is to end poverty in the areas where the firm purchases raw materials. The firm accomplishes its goals by rebuilding communities where it buys materials and purchasing from communities in need where a fair price for their harvests ensures healthcare, clean water systems, housing, fair wages, and education for children.

Endnotes/References

Part 1: Strategic Business Giving

1. Azari, Aaron. Colorado State Bank and Trust. Telephone inter view conducted on July 21, 2005.

The Nuts & Bolts of Community Involvement

1. The Conference Board. Aburdene, p.5
2. The McKinsey Quarterly. February 2008. The state of corporate philanthropy: A McKinsey global survey. Pg. 9.
3. Kartalia. Date Unknown. Primer: Corporate Social Responsibility. Entegra Corporation: Risk Solutions for Companies that Care.
4. Giving USA 2010: The Annual Report on Philanthropy for the Year 2009. Executive Summary pp. 18. Giving USA Foundation.
5. Bair, Chip. Beau Jo's Pizza. Telephone interview, August 22, 2005.
6. Simone, Maria. Signature Accents. Telephone interview, June 6, 2005.
7. Houlihan, Michael. Barefoot Cellars. Telephone conversation, December 17, 2010
8. Simons, Chelsea. Annie's Homegrown. Telephone interview, August 29, 2005.
9. Ulmer, Tracy. The Denver Post. Telephone interview, July 17, 2005.

The Business Benefits of Community Involvement

1. Lambert, Andy. Peace Coffee. Telephone interview, July 21, 2005.
2. Schilling, Frederick. Dagoba Organic Chocolate. Telephone interview, June 29, 2005.
3. Boston College Center for Corporate Citizenship. 2004. 2004 Corporate Giving Standard Survey Results.http://www.bcccc.net/index.cfm?fuseaction=Page.viewPage&pageID=1094 Accessed 9/14/2006.

4. McKinsey & Company. 2008. The State of Corporate Philanthropy: A McKinsey Global Survey. The McKinsey Quarterly.
5. Eisner, David. Telephone interview, October 15, 2008.
6. Wicks, Judy. White Dog Café. Telephone interview, June 22, 2005.
7. McKinsey & Company. 2008. The State of Corporate Philanthropy: A McKinsey Global Survey. The McKinsey Quarterly.
8. Cone, Inc. 2010. Cone Cause Evolution Study. Pg. 5.
9. Points of Light Foundation and Allstate Foundation. 2000. The corporate volunteer program as a strategic resource: The link grows stronger. Washington, D.C.: The Points of Light Foundation.
10. Burke, Edmund M. 1999. Corporate community relations: the principle of the neighbor of choice. Greenwood Publishing Group. Pg.25.
11. McKinsey & Company. 2008. "The state of corporate philanthropy: A McKinsey global survey." Published in The McKinsey Quarterly February 2008.
12. Nihon Keizei Shimbum/Bozell Worldwide as quoted in: Weeden, Curt. 1998. Corporate Social Investing: The Breakthrough Strategy for Giving and Getting Corporate Contributions. San Francisco: Berrett-Koehler Publishers, Inc. Pg.
13. Boston College Center for Corporate Citizenship and Reputation Institute. 2008. Building reputation here, there and everywhere.
14. Brumbarger, Ron. BitWise Solutions. Telephone interview, October 24, 2005.
15. Raines, Karla. Corona Insights. Telephone interview, June 22, 2005.
16. Eisner, David. Telephone interview, October 15, 2008.
17. Cone, Inc. 2010. Cone Cause Evolution Study. Pg. 5.
18. Ibid. pg. 6.
19. Cone, Inc. 2010. 2010 Cone Holiday Trend Tracker FactSheet.
20. Ibid.
21. Ibid. Pg. 12.
22. Cone, Inc. 2007.
23. Cone, Inc. 2010. Cone Cause Evolution Study. Pg. 6.

24. Ibid.
25. Sears.
26. Bauer, Matt. BetterWorld Telecom. Telephone interview, June 9, 2005.
27. Stander, Jennifer. Endangered Species Chocolate. Telephone interview, July 25, 2005.
28. Drake, Tim 2006. I Want to Make a Difference: Discover a Purpose in Life and Change Things for the Better. Cyan Communications.
29. Points of Light Foundation and Allstate Foundation. 2000. The corporate volunteer program as a strategic resource: The link grows stronger. Washington, D.C.: The Points of Light Foundation.
30. Cone, Inc. 2010. Cone Cause Evolution Study. Pg. 21.
31. Cone, Inc. 2010. Cone Cause Evolution Study. Pg. 8.
32. Cone, Inc. 2006. 2006 Millennial Cause Study.
33. Deloitte & Touche USA and the Points of Light Foundation & Volunteer Center National Network. 2006. Volunteer IMPACT Survey.
34. Business for Social Responsibility. Xxxxx
35. Walker Information Inc. and the Council on Foundations. 2003. The Walker Loyalty Report: Volunteerism, Philanthropy, and US Employees.
36. McKinsey & Company. 2008. "The state of corporate philanthropy: A McKinsey global survey." Published in The McKinsey Quarterly, February 2008.
37. T'Kach, Mary. Aveda. Telephone interview conducted September 9, 2005.
38. Ibid.
39. Cone, Inc. 2010. Cone Cause Evolution Study. Pg. 8.
40. Lampman, Jane. 2005. Trend-watcher sees moral transformation of capitalism. The Christian Science Monitor, October 3, 2005.
41. Ibid.
42. Ibid.
43. Social Investment Forum Foundation. 2010. Report on Socially

Responsible Investing Trends in the United States. http://www.socialinvest.org/news/releases/pressrelease.cfm?id=168.

44. Boston College Center for Corporate Citizenship. 2007. What Do Surveys Say About Corporate Citizenship?
45. Financial Times. 6/2/2000
46. Simone, Maria. Signature Accents. Telephone interview, June 6, 2005.

The New Giving Paradigm

1. Hannigan, Mike. Give Something Back Office Supplies. Telephone interview, July 22, 2005.
2. Keys, Tracey, Thomas W. Malnight, and Kees van der Graaf. December 2009. Making the most of corporate social responsibility. McKinsey Quarterly.
3. Ibid. Pg. 3.
4. Austin, James E. 2000. The Collaboration Challenge: How Nonprofits and Businesses Succeed Through Strategic Alliances. San Francisco: Jossey-Bass Publishers. Pages 36-37.
5. Eisner, David. Telephone interview, October 15, 2008.
6. Sisodia, Raj, Jag Sheth, and David B, Wolfe. 2007. Firms of Endearment: How World Class Companies Profit from Passion and Purpose. Upper Saddle River, NJ: Wharton School Publishing. Pg. xxiii.
7. Ibid. Pg. xxv.
8. Easterbrook, Gregg. 2003. The Progress Paradox: How Life Gets Better While People Feel Worse. Random House. Pg. 317.
9. GolinHarris. 2006. Americans Send the Message: "Get Down to Business on Corporate Citizenship." http://www.golinharris.com.hk/breakthrough10/global.htm. Accessed 11/15/2010.
10. Clinton, Bill. 2007. Giving: How Each of Us Changes the World. New York: Alfred A. Knopf. Pg. 152.
11. Aburdene, Patricia. 2005. Megatrends 2010: The Rise of Conscious Capitalism. Charlottesville, VA: Hampton Roads Publishing Company.

12. Hawken, Paul. 2007. Blessed Unrest: How the Largest Movement in the World Came into Being and Why No One Saw It Coming.

The Continuum of Community Involvement

1. Batstone, David. 2003. Saving the Corporate Soul & (Who Knows) Maybe Your Own. San Francisco: Jossey-Bass, Inc. Pg. 80. (Endnotes)

Part II: Developing Your Strategy for Good

1. Bauer, Matt. BetterWorld Telcom. Telephone interview, June 9, 2005.

Getting into Partnership

1. Newman, Jessica. Rock Bottom Foundation. Telephone interview, July 18, 2005.
2. Austin, James E. 2000. The Collaboration Challenge: How Nonprofits and Businesses Succeed Through Strategic Alliances. San Francisco: Jossey-Bass Publishers.
3. Hanigan, Mike. Give Something Back Office Supplies. Telephone interview, July 22, 2005.
4. Sagawa, Shirley and Eli Segal. Common Interests, Common Good.
5. Burda, Bená. Maggie's Functional Organics. Telephone interview, July 22, 2005.

The Seven Steps of Business Giving

Step 1: Build Commitment Within Your Company

1. Weiser, John and Simon Zadek. 2000. Conversations with Disbelievers. The Ford Foundation. Pg. 4. http://www.brodyweiser.com/pdf/convdisb.pdf (Accessed 11/6/2010)
2. Ibid. Pg. 4.
3. Ulmer, Tracy. The Denver Post. Telephone interview, July 15, 2005.
4. Berzins, Mark. Little Pub Company. Telephone interview, August 17, 2005.
5. Abrams, Judy. Landscapes Within. Telephone interview conducted December 2, 2005.
6. Hannigan, Mike. Give Something Back Office Supplies. Telephone interview conducted July 22, 2005.
7. Bauer, Matt. BetterWorld Telecom. Telephone interview, June 9, 2005
8. Goldman, Seth. Honest Tea. Telephone interview, July 19, 2005.

Step 2: Review Past Community Involvement

1. Batstone, David. 2003. Saving the Corporate Soul & (Who Knows) Maybe Your Own. San Francisco, CA: Jossey-Bass. Pg. 99.
2. Macy's Department Stores. Giving Back to Our Communities. http://www.macysinc.com/community. Accessed 11/10/2010.
3. Macy's Department Stores. Employee Volunteerism. http://www.macysinc.com/community/employee_volunteerism.aspx Accessed 11/10/2010
4. Independent Sector. Value of Volunteer Time. http://independentsector.org/volunteer_time Accessed 11/10/2010.
5. Taproot Foundation. 2010. National Conference on Volunteering and Service: Pro Bono Dollar Valuation Table.
6. Bureau of Labor Statistics. Wages by Area and Occupation. http://www.bls.gov/bls/blswage.htm Accessed 11/10/2010
7. Independent Sector. Value of Volunteer Time. http://www.independentsector.org/volunteer_time. Accessed 11/20/2010

Step 3: Inventory Your Values and Goals

1. Stander, Jennifer. Endangered Species Chocolate. Telephone interview, July 25, 2005.
2. Azari, Aaron. Colorado State Bank and Trust. Telephone interview, July 21, 2005.
3. Berzins, Mark. Little Pub Company. Telephone interview, August 17, 2005.
4. Ibid.
5. Ulmer, Tracy. The Denver Post. Telephone interview, July 15, 2005.
6. Joseph, John. Joseph Jewelers. Telephone interview, August 17, 2005.
7. Ulmer, Tracy. The Denver Post. Telephone interview, July 15, 2005.
8. McIntyre, Diane. Dreyer's Ice Cream Foundation. Telephone interview, September 23, 2005.
9. Simpson, Bryan. New Belgium Brewery. Telephone interview, July 20, 2005.
10. Waller, Tony. State Farm Insurance. Telephone interview, July 18,

2005.

11. Phillips, Rachel. Sambuca Restaurants. Telephone interview, July 19, 2005.
12. Feeney, Ellen. Telephone interview, October 28, 2005.
13. Ibid.
14. Erickson, Gary. Clif Bar. Telephone interview, September 21, 2005.
15. Weiss, Jodi. PeaceKeeper Cause-Metics. Telephone Interview conducted July 22, 2005.
16. Benioff, Marc and Karen Southwick. 2004. Compassionate Capitalism: How Corporations Can Make Doing Good an Integral Part of Doing Well. Franklin Lakes, NJ: Career Press. Pg. 98.
17. Erickson, Gary. Clif Bar. Telephone interview, September 21, 2005.
18. CECP. 2010. Corporate Giving Standard: Giving in Numbers. Pg. 16.
19. 1 Percent for the Planet. About Us. http://www.onepercentfortheplanet.org
20. Two Percent Club. Welcome to the Club. http://www.twopercentclub.org/ Accessed 11/10/2010.
21. Cone, Inc. 2010. Cone Cause Evolution Study. Pg. 15.
22. Kimpton Hotels & Restaurants. About Kimpton Cares/Charities. http://www.kimptonhotels.com/programs/kimpton-cares-interview.aspx. Accessed 11/8/2010.
23. Council on Foundations. http://www.cof.org.
24. Ulmer, Tracy. The Denver Post. Telephone interview, July 15, 2005

Step 4: Select Causes and Partners You Care About

1. Brumbarger, Ron. BitWise Solutions. Telephone interview, October 24, 2005.
2. Berzins, Mark. Little Pub Company. Telephone interview, August 17, 2005.
3. Ibid.
4. Abrams, Judy. Landscapes Within. Telephone interview, December 2, 2005.
5. Azari, Aaron. Colorado State Bank and Trust. Telephone interview, July 21, 2005.

6. Cone, Inc. 2010. Cone Cause Evolution Survey. Pg. 16.
7. Leondakis, Niki. Kimpton Hotels & Restaurants. Telephone interview, July 21, 2005.
8. Muzyka, Zhena. Zhena's Gypsy Tea. Telephone interview, August 18, 2005.
9. Brumbarger, Ron. BitWise Solutions. Telephone interview, October 2005.
10. North, Rodney. Equal Exchange. Telephone interview, June 30, 2005.
11. Ibid.
12. Hirshberg, Gary. Stonyfield Farm. Telephone interview, October 5, 2005
13. Ibid.
14. Eisner, David. Telephone interview, October 15, 2008.
15. Hirshberg, Gary. Stonyfield Farm. Telephone interview, October 5, 2005.
16. Linkow, Jason. Metafolics Salon. Telephone interview, September 27, 2005.
17. Ulmer, Tracy. The Denver Post. Telephone interview, July 15, 2005.

Step 5: Grow Win-Win Relationships

1. Raines, Karla. Corona Insights. Telephone interview, June 22, 2005.
2. Hirshberg, Gary. Stonyfield Farm. Telephone interview, October 5, 2005.
3. North, Rodney. Equal Exchange. Telephone interview, June 30, 2005.
4. Ibid.
5. Barnum, Gregor. Seventh Generation. Telephone interview, August 16, 2005.
6. Adams, Clayton. State Farm Insurance. Telephone interview, July 18, 2005.
7. Points of Light Foundation. 2005. Building Partnerships that Work: Nonprofit Organizations and Employee Volunteers.
8. Leondakis, Niki. Kimpton Hotels & Restaurants. Interview

conducted on July 21, 2005.

9. Hall, Amy. Eileen Fisher. Telephone interview, July 25, 2005.
10. Barnum, Gregor. Seventh Generation. Telephone interview, August 16, 2005.
11. Sage, John. Pura Vida Coffee. Telephone interview, September 23, 2005.
12. Goldman, Seth. Honest Tea. Telephone interview, July 19, 2005.
13. T'Kach, Mary. Aveda. Telephone interview, September 6, 2005.
14. Goldman, Seth. Honest Tea. Telephone interview, July 19, 2005.
15. North, Rodney. Equal Exchange. Telephone interview, June 30, 2005.
16. Adams, Clayton. State Farm. Telephone interview, July 18, 2005.
17. Newman, Jessica. Rock Bottom Foundation. Telephone interview, July 18, 2005.
18. Sheridan, Leslie. The Added Edge. Telephone interview, June 10, 2005.

Step 6: Measure Success

1. Feeney, Ellen. Telephone interview, October 28, 2005.
2. Center for Community Relations. 2000. Making the Business Case: Determining the Value of Corporate Community Involvement. Chestnut Hill, MA: Boston College.
3. Batstone, David. 2003. Saving the Corporate Soul & (Who Knows) Maybe Your Own. San Francisco, CA: Jossey-Bass. Pg. 99.
4. Erickson, Gary. Clif Bar. Telephone interview, September 21, 2005.
5. Brumbarger, Ron. BitWise Solutions, Inc. Telephone interview, October 24, 2005.

Step 7: Share Your Story

1. Linkow, Jason. Metafolics Salon. Telephone interview, September 27, 2005.
2. Cone, Inc. 2010. Cone Cause Evolution Study. Pg. 5.
3. Cone, Inc. 2010. Cone Cause Evolution Study. Pg. 24.
4. Hirshberg, Gary. Stonyfield Farm. Telephone interview, October 5, 2005.

5. Austin Community Action Network. 2005. Good Community is Good Business. Small Business Edition 2005.
6. Ulmer, Tracy. The Denver Post. Telephone interview, July 15, 2005.
7. Berzins, Mark. Little Pub Company. Telephone interview, August 17, 2005.
8. Ibid.

Part III: Strategic Ways to Give

1. Hannigan, Mike. Give Something Back Office Supplies. Telephone interview, July 22, 2005.

Dollars In-Kind, People & Commerce

Charitable Dollars

1. Bowen, Lisa. Tweezerman. Telephone interview, September 30, 2005.
2. BetterWorld Telcom. 2008. BetterWorld telecom Corporate Citizenship Report. Pg. 7. http://betterworldtelecom.com/pdf/CSR_Report2008.pdf.
3. Patagonia. Environmental Grants. http://www.patagonia.com/us/patagonia.go?assetid=2927. Accessed 11/21/2010.
4. Newman, Jessica. Rock Bottom Foundation. Telephone interview, July 18, 2005.
5. Simpson, Bryan. New Belgium Brewing. Telephone interview, July 20, 2005.
6. Muzyka, Zhena. Zhena's Gypsy Tea. Telephone interview, August 18, 2005.
7. Kresge Foundation. Challenge Grant. http://www.kresge.org/index.php/our_funding_methods/challenge_grant_program/. Accessed 10/15/2010
8. Simons, Chelsea. Annie's Homegrown. Telephone interview, August 29, 2005.
9. Qwest. About Qwest: Volunteerism. http://www.qwest.com/about/company/community/volunteerism.html Accessed 11/21/2010.
10. Ibid.
11. PSEG. Community: Employee Grants and Volunteerism. http://

www.pseg.com/info/community/employee/volunteer.jsp#anchor0. Accessed 11/22/2010.

12. Clinton, Bill. Giving: How Each of Us Can Change the World. New York: Alfred A. Knopf.
13. Dakin, Karl. Karl Dakin. Telephone interview, June 29, 2005.
14. Ibid.
15. Hannigan, Mike. Give Something Back Office Supplies. Telephone interview, July 22, 20105.
16. Benioff, Marc and Karen Southwick. 2004. Compassionate Capitalism. Franklin Lakes, NJ: Career Press. Pp. 94-95.
17. Ibid. Pg.95.
18. Entrepreneurs Foundation of Central Texas. Our Success: Realized Companies. http://www.givetoaustin.org/oursuccess/realized.html. Accessed 11/21/2010.
19. Ibid.
20. Macy's Department Stores. Helping Our Customers Give Back. http://www.macysinc.com/community/helping_our_customers_give_back.aspx. Accessed 11/10/2010.
21. Ibid.
22. (http://uk.trendmicro-europe.com/housecall/v6.5/charity/schools_online.php Accessed 12/10/2007)
23. Hall, Amy. Eileen Fisher. Telephone interview, July 25, 2005.
24. Bowen, Lisa. Tweezerman. Telephone interview, September 30, 2005.
25. Xcel Energy. Employee Giving and Volunteerism. http://www.xcelenergy.com/SiteCollectionDocuments/docs/2010-CRR/index.aspx. Accessed 11/28/2010.
26. Microsoft. Microsoft 2010 Citizenship Report: Employee Community Involvement. http://www.microsoft.com/about/corporatecitizenship/en-us/our-commitments/reporting/operating-responsibly/our-people/employee-community-involvement/ Accessed. 11/21/2010.
27. IBM Matching Grants Programs. http://www.ibm.com/ibm/

ibmgives/grant/giving/match.shtml. Accessed 10/15/2010.

28. America's Charities and the Consulting Network. 2006. Campaigns at the Crossroads - Changing Direction: Developing Employee-Friendly Workplace Campaigns with Technology and Best Practices Pp. iii https://www.charities.org/ChangingDirectionsPDF/ChangingDirections.pdf. Accessed 10/15/2010
29. America's Charities and the Consulting Network. 2006. Campaigns at the Crossroads - Changing Direction: Developing Employee-Friendly Workplace Campaigns with Technology and Best Practices Pp. 8. https://www.charities.org/ChangingDirectionsPDF/ChangingDirections.pdf. Accessed 10/15/2010
30. Ibid.
31. Microsoft. Microsoft 2010 Citizenship Report: Employee Community Involvement. http://www.microsoft.com/about/corporatecitizenship/en-us/our-commitments/reporting/operating-responsibly/our-people/employee-community-involvement/ Accessed. 11/21/2010.
32. CH2MHILL, http://www.ch2m.com/corporate/about_us/community_investment/water-for-people.asp. Accessed 10/15/2010

In-Kind Contributions

1. Goldman, Seth. Honest Tea. Telephone interview, July 19, 2005.
2. Leondakis, Niki. Kimpton Hotels & Restaurants. Telephone interview, July 21, 2005
3. T'Kach, Mary. Aveda. Telephone interview, September 6, 2005.
4. Crocs, Inc. Crocs Cares. http://company.crocs.com/our-company/crocs-cares/, Accessed 11/21/2010.
5. Gifts In Kind International. 2008 Annual Report. http://www.giftsinkind.org/images/pdfs/2008_gik_annual_report.pdf. Accessed 11/21/2010.
6. Waste to Charity. Business Donations. http://www.wastetocharity.org/donations.htm. Accessed 11/21/2010.
7. Providers' Resource Clearinghouse. Sustaining Colorado Nonprofit Organizations, Agencies, and the Community. http://www.

prccolorado.org/. Accessed 11/21/2010.

8. Phllips, Rachel. Sambuca Restaurants. Telephone interview, July 19, 2005.
9. Elder, Ramon. Virginia Village Texaco. Telephone interview, June 23, 2005.
10. Chesapeake Energy. About. http://www.chk.com/About/Pages/Default.aspx. Accessed 11/23/2010.
11. Sharrock, Nancy. Oklahoma Community Service Commission. Telephone interview, November 23, 2010.
12. Berzins, Mark. Little Pub Company. Telephone interview, August 17, 2005.
13. Hannigan, Mike. Give Something Back Office Supplies. Telephone interview, July 22, 1005.

People

1. Joseph, John. Josephs Jewelers. Telephone interview, August 17, 2005.
2. Winter, Nita. Nita Winter Photography. Telephone interview, June 29, 2005.
3. Ibid.
4. HandsOn Network. Corporate Volunteer Council Network. http://www.handsonnetwork.org/companies/corporatevolunteercouncils. Accessed 12/4/2010.
5. Corporation for National and Community Service Resource Center. Pro Bono FAQ. http://www.nationalserviceresources.org/probonofaq#difference. Accessed 12/4/2010.
6. Deloitte and the Points of Light Foundation. 2006 Deloitte / Points of Light Volunteer IMPACT Study. http://www.pointsoflight.org/about/mediacenter/releases/2006/04- 24.cfm
7. Corporation for National and Community Service.
8. Ibid.
9. Corporation for National and Community Service. A Billion + Change. http://www.nationalservice.gov/about/initiatives/probono.asp. Accessed 12/4/2010.

10. Boston College Center for Corporate Citizenship. 2009. Staying the course: The 2009 Community Involvement Index.
11. Barnett, Jeanie. Tweezerman. Telephone interview, August 17, 2005.
12. Ibid.
13. Xcel Energy. Employee Giving and Volunteerism. http://www.xcelenergy.com/SiteCollectionDocuments/docs/2010-CRR/index.aspx. Accessed 11/28/2010.
14. BetterWorld Telecom. Commitment. http://betterworldtelecom.com/commitment/ .Accessed 12/12/2010.
15. BetterWorld Telcom. 2008. BetterWorld telecom Corporate Citizenship Report. Pg. 7. http://betterworldtelecom.com/pdf/CSR_Report2008.pdf
16. T'Kach, Mary. Aveda. Telephone interview, September 6, 2005.
17. Boston College Center for Corporate Citizenship. 2009. Staying the course: The 2009 Community Involvement Index.
18. HP. Employee Volunteerism and Giving. http://www.hp.com/hpinfo/globalcitizenship/society/social/volunteerism.html. Accessed 11/23/2010.
19. Boeing Bluebills. Welcome Page. http://www.bluebills.org. Accessed 11/23/2010.
20. Honeywell Retiree Volunteer Program. The HRVP Story. http://eclub.honeywell.com/eclub/hrvp_story.htm. Accessed 11/23/2010.
21. Boston College Center for Corporate Citizenship. 2009. Staying the course: The 2009 Community Involvement Index.
22. Linkow, Jason. Metafolics Salon. Telephone interview, September 27, 2005.
23. Goldman, Seth. Honest Tea. Telephone interview, July 19, 2005.
24. Clark, Hannah. May 31, 2006. Beyond Philanthropy. http://www.forbes.com/2006/05/31/philanthopy-executive-loaner-cx_hc_0531beyondphilanthropy.html. Accessed 12/3/2010.
25. Clark, Hannah. May 31, 2006. Beyond Philanthropy. http://www.forbes.com/2006/05/31/philanthopy-executive-loaner-cx_hc_0531beyondphilanthropy.html. Accessed 12/3/2010.

26. Terry, Sarah. May 13, 2002. Executives on loan. The Christian Science Monitor. http://www.csmonitor.com/2002/0513/p15s02-wmcr.html. Accessed 11/23/2010.
27. Kropf, Annemarie. May 7, 2004. Executives get new perspective with 'loan' program CNY Business Journal. http://findarticles.com/p/articles/mi_qa3718/is_200405/ai_n9412667/. Accessed 11/23/2010.
28. Arndt, Michael. January 9, 2006. Nice work if you can get it. Bloomberg Business Week. http://www.businessweek.com/magazine/content/06_02/b3966083.htm. Accessed 12/3/2010.
29. Chura, Hillary. April 22, 2006. Sabbaticals Aren't Just for Academics Anymore. The New York Times. http://www.nytimes.com/2006/04/22/business/22sabbaticals.html. Accessed 11/23/2010.
30. Xerox. Social Service Leave background and quotes from past participants. http://news.xerox.com/pr/xerox/pagedoc/nr_XeroxSSL_Backgrounder_2007.pdf. Accessed 12/4/2010.
31. Accenture. Communities and Giving. http://www.accenture.com/Global/About_Accenture/Company_Overview/Corporate_Citizenship/Financial/Communities_and_Giving.htm. Accessed 12/3/2010.
32. Patagonia. Environmentalism: What We Do. http://www.patagonia.com/us/patagonia.go?assetid=2329 Accessed. 11/21/2010.
33. Batstone, David. 2003. Saving the Corporate Soul &(Who Knows) Maybe Your Own. San Francisco: Jossey-Bass, Inc. Pg. 83.

Commerce Connections

1. Cone, LLC. 2006 Millennial Cause Survey. http://causemarketingforum.com/page.asp?ID=473. Accessed 12/4/2010.
2. Cone, LLC. 2008. Past. Present. Future.: The 25th Anniversary of Cause Marketing. http://www.coneinc.com/content1187.
3. Muzyka, Zhena. Zhena's Gypsy Tea. Telephone interview, August 18, 2005.
4. Sheridan, Leslie. The Added Edge. Telephone interview, June 10, 2005.

5. Bair, Chip. Beau Jo's Pizza. Telephone interview, August 22, 2005.
6. Hall, Amy. Eileen Fisher. Telephone interview, July 25, 2005.
7. T'Kach, Mary. Aveda. Telephone interview, September 6, 2005.
8. Macy's Department Stores. Helping Our Customers Give Back. http://www.macysinc.com/community/helping_our_customers_give_back.aspx. Accessed 11/10/2010.
9. Curtis, John. Energy Products. Telephone interview, September 29, 2005.
10. Ibid.
11. Winter, Nita. Nita Winter Photography. Telephone interview, June 29, 2005.
12. Ibid.
13. Dakin, Karl. Telephone interview, June 29, 2005.
14. Bair, Chip. Beau Jo's Pizza. Telephone interview, August 22, 2005.
15. The Kroger Company. Neighbor to Neighbor. http://www.kingsoopers.com/company_information/community/Pages/neighbor_to_neighbor.aspx. Accessed 12/5/2010.
16. Bauer, Matt. BetterWorld Telecom. Telephone interview, June 9, 2005.
17. BetterWorld Telecom. Partners. http://betterworldtelecom.com/partners/. Accessed 12/12/2010.
18. Make-up Artist Cosmetics. Viva Glam. http://www.maccosmetics.com/cms/giving_back/vivaglam.tmpl Accessed 11/2/2010
19. (RED). The (RED) idea. http://www.joinred.com/red/. Accessed 12/4/2010.
20. Kamentz, Amy. September 1, 2008. Clorox goes green. Fast Company. http://www.fastcompany.com/magazine/128/cleaning-solution.html. Accessed 12/5/2010.
21. BTS Communications. Like No Other Agency in the Country. http://www.beittshuvah.org/BTS-COMMUNICATIONS. Accessed 11/28/2010.
22. Ben & Jerry's. Our Brownies. http://www.benandjerry.com.au/

activism/inside-the-pint/greyston/ Accessed 11/21/2010.

23. Greyston Foundation. Welcome to Greyston! http://www.greyston.org/index.php?who_we_are. Accessed 11/21/2010.
24. Aveda. The Story of Brazilian Urukum. http://www.aveda.com/aboutaveda/uruku.tmpl. Accessed 11/2/2010.
25. T'Kach, Mary. Aveda. Telephone interview, September 6, 2005.
26. Schilling, Frederick. Dagoba Organic Chocolate. Telephone interview, June 29, 2005.
27. Haji, Priya. World of Good. Telephone interview, November 8. 2010.
28. Harvard Business School. Common Interest Common Good. December 21, 1999. http://hbswk.hbs.edu/archive/1216.html. Accessed 11.28.2010.
29. Harris, John. Belcaro Paint and Decorating Center. Telephone interview, July 25, 2005.
30. Adams, Clayton. State Farm. Telephone interview, July 18, 2005.
31. Lambert, Andy. Peace Coffee. Telephone interview, July 21, 2005
32. Ticketmaster. http://www.ticketmaster.com/promo/w02efd/?dma_id=264. Accessed 12/4/2007.
33. Muzyka, Zhena. Zhena's Gypsy Tea. Telephone interview, August 18, 2005.
34. FundingFactory. How Fundraising with FundingFactory Works. http://fundingfactory.com/programs/recycling/ Accessed 11/21/2010.

Call to Action

1. Erickson, Gary. Clif Bar & Company. Telephone interview, September 21, 2005.
2. Hirshberg, Gary. Stonyfield Farm. Telephone interview, October 5, 2005.

Index

About the Author

Susan Hyatt is the founder and CEO of CORE THOUGHT, a private consulting company that provides small and mid-sized companies with ideas and tools for actively managing their community impacts and giving strategies. Leveraging 20 years of experience in corporate social responsibility, business philanthropy, organizational development, and nonprofit resource development and partnerships, Susan helps clients transform their good intentions into real impact in their communities and on their bottom line.

Her clients have included CARE, Habitat for Humanity, Save the Children, Pathfinder International, Heifer International, the US Agency for International Development, and dozens of businesses and local, state, and national agencies.

Susan specializes in community involvement audits, strategic planning to integrate community and business goals, and designing unique all-win community involvement initiatives. She loves clients who are motivated by the business value created by social responsibility and are committed to Doing Good AND Doing Well.

Susan previously worked extensively with the Corporation for National and Community Service (CNCS) for fourteen years providing consulting, facilitation, curriculum design, and training to Governors' Commissions on National and Community Service, AmeriCorps State and National, VISTA, Learn and Serve America, and Senior Corps (FGP, SCP, and RSVP). She's created state and national programs on topics such as leadership, board development, performance measurement and program evaluation, and strategic public-private and trisector partnerships.

Susan holds a Master's degree in Community/Public Health Nutrition with a specialization in international development from Virginia Polytechnic Institute and State University. She completed her PhD work in Sociology at Colorado State University in social change and organization development. She was a Fulbright Scholar to the Sociology Department at the University of Helsinki, Finland, and an AAAS Science, Engineering and Diplomacy Postdoctoral Fellow at the U.S. Agency for International Development in Washington, DC. She is also a certified professional effectiveness coach. Susan lives in Denver, Colorado and proudly drives a Prius.

To connect with Susan:

Twitter	@Susan_Hyatt
LinkedIn	www.linkedin.com/in/susanhyatt
Facebook	www.facebook.com/SusanHyatt303
YouTube	www.youtube.com/user/suehyatt

Services

CORE THOUGHT is a corporate social responsibility (CSR) consulting and training company specializing in strategic business and nonprofit/non-governmental organization partnerships that benefit local communities – both in North America and around the world. CORE THOUGHT provides the cutting edge training, tools, expertise, and best practice examples needed to effectively design and manage community investment programs that are in alignment with organizational vision, values, and goals.

Business Services:

Community Investment Appraisal – Clarify how your company can make more effective future community investments by reviewing your company's current and past giving – focus areas, goals, resources, level of involvement, etc. - to assess tangible and intangible impacts and identify areas for continuous improvement.

Strategy for Good Planning Facilitation – Formalize and/or update your company's community investment vision, mission and goals, inventory unique company strengths and available resources, and identify community investment program focus areas and ways to maximize employee participation.

Strategic Partnership Development Coaching – Identify and research potential nonprofit partner organizations, assess goodness of fit, develop the relationship, and design joint community programming.

Community Investment Systems Consulting – Create more effective and efficient systems for grant making, employee volunteer programs and/or general management of your community investment portfolio to make the most of scarce company resources and provide accurate data for decision-making.

Nonprofit Services:

Sustainability and Resource Development Training– Discover how to design strategic partnerships with businesses, grow your partnerships for long-term sustainability, and use your board and volunteers to get support for program activities.

Performance Measurement and Evaluation – Assess whether or not your business partnerships are producing desired results, measure the impact of your nonprofit programs on the community, and leverage your results for additional support.

Leadership and Organization Development Training– Strategic planning, retreat facilitation, board and staff development training, teambuilding, and organizational and staffing analyses. Selected training topics include Leadership Skills for the 21st Century, Engaging Board Members to Make Your Nonprofit Soar, and Nonprofit Stewardship.

To take advantage of Susan Hyatt's expertise in building strategic nonprofit connections, contact her online at **www.core-thought.com.**

Nonprofit Toolkit

Looking for a way to support your favorite nonprofit? The Nonprofit Toolkit teaches organizations how to effectively work with businesses to maximize their profits and partnerships. Why not buy them a copy of the Nonprofit Toolkit: Designing Strategic Partnerships with Businesses?

This toolkit is just one way to support your nonprofit in expanding their impact.

STRATEGIC PARTNERSHIPS TOOLKIT OVERVIEW:

Many nonprofits have limited experience thinking of business relationships as being a two-way street or viewing themselves as assets capable of addressing business needs. Instead, when talking to business people, they focus on self-promotion and their own needs.

However, to create a long-term, sustainable partnership or connection, both sides must benefit just like in any other lasting relationship. What's more, businesses and nonprofits often have trouble communicating with each other about expectations, roles, and desired outcomes for their joint efforts in the community. It's as if they come from two different worlds.

To order a toolkit for your organization simply complete this form and email or fax it back to CORE THOUGHT.

ORDER FORM:

Name: ____
Company Name: ______________________________________
Billing Address: _____________________________________
____
Phone: ____
Email: ____

Shipping Information (if different than above):
Name:____
Address:____
____
Phone: ____
Email: ____

Payment Information:
Credit Card: Mastercard or Visa
Credit Card #: _____________________________________
CVV Code: ____________ Expiration: _____________

Order:	Qty	Price
Nonprofit Toolkit: Designing Strategic Partnerships with Businesses	_____	$149.95
Strategy for Good: Business Giving Strategies for the 21st Centry	_____	$19.95
Total Amount:	_______________	

Fax to 866-255-8458
Email to admin@core-thought.com

***For wholesale book prices, please inquire with CORE THOUGHT.**

Royalty Recipients

The author is donating a portion of proceeds from the sale of this book to the following nonprofit organizations:

Social Venture Partners International is an international network of 26 Social Venture Partner (SVP) organizations with 2,000+ Partners in the USA, Canada and Japan, who have contributed $36 million in grants and countless hours of strategic volunteering to more than 397 nonprofit organizations. All SVPs share the dual mission of seeking to catalyze significant, long-term positive social change in their communities through philanthropy development and capacity building. *www.svpi.org*

Net Impact inspires, educates, and equips individuals to use the power of business to create a more socially and environmentally sustainable world. Spanning six continents, their membership of 20,000+ people in 280 chapters makes up one of the most influential networks of professionals and students in existence today. Net Impact members are current and emerging leaders in CSR, social entrepreneurship, nonprofit management, international development, and environmental sustainability who are actively improving the world. *www.netimpact.org*

1% for the Planet is helping to tilt the scales of giving toward the thousands of under-funded nonprofits dedicated to the pursuit of sustainability, to preserving and restoring our natural environment. Membership consists of more than 1,400 businesses in 38 countries that have committed to donating 1% of sales to support the environment. Together, they give over $15 million annually to over 2,000 environmental organizations worldwide. To date, 1% for the Planet has initiated over $50 million in environmental giving. *www.onepercentfortheplanet.org*

Made in the USA
Lexington, KY
15 January 2015